LETTERS OF INDUSTRIAL LAW

the executive's practical guide to
the Industrial Relations Act

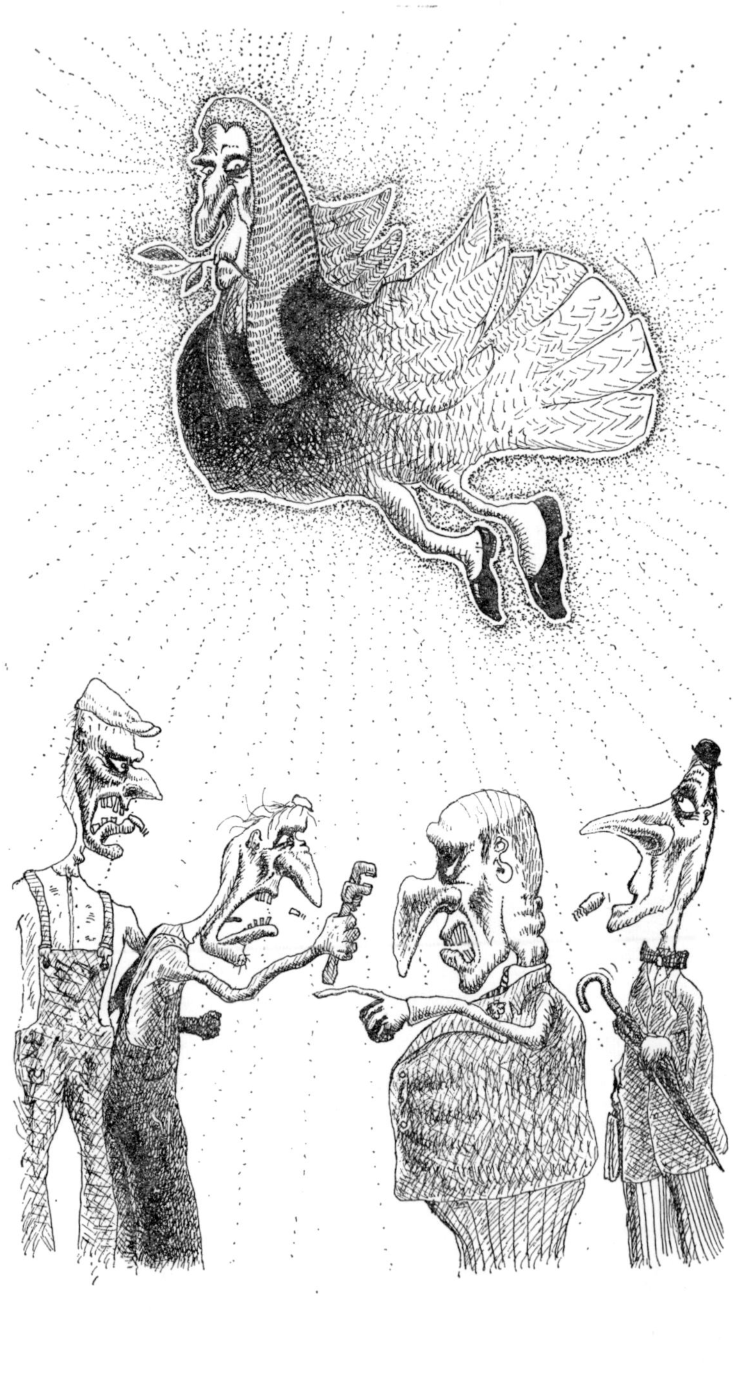

EWAN MITCHELL

Letters of Industrial Law

the executive's practical guide to the Industrial Relations Act

---

Cartoons by Nigel Francis

BUSINESS BOOKS LIMITED

London

First published 1972

ISBN 0 220 66858 2

This book has been set in Times (327) 10 on 11 pt and printed in Great Britain by C. Tinling & Co. Ltd., London and Prescot, for the publishers, Business Books Limited, (registered office: 180 Fleet Street, London EC4) publishing office: Mercury House, Waterloo Road, London SE1

MADE AND PRINTED IN GREAT BRITAIN

FOR

LAURA

—my favourite smallest daughter—

with my love

OTHER BOOKS BY EWAN MITCHELL

Your Factory and the Law

The Retailer's Lawyer

The Sales Executive's Lawyer and Businessman's Guide to the Laws of Buying and Selling

Your Office and the Law

Motorists—Know Your Law

The Lawyer and His World

Farming and the Law

You and the Law

All You Need to Know About the Law

Your Property and the Law and Investor's Legal Guide

The Businessman's Guide to Speech-making and to the Laws and Conduct of Meetings

The Director's Lawyer and Company Secretary's Legal Guide

Coping with Crime—The businessman's guide to dealing with stealing, spying, fraud, false trade descriptions and other common commercial crimes

Letters of the Law—an encyclopaedia of draft letters with legal implications

The Businessman's Guide to Letter-writing and to the Law on Letters

The Businessman's Legal Lexicon

The Business and Professional Man's Lawyer

The Employer's Lawyer

The Businessman's Guide to Travel

Contents

Preface

ONE INEVITABLE result of the *Industrial Relations Act, 1971*? That executives are having to write vitally important letters on new and complicated themes.

Take collective bargains, for instance. In the absence of some agreement to the contrary, if these are made in writing and after the commencement of the Act, they will be conclusively presumed to be intended by the parties to have legally binding effect. But there is a proviso—you can exclude this, if you wish. How? What is meant by an agreement 'in writing', anyway? And *should* you exclude these terms, if you can?

Or take the rules on 'unfair dismissal'—which may result in an employee obtaining as much as £4,160 as compensation. There are (literally) masses of letters which an employer, personnel manager, factory manager or other executive may have to write—letters which, in the past, were better left unwritten. Today, if you wish to protect the company's position—or your own (as employer's representative or as employee)—writing the correct letter at the right time may prove crucial.

Then there are 'agency shop agreements' and agreements concerning 'sole bargaining agencies'. These will inevitably be in writing. You will have to cope with correspondence to conciliation officers and union officials. There will be requests for—and (whole or partial) refusal of—information. You will have to bargain, in writing, with individual employers regarding claims for unfair dismissal and with unions, either seeking to avoid the effects of the Act, or (on occasion) to rely upon it.

You may, of course, concoct your own series of letters, dealing with these problems. Indeed, until this book appeared you would probably have had to. But precedents carefully prepared and adapted to your own use should provide you with an invaluable guide, saving you time, anxiety—and money.

Still, just as no two individuals—or legal cases, for that matter—are identical, so it is unlikely that you will be able to use a precedent letter without translating it to your own needs. By all means help yourself to letters in this book and use them as standard documents. But mind how you adapt.

In order to explain the use of letters, you have to understand why they are drafted in any particular form. For this purpose, I have included with each Part and Chapter and with most individual letters, explanatory notes. These of themselves amount to (I believe, a unique) 'potted' version of those parts of the Act which you are most likely to meet, in practice.

I have included, of course, some of the letters which you hope never to have to use—for example, requests to the Secretary of State that he invoke the emergency powers given to him, to apply to the Court for a '60-day cooling-off period' or for a compulsory strike ballot. And the book—unlike the Act—is fully indexed. I have also numbered the letters, so that if you have any difficulty in finding what you want in the index, you should discover it without difficulty in the Contents pages.

To include the entire Act and Schedules as an appendix, would make this book unduly weighty. I have therefore extracted those sections which specifically apply to the draft letters—and those portions of the Act which you are most likely to meet in practice. I have excluded most of Part 4—which deals with the Registration and conduct of trade unions and employers' associations; and most of Part 6—with its detailed rules for the National Industrial Relations Court, Industrial Tribunals, Commission on Industrial Relations and Industrial Arbitration Board. I have also excluded most of the technical (and often necessarily repetitious) rules laying down the procedures governing applications to Court and Tribunal and transfer to and from the Commission on Industrial Relations. Nor have I thought it worth including all 9 Schedules.

So in the book, I have tried to extract those areas of the new law which the executive and businessman must contend with—and many of which are almost entirely unpublicised. I have digested and explained them—as well as providing letters based upon them. And in Appendix 1, I have included Sections to which you are likely to want to refer. Appendix 1 (like the rest of the book) is included in the index.

Further, to keep this book down to a reasonable size, I have dealt only with problems and situations arising directly from the Act. You will find more general letters in my companion volume: *Letters of the Law—the Businessman's Encyclopaedia of Draft Letters with Legal Implications**. These include more general letters of hiring and appointment; restraint clauses; letters from dismissed or suspended employee or director; reference letters and others involving contracts

* Business Books, £4·75

of service, employers and employees; agents, advisers and independent contractors; debts and debtors; and banks and loans. So if you find these letters useful, you may wish to supplement them from *Letters of the Law.*

Finally, some notes on the use of this book.

While every care has been taken in the preparation of these precedents and of the chapters and notes which accompany them, the author and publishers wish to emphasise the following:

1 The precedents are guides, to be used or adapted to suit particular circumstances; care must be taken by the writer in so doing.

2 The law (both as laid down by Parliament and interpreted by the Courts) is subject to change—not least in the interpretation of words. And much of the Act is obscure and will require considerable interpretation. The Courts and Tribunals are unlikely to be out of work. This legislation will not only be (as often described) a 'lawyer's paradise', but also a letter-writer's nightmare.

3 It is confidently expected that judicious use of this book will save many unnecessary visits to solicitors (and, indeed, that the precedents may prove useful to solicitors themselves). But in the event of legal disputes arising or coming into prospect, for the non-lawyer there is no substitute for the advice and assistance of an experienced solicitor in possession of all the facts. Indeed, in certain cases you may wish to adapt precedents in this book for your regular use and it may be advisable to invite your solicitor to cast a careful eye over your revised draft.

4 Because of the foregoing—and as a further encouragement to care in the use of these drafts—it must be emphasised that no legal responsibility can be accepted either by the author or by the publishers in respect thereof, or arising in any way whatsoever from the use or adaptation thereof, in whole or in part, in any circumstances whatsoever. (The above statement is known, in law, as a 'disclaimer' —and is a form of 'contracting out'—a subject fully dealt with in the book, in its industrial relations context.)

5 The Code of Industrial Relations is supplementary to the Act—and has its own chapter. In the main, it sets out elementary (and often incredibly obvious) rules on the conduct of Industrial Relations.

6 The Act contains no less than 170 Sections and 9 Schedules. I

include the bulk of it in Appendix 1, by kind permission of HM Stationery Office. If you do not understand it, be not dismayed—the odds are that the Section that worries you will worry everyone else as well.

7 In order that each Chapter may be as comprehensive as possible, some repetition of the more important points and Sections is inevitable.

So here—fully annotated—are well over 200 precedents, which I hope will save you time, effort, worry and expense. With them—and with the Act and with the Code and with the Regulations to be made and the interpretations to be placed on all three by the Industrial Court and Industrial Tribunals—I wish you good luck!

I am very grateful indeed to Messrs. Brian Clapham, Don Chappell, Alun Evans and Peter Hill, and to my wife, for their encouragement, help and guidance; and to Nigel Francis for his brilliant illustrations.

EWAN MITCHELL

The Temple
London, EC4
February 1972

CONTRACT
CONTR
50 YEARS NOTICE (FROM TODAY)

Part One

Unfair Industrial Practices, Collective Agreements and Workers' Rights

Introduction

'Unfair Industrial Practices'

THE INDUSTRIAL RELATIONS ACT, 1971 (which I shall now call 'the Act') has created a whole new category of offences—neither civil nor criminal, but with some of the attributes of both. These are called 'unfair industrial practices', and you will meet them throughout the book. This Part, though, collects together some letters, designed for your use when you wish to allege that an unfair industrial practice has been committed; to deny that your actions were 'unfair'—industrially or otherwise; to threaten proceedings; or to react against such threats.

But first, some basic essentials, necessary in order to understand the whole basis of the new 'legal framework'.

The Act is designed to bring industrial relations—with the implied consent of the parties, whenever such consent is not expressly excluded—within the realms of the general laws on contract. Section 34 provides that where a collective agreement does not contain a provision—however expressed 'that the agreement or part of it is intended not to be legally enforceable', then it 'shall be conclusively presumed to be intended by the parties to it to be a legally enforceable contract' (see Chapter 4).

Now, if the parties 'contract out', by making it a term of their collective bargain that it shall not be legally enforceable, the situation remains as before—for better or for worse. But if the agreement is legally enforceable, Section 36 comes into play:

'It shall be an *unfair industrial practice* for any party to a collective agreement—

(*a*) where the agreement is a legally enforceable contract, to break the agreement, or
(*b*) where part (but not the whole) of the agreement is a legally enforceable contract to break that part of the agreement.'

The party who breaks the agreement is guilty of committing an 'unfair industrial practice'. He will not be taken before a criminal court—he has not committed a crime. Nor will he be taken to the High Court (which, in general, deals with matters involving over £750), nor to a County Court. The aggrieved party may claim the appropriate remedy (usually an injunction and damages) from the Industrial Court.

Again, Section 36 (2) says that where there is a legally enforceable contract, 'it shall be an *unfair industrial practice* for any party to the agreement not to take all such steps as are reasonably practicable for the purpose—

(*a*) of preventing persons acting or purporting to act on behalf of that party from taking any action contrary to an undertaking given by that party and contained in the collective agreement or in that part of the agreement, as the case may be;

(*b*) where the party in question is an organisation, of preventing members of the organisation from taking any such action; and

(*c*) where any action has been taken as mentioned in paragraph (*a*) or (*b*) of this Sub-Section, of securing that the action is not continued and that further action as mentioned in those paragraphs does not occur.'

So not only must a party to the agreement comply with its terms, but it must also take 'reasonably practicable' steps to prevent those whom it controls or for whom it acts, from breaking the agreement. Failure to take such steps will itself be an 'unfair industrial practice'.

Breach of a legally enforceable agreement may lead to the Industrial Court. So may (for instance) attempts 'knowingly to induce or attempt to induce an employer to enter into an agency shop agreement in respect of workers of any description after an application relating (wholly or in part) to workers of that description has been made' to the Court; or 'for any person (including any trade union or other organisation of workers or any official of a trade union or of such an organisation)' to apply pressure on an employer to infringe the rights of workers. These are only examples of several dozen new 'unfair industrial practices' which would be dealt with by the Industrial Court.

For their part, the Industrial Tribunals are given power over disputes arising from Section 5 (workers' rights—Chapter 13) and Section 22 (unfair dismissal—Part 2).

Section 5, you will recall, gives every worker the right as between himself and his employer to be a member of such trade union as he may choose or—subject to agency shop agreements or approved closed shop agreements—not to join a union. And where there is an agency shop agreement in force, the worker may pay the 'appropriate contribution' to a registered trade union in lieu of membership—or, if he can prove 'conscientious objection' to making such payment to the union, he may pay to a charity instead.

Now, Section 5 (2):

'It shall . . . be an *unfair industrial practice* for any employer, or for any person acting on behalf of an employer—

(*a*) to prevent or deter a worker from exercising any of the rights conferred on him' by the Section, or

'(*b*) to dismiss, penalise or otherwise discriminate against a worker by reason of his exercising any such right', or, with certain exceptions,

'(*c*) to refuse to engage a worker on the grounds that, at the time when he applied for engagement, he was a member of a trade union or of a particular trade union, or that he was not then a member of a trade union or other organisation of workers or of a particular trade union or other organisation of workers or of two or more particular trade unions or other such organisations.'

Where an employer acts in breach of a worker's rights, he will not find himself in the dock. Nor will he be brought before an ordinary court. He will be taken to an Industrial Tribunal.

Similarly, Section 22 provides that in any employment from which the employee has the right not to be 'unfairly dismissed' (for exclusions, see Chapter 7), 'it shall be an *unfair industrial practice* for an employer to dismiss an employee unfairly.'

An aggrieved employee may bring his claim for compensation for unfair dismissal to an Industrial Tribunal. Here is no old-fashioned 'cause of action'—an allegation of a breach of contract. . . . Instead there is a new concept—the employer (it is alleged) has indulged in an 'industrial practice' which is 'unfair'.

* * *

Once a complaint is brought before the Industrial Court or an Industrial Tribunal, that Court or Tribunal has very considerable powers. In some cases these are even greater than those of the High Court. For instance, an Industrial Tribunal may recommend that an employer re-engage an employee who has been unfairly dismissed (see Chapter 12)—a power which no Court has previously been able to exercise—although, in practice, Judges have sometimes dropped firm hints to those representing an employer that this might be a sensible way in which to keep down the damages in a claim for wrongful dismissal.

As always when new Courts are set up or old ones given fresh strength, the legislation concerned lays down the powers of the Courts.

Section 116 gives both the Court and an Industrial Tribunal the right to award *compensation.* In general, this is to be such a sum as the Court or Tribunal 'considers just and equitable in all the circumstances having regard to the loss sustained by the aggrieved party in consequence of the matters to which the complaint relates, insofar as that loss was attributable to action taken by or on behalf of the party in default'.

This loss is taken to include 'any expenses reasonably incurred' by the aggrieved party in consequence of the matters to which the complaint relates, and 'loss of any benefit which he might reasonably be expected to have had, but for those matters'. But he must mitigate his loss as best he can, and the Court or Tribunal will take itno account the extent to which his loss was 'caused or contributed to' by any action of his (details in Chapter 6).

Limits on the Court's power to award compensation against a registered trade union are (approximately) a maximum of £1 per head of membership: in the case of a registered trade union with a membership of less than 5,000, the limit is £5,000; if the union has a membership of 5,000 or more but less than 25,000, it goes up to £25,000; if the membership is 25,000 or more but less than 100,000, then the limit is £50,000; and where the union has a membership of 100,000 or more, then the limit is £100,000.

But note: this upper limit is confined to registered trade unions—including any organisation of workers which is entered in the Provisional Register at the particular time. There is no limit for unregistered unions.

Again, Section 118 lays down the limit of £4,160—or 104 weeks' pay at a maximum of £40 a week—for the employee who is 'unfairly dismissed'.

Section 101 (3) gives the Industrial Court other powers where it finds that there has been an 'unfair industrial practice'. In general, it may grant the following remedies:

'(*a*) an order determining the rights of the complainant and of the respondent in relation to the action specified in the complaint;
(*b*) an award of compensation, to be paid by the respondent to the complainant, in respect of that action; and
(*c*) an order directing the respondent to refrain from continuing to take that action, and to refrain from taking any other action of a like nature in relation to the complainant.'

In other words, compensation may be awarded—which, as we have already seen, is often limited. It may make a declaration, setting out the rights of the parties. Above all, it may grant an injunction, restraining any continuation or repetition of the 'unfair industrial practice' complained of. It is this last power which, in the long run, may prove the Court's strongest weapon.

As to declarations, these may help the parties to carry out their agreements by interpreting words or phrases or the meaning of the agreement concerned. In legal terms, this is described as 'the construction' of a document.

Alternatively, the Court may declare that one or other of the parties is correct—or incorrect—in the view (or the action) that it has taken. A declaration of itself does not impose new obligations on either of the parties, it only sets out what those obligations are.

On the other hand, an injunction amounts to a ban on particular behaviour. Failure to comply with such a ban would be a contempt of court. Like a refusal to meet a fine, it could lead the contemnor into prison.

If a Court is to do its job properly, it must have a residual power in order to enforce its orders. That power lies in the judge's right to commit to prison any person who flouts his legitimate authority. Once that authority is ignored, the law falls into disrepute.

That, in my view, is one of the greatest defects in the Act. Although 'an unfair industrial practice' is not a 'crime'—and although the Act itself makes no provision for anyone to be sent to jail—there is more than one path to the prison door.

Suppose, for instance, that a Court declares that a union (registered or otherwise) has acted unfairly. It grants to the employer an injunction, restraining the union (or 'organisation of workers', if the union is not registered) from continuing such action as the Court has held to be wrongful or 'unfair'. If the union leaders then act in breach of that order, they are in contempt of court. I repeat: the Court may then send the 'contemnors' to prison.

In my view, if a Court's order is persistently flouted, a Judge will have no alternative other than to commit the offenders to jail. At that stage, what happens to good industrial relations?

In my opinion, wise employers will keep as far away as possible from the new 'legal framework'. They will not bring complaints for 'unfair industrial practices' because they can afford neither to lose nor to win. If they lose, they would obviously have been better off not to have brought the claim in the first place. If they win, then they must hope that the workers' leaders concerned will obey the order because if they do not, then they may be sent to prison. In those circumstances, will the employer's business stay open, or will the men whom the jailed leaders represent bring the business to a halt? And when the leaders emerge from prison, what then will be the state of industrial harmony within the factory, works or other 'undertaking'?

You will find some of these observations appear also in Chapter 22. For that, I make no apology. In my opinion, these problems lie at the very heart of the application of this Act. You may decide to disregard my views and to use the Act to give muscle to your industrial arm. That is a matter entirely for you. It is a free country. But at least you have been warned, and you will go into legal battle with your eyes wide open.

Now for the letters . . .

* * *

Chapter 1

Letters Before Complaints—Employers to Unions

1 In anticipation of agency shop ballot

Dear Mr Brown,

The management takes a very serious view of the action which is apparently being taken by your Union, in threatening to call a strike regarding the proposed agency shop in the ______ plant/factory/office/shop, in respect of which an application has been made under Section 11 of the Industrial Relations Act. We are advised that this sort of pressure to anticipate the result of a ballot amounts to an unfair industrial practice, under Section 16 of the Act. I trust that you will give this matter your most serious consideration.

If you would like to discuss the situation with me, please do not hesitate to contact me.

Yours sincerely,

2 Agency shop agreement with one union—letter to another

Dear Mr Green,

Whether you (or for that matter, whether I) like it or not, a ballot has been held; and over two-thirds of those employees voting were in favour of an agency shop agreement being made with the ______ and the ______ Unions. In view of the exclusion of your Union, the management cannot possibly make the agreement with you—and your threatening to call a strike is clearly an attempt to induce the management not to perform a duty imposed on the Company by Section 13 (1) of the Act. In other words, we are bound to abide by the result—and so are you. In the circumstances, I do most earnestly hope that the threat will be withdrawn.

Yours sincerely,

3 To 'organisation of workers'—no agency shop possible

Dear Mr White,

As you well know, your decision not to register has made it impossible for the Company to enter into an agency shop agreement with you. Equally, the result of the ballot last week showed a majority of those workers eligible to vote as being in favour of such an agreement with the ______ and the ______ Unions, both of which are registered.

You have now threatened to take steps to interfere with our production, and this would certainly amount to 'an irregular industrial action short of a strike'. We must call upon you to desist. You would undoubtedly be committing 'an unfair industrial practice'.

Of course, we are not happy about this whole affair—and we would much prefer your inclusion in any arrangement. But all this is beyond our power to control. I can assure you that if you do change your mind about registration, we will use our best endeavours to obtain agreement from the other Unions to your joining in the total agency shop agreement. And if that fails, then maybe further application can be made in due course to the Court.

Meanwhile, we shall be glad to cooperate with you in any way that is within the law, so as to maintain the good relations which we have always cherished in the past, between your organisation and our Company.

Yours sincerely,

4 Company cannot intervene in inter-union dispute

Dear Mr Green,

We appreciate the reasons why your (craft) Union should be concerned at the proposed Union shop agreement. And by putting the matter before the Industrial Court, so that there could be a ballot, we have done all that we can in the matter. But our hands are tied—and we trust that no dispute between your Union and the Union of ______ and the Union of ______ will affect production—and hence the livelihood of all those who work here.

You will appreciate, I am sure, that it would be an unfair industrial practice for us to take any steps in the teeth of the result of the ballot—or for you to do so. So let us meet, to see whether we cannot deal with this very unhappy business, in an amicable fashion.

Yours sincerely,

5 Breach of agreement, legally enforceable* in part

Dear Mr Jones,

You will recall that both your Union and our Company agreed that the part of the collective agreement referring to —— should be legally enforceable. Therefore—with everyone's eyes open to the consequences—it was accepted that we would not include the usual words stating that the part concerned was intended not to be legally enforceable.

Unfortunately, you have now seen fit to break that agreement in the following respects:

(a) . . .
(b) . . .
(c) . . .

In the circumstances, the Company would be within its lawful right in seeking to have the agreement legally enforced. In other words, we could take it to the Industrial Court.

As you know, we always much prefer to sort out these matters in an amicable fashion if this is at all possible. And, despite the agreement, I think that you and I could deal with these problems very well, without the intervention of the Courts. Happily, we shall be meeting on Tuesday. I shall be pleased to discuss the matter further with you then.

Yours sincerely,

NOTE:
In my opinion, it is rare that personal contact does not *provide the best way out of trouble. Letters should be used, where possible, to open the door to personal communication. There are, of course, occasions when one has to indicate in writing that patience has come to its premature end. Thus:*

6 Patience exhausted—application to court is next step

Dear Mr Green,

We have met many times, but without result. You well know that your Union has been guilty of a series of 'unfair industrial practices'. The management has exercised the utmost patience and restraint. But production is now seriously affected and you leave us with no alternative other than to apply for an injunction. Unless I hear from you by tomorrow noon with some reasonable proposal, this unhappy step will have to be taken.

Yours sincerely,

* Legally enforceable collective agreements are fully dealt with in Chapter 4.

7 For more meetings, you must come to us

Dear Mr Smith,

I have now made many overtures, suggesting that we meet. I have, on behalf of the management, presented various possible solutions to the present situation. However, my efforts have failed—and you would appear actually to want us to take this matter before the Industrial Court.

This attitude surprises us, because you have always maintained that industrial relations are matters properly to be dealt with around the bargaining table, and not in a court of law. As I understand it, this was one of your main reasons for opposing the Industrial Relations Act. To a large extent, we agreed with you. But whether we like it or not, the Act is there—and your present attitude seems to indicate that you would like to leave us with no alternative other than to seek our legal remedy—with all that that means, both for your Union and for my Company.

If production is to be brought to a halt in any event, then we shall have to go to Court. If you would like a further meeting, then please contact me—the matter is in your hands—but only until next______. Thereafter, we shall take such steps as are necessary in order to protect the Company's business.

Yours sincerely,

8 No more meetings

Dear Mr Green,

Our meetings have got us absolutely nowhere. We are now applying to the Court. We deeply regret that matters have reached this sorry pass. But you leave us with no alternative.

Yours sincerely,

NOTE:

It may be that your bluff will be called. The Unions will appreciate the dangers involved for you, if you see fit to take matters to Court. So mind how you go.

9 Dispute concerning sole bargaining agent

Dear Mr Brown,

May I remind you of Section 54 (4) (b) of the Industrial Relations Act? It is an unfair industrial practice for any person including a trade union or other organisation of workers or any official of a trade union or of such an organisation to call, organise, procure or finance a strike or any irregular industrial action short of a strike, while the Court is considering a dispute regarding the recognition of a sole bargaining agent.

In the present instance, you agreed with us that this dispute could only be sorted out by the Court—and that we, as a Company, should not attempt to interfere as essentially the argument was one between you and your fellow Unions. But now that production is being disrupted, surely you cannot expect us to continue to keep in the background? After all, our job is to keep the Company going—and if we are to have any funds to bargain with when the dispute is over, we must keep the business afloat.

I feel sure that, on reconsideration, you will appreciate our difficulties—and—either individually or together with your Trade Union colleagues—we must try to reach a sensible settlement. My door is always open to any of you, at any time. Let us not have this disagreement dragged into Court, along with the major problem with which the Court is already dealing.

Yours sincerely,

10 Allegation of disclosure of information

Dear Mr Smith,

It is not in fact an unfair industrial practice to reveal information passed on to you in the course of collective bargaining, in accordance with the Company's obligations under Section 56 of the Industrial Relations Act. But a person who discloses information in such circumstances is liable to be fined up to £400, 'on summary conviction'. In other words, we are told that this is one of the few matters in the Industrial Relations Act which can give rise to criminal proceedings.

I must warn you that if there is any repetition of the 'leaks' which I discussed with you this morning, I am instructed to place the matter immediately in the hands of the authorities.

Yours sincerely,

NOTE:
'On summary conviction' means—if convicted by a Magistrates' Court, i.e. without going to trial by jury.

11 Employers—to federation

Dear Sirs,

You have seen fit 'by way of arbitrary or unreasonable discrimination' to exclude our Company from your Federation. There is no reason for this—we can only put it down to personal prejudices.

May we remind you of Section 70 of the Industrial Relations Act? It is an unfair industrial practice for any organisation of employers, or any official of or person acting on behalf of such an organisation, to take or threaten to take any action in contravention of the principles referred to in Section 69 of the Act—which in its turn inter alia bans unlawful discrimination against potential members. Perhaps you will consult your lawyers and give this matter your careful consideration. We shall be pleased to have an early reply, failing which we shall have no hesitation in following the advice given to us by our lawyers and taking your Federation before the Industrial Court.

Yours faithfully,

12 To unregistered trade union, threatening to induce breach of contract

Dear Mr Brown,

When your Union decided not to register, I presume that it bore in mind Section 96 of the Industrial Relations Act, which protects registered unions and their representatives who induce another person to break a contract to which that other person is a party—but which provides no such protection to an organisation of workers which is not registered under the Act.

You have been attempting to induce our employees to strike without giving proper notice. And in view of the excellent relationship which has always existed between our employees and ourselves, we bitterly resent this attitude and must ask you to desist from your attempts to disrupt production in this works.

Yours faithfully,

NOTE:

(1) *The various Trade Disputes Acts are repealed. Only registered unions are, in general, given equivalent protection.*

(2) *The fact that a union is unregistered does not mean that you are likely to get much joy if you take it to Court. You are then faced with very similar risks to those incurred by employers who bring complaints against registered unions—delays in procedures; inevitable increase in ill will; and above all, the danger not merely of losing the proceedings, but of winning them—please see the Introduction to this Chapter for details.*

(3) *Having regard to the dangers of sabre rattling, the letters in this Chapter are couched in moderate terms.*

13 Alleged industrial action in support of unfair industrial practice

Dear Mr Brown,

In organising a strike in the present circumstances, your Union is seeking to assist the Union of ——, which in our view is itself behaving in a manner which constitutes an unfair industrial practice, under Section 96 of the Industrial Relations Act. Please would you now desist?

Yours sincerely,

NOTE:

The small word 'please' is worth using.

14 Sympathy strikes

Dear Mr Green,

You are seeking to prevent the distribution of goods manufactured by X Limited, in order to support the workers in that factory. We are not ourselves involved in that dispute, but as distributors our business is very considerably affected by your action. Clearly, you are intending to prevent us from carrying out our contracts with X Limited—and you are what the Industrial Relations Act calls 'an extraneous party' to the industrial dispute going on at X Limited's works. You are not a party to that dispute, nor have you 'taken action in material support of a party to it'.

In the opinion of our lawyers, your Union is in breach of

Section 98 of the Industrial Relations Act and is committing an unfair industrial practice by engaging in this sympathy strike. I would urge you to consider the matter in that light, if you have not already done so. And please bear in mind that it is not only the business of the Company that is at stake, but also the future wages of your own members—wages which we have been hoping to increase, if we were only able to maintain our services.

Yours sincerely,

NOTE:

(1) *Unions are concerned with the livelihood of their members—but solidarity, sentiment and even self-interest may induce a Union to engage in sympathetic strike action. After all, the next time its members may need help.*

(2) *In any event, it is worth reminding Union representatives of the economic facts of the Company—including any hope of raising pay—a hope which may be blighted if the dispute continues.*

(3) *The fact that the union itself is short of funds and hence unable to provide adequate strike pay, or sufficient pay for a prolonged period —is a matter which both the union and its members will know and appreciate, and which it is neither necessary nor tactful for you to mention.*

(4) *Before sending a letter of this kind, consult the company solicitors.*

Chapter 2

Letters from Unions—Alleging Unfair Industrial Practices

15 Dismissal—for 'agitation'

Dear Mr Brown,

We have received a most serious complaint concerning your company, from our member, Mr J. Jones. He alleges that you have called him an 'agitator', and seen fit to threaten him that if he carries on his union activities, he will be dismissed.

May I remind you that Section 5 of the Industrial Relations Act gives a worker the right to belong to a registered trade union such as mine, and to take part in its activities? And any employer who discriminates against a worker by reason of his exercising any such right is guilty of an unfair industrial practice.

Mr Jones has told me that you have attempted to induce him to leave your company. I trust that you will not take any further improper action in order to induce him so to do.

Yours faithfully,

16 Alleged attempt to induce union not to apply for agency shop

Dear Sir,

Knowingly to attempt to induce a trade union not to make an application under Section 11 of the Industrial Relations Act for an agency shop agreement, by threatening a lock-out, is an unfair industrial practice. In the circumstances, unless your threat is withdrawn in the present case, immediate application will be made to the Court for the appropriate injunction.

Yours faithfully,

NOTE:

(1) *Initially, it is unlikely that unions will make use of the procedures laid down by the Act. Later, they may well do so—in which case,*

employers may find themselves in just as sad a plight as if they themselves had brought the proceedings (*win or lose*).

(2) *If you receive the above type of letter, take it to your lawyers forthwith. The union may be a lot more willing to have its bluff called than you are, in similar circumstances.*

(3) *Both because this is essentially a book for employers—and because of the unlikelihood of trade unions using the Court in this way, to make complaints—this Chapter is a brief one.*

Chapter 3

Replies to Threats of Complaints

17 Employers to unions—troubled protest

Dear Mr Green,

Thank you for your letter. I was extremely perturbed to learn that you feel that the circumstances are now so serious that you wish to take the dispute over the meaning of our collective bargain, to a court of law for interpretation. Surely we can sort matters out between ourselves, with a little more patience and goodwill? I would be pleased to see you, if you would like to contact me.

Yours sincerely,

18 Management to union—calling the bluff

Dear Mr Jones,

If you wish to go to court, we cannot stop you.

Yours sincerely,

19 Management to union—please think again

Dear Mr White,

Before you plunge into litigation, may I respectfully suggest that you and your colleagues might reconsider the following points?

(a) . . .
(b) . . .
(c) . . .

Yours sincerely,

20 Suggested meeting outside door of court

Dear Mr Brown,

The only people who are absolutely certain to emerge victorious from our current battle are the lawyers. We are bound to meet inside the Court tomorrow morning. I shall be there half an hour early, just in case you might care to meet me outside.

I assure you that in spite of what has happened—and without prejudice to our views as to the merits—there is a fund of goodwill in the company, for your union in general and for yourself in particular.

Yours sincerely,

NOTE:

(1) *Few laymen really approve of lawyers—until they need them. So if you cannot join with your opposition in mutual love, perhaps mutual dislike of lawyers might do the trick! Or even if you are fond of men of law, no one enjoys paying legal costs.*

(2) *Even the most unreasonable of men sometimes turn friendly, when they are actually within sight of the witness box. Only a few exhibitionists really enjoy being cross-examined. And anyway, there is something salutory about hanging around in draughty court corridors —with the prospects of useless, aggravating, boring, protracted further hours of (extremely expensive) misery, in precisely the same place.*

(3) *Even if you decide not to write a letter of this sort, you might bear in mind that probably the majority of cases which actually reach the door of the court are settled without adjudication by the judge. No one at present knows the percentage—but statistics are (as we go to press) in the course of preparation.*

21 Denial of justification for complaint

Dear Mr Brown,

There is a misunderstanding. Your complaint is unjustified, for the following reasons:

(a) . . .
(b) . . .
(c) . . .

If you see fit to proceed with your complaint, then your application will be most strenuously opposed.

Without prejudice to our views, we are perfectly prepared to meet you to see whether some compromise arrangement can be arrived at. We maintain our view that this form of litigation is of no use to anyone—except, perhaps, to the lawyers.

I shall telephone your office, tomorrow morning, to see whether you and I cannot hammer out some sensible arrangement.

With my best wishes to you personally,

Yours sincerely,

NOTE:

(1) *Litigants are always afraid of 'showing weakness', by apparently seeking a settlement. So olive branches are usually waved rather gently.*

(2) *On the other hand, hostility and aggression tend to breed a like response. So moderate letters are normally sensible, when industrial relations are concerned—even in reply to thoroughly aggressive outbursts. Such letters show maturity as well as restraint—and are far more likely to lead to satisfactory results than the venting of steam. This may make you feel better to 'get it off your chest', but aggressive responses are bad medicine, in almost every case.*

(3) *Letters like the above—which make it plain that there is no ill-will between the writer of the letter and its recipient—may pave the way to future good relations. It is important, where possible, to distinguish between a man's views and his personality. One of the joys of both Parliament and the Courts, from the viewpoint of Parliamentarians and lawyers, is the comradeship and friendliness which exists outside political or legal battle (as the case may be). Life is sufficiently short and unpleasant without forming personal animosities against opponents. And the same should also apply in the world of industrial relations.*

If you say something unkind, stupid, aggressive or hurtful, then it may be forgotten—or, perhaps, explained away as a misunderstanding. Or the hearer may even convince himself that he has misheard. Not so if you put your remark into writing. It is then available to be mulled over—not only by the recipient but also by others.

(4) *There are colleagues who have to see the letter—and if you humble the recipient, you will do so in the eyes of others—and make it harder for him to lift his head and hence to compromise. And you will also do so in the eyes of the Court—unless the letter is marked 'without prejudice' (see Letter 69). When dealing with complaints made to the Industrial Court or to an Industrial Tribunal, precisely the same principals apply when you put pen to paper as they do when you are coping with ordinary litigation. The effect which your letter has on its immediate reader is doubtless important—but you should have your sights fixed on the future—and in particular on the effect which the*

letter is likely to have on the Court, i.e. on the individual or people who will eventually decide your case, one way or the other. Thus:

22 Letter will be referred to the court

Dear Mr Green,

I really am surprised at the way in which you have seen fit to write to me. I hope, that on reflection, you will regret the intemperate language you have used—and the accusations which you have seen fit to make against my company and myself. These are completely without foundation.

Your letter, of course, will be brought to the attention of the Court, in due course. I am sure that it will make as bad an impression upon the judge and his colleagues as it has done upon me and mine.

I do appreciate, though, that you are working under considerable stress at the moment. In the circumstances, I shall not reply in kind. However, I wish to deal with certain specific allegations of fact:

(a) . . .
(b) . . .
(c) . . .

Despite the nature of your letter, we are still prepared to meet with you and your colleagues—and to attempt to re-establish the sort of atmosphere within which good industrial relations may prevail, to the benefit of your members as well as that of the company.

Yours sincerely,

23 When negotiations are at an end

Dear Mr Brown,

I have read your letter with care. I have already dealt with your allegations, many times—I would refer you in particular to my letters of the ______, the ______, and the ______.

No useful purpose would be served by prolonging this correspondence. Unfortunately, it appears that this matter will now have to be decided by the Court.

Yours sincerely,

24 In brief . . .

Dear Mr Brown,

We must let the Court decide. Alas!

Yours sincerely,

25 The door re-opened

Dear Mr Black,

My door will always be open to you—and you will be welcome to come in for a chat—in the future, as in the past. There must be some way out of this horrible mess—for the sake of your people, as well as mine.

Yours sincerely,

Chapter 4

Collective Agreements—and Contracting Out of Legal Enforceability

Section 34 (1) of the Act provides:

'(1) Every collective agreement which—
   (a) is made in writing after the commencement of this Act and,
   (b) does *not* contain a provision which (however expressed) states that the agreement or part of it is intended *not* to be legally enforceable,

shall be conclusively presumed to be intended by the parties to it to be a legally enforceable contract.'

Conversely, of course, if the collective agreement contains a provision which (however expressed) states that the agreement or part of it is intended not to be legally enforceable, then it will not be an 'unfair industrial practice' to break it.

It is sometimes said that Unions who wish agreements not to be legally enforceable are trying to put themselves outside the law. In practice, many lawyers spend much of their time in helping business people to avoid the effects of their contracts which they have come to regret—or in helping them to cancel such contracts as cheaply as possible. Sauce for the goose is also sauce for the gander. . . . And in the case of Section 34, the gander is unlikely to agree to legal enforceability in the first place.

It follows that if a registered trade union, or an unregistered 'organisation of workers', is only prepared to make a collective bargain with you if you agree to non-legal-enforceability, Section 34 is (in that instance) a dead letter.

In any event, you may not want Section 34 to apply. After all, do you really wish your industrial disputes to be tied up in the procedures of the law—with the delays and difficulties and expense which that normally involves?

Again, if you lose your case, you would obviously be better off not to bring it. But could you afford to win? If, for instance, you do succeed and the Court makes an order which the workers' representatives refuse to obey, they will be in contempt of court. Presumably, if this contempt continues, they will be jailed until the contempt is 'purged'? How long will that be? Will the rest of your workers stay on the job while their leaders are in prison? And anyway, you will have to work with the leaders eventually—so is it worth your while to put your agreement within the new 'legal framework'?

All this is a matter for you—to be thought out very carefully. If you decide that you wish legal enforceability, then you merely keep silent—and if the workers' representatives do the same, the collective agreement will have legally binding effect. A breach can lead the party in default to the Industrial Court.

In case, however, you would prefer to steer clear of the law—or in case you have to do so because the other side is not prepared to enter into an enforceable agreement—here are a few suggestions for 'exclusion clauses'.

Also, note that collective bargains may be 'in writing' if they are contained in the agreed Minutes of meetings at which collective bargains were arrived at—or in an exchange of letters.

26 Clause contracting out of legal enforceability

Dear Mr Green,

I enclose herewith a Minute setting out my understanding of the terms agreed between us last night. If this accords with your recollection and that of your colleagues, please will you sign it and return it to me.

This agreement (as stated at the foot thereof) is not intended to be legally enforceable.

Yours sincerely,

NOTE:

Non-enforceability clauses will generally be included at the beginning of written agreements, rather than in letters. But letters, such as those that now follow, will be useful stand-bys.

27 Alternative provisions, excluding legal enforceability

Dear Mr Brown,

Thank you for your letter, setting out the terms of the collective agreement arrived at between the ——— Union and the Company, at the meeting last night. I confirm that it is not the intention of the parties that any part of the agreement should be legally enforceable. (*Alternatively:* I confirm that the part of the agreement dealing with (and/or contained in paragraphs — to —) of your letter are not intended to be legally enforceable).

With best wishes,

Yours sincerely,

28 Note at foot of minutes

Dear Mr Franks,

You appear to have omitted to put a note at the foot of the Minutes of our meeting, containing the agreed term that the bargain is not intended to be legally enforceable. I suggest that we simply add the following words:

It is not the intention of the parties that any portion of the above bargain should be legally enforceable.

Yours sincerely,

NOTE:

It is not at all clever to allow an agreement to become legally enforceable by mistake—or due to a clerical error on the part of the Unions or their representatives. Industrial relations are basically founded on good personal relations.

29 Part only to be legally enforceable

Dear Mr Green,

I confirm that the portion of our written agreement, arrived at this morning, which deals with ——— is not intended to have legally enforceable effect.

Yours sincerely,

30 Reminder of legally enforceable effect

Dear Mr Black,

I note that your Union is intending to ——. May I remind you that we agreed that the collective bargain concerned should *not* contain any term to avoid the presumption of legal enforceability? Hence a breach of that agreement is an unfair industrial practice.

Obviously, we would like to sort out the dispute in an amicable fashion and without taking the matter to the Court. Would you care to see me about it? If you would kindly telephone to make an appointment, I will be glad to meet you, at our mutual convenience.

With kind regards,

Yours sincerely,

NOTE:

(1) *Section* 36 (1) *makes it an unfair industrial practice 'for any party to a collective agreement where the agreement is a legally enforceable contract to break the agreement'.*

(2) *I think it* very *unlikely that workers' representatives will—at least in the initial stages of the operation of the Act—agree to legal enforceability. Hence the above may prove to be a 'dead letter'—in the same way as the Section itself.*

31 Graceful acceptance of non-legal-enforceability

Dear Mr Green,

We agree that we should contract out of legal enforceability, in accordance with the right given by Section 34. Like you, we feel that it would be better to maintain full flexibility in our arrangements. And we know that we can rely upon our Union to honour its agreements—and you know that you can rely upon us to be available to sort out difficulties which may arise in practice, in an amicable and swift manner.

With best wishes,

Yours sincerely,

32 Agreement to non-enforceability—with regret

Dear Mr Brown

We appreciate—although we do not accept—your reasons regarding the potential legal enforceability of our collective bargains. With some reluctance, we are prepared to contract out of such enforceability. You will appreciate, of course, that this not only places restriction on our potential use of the good offices of the Court in the interpretation and (if unfortunately necessary) in the enforcement of such agreements—but it also means that you would not be able to use the Court against the Company, if and when the situation arose. We would have thought that the Courts would provide useful service, potentially to either parties or both. Perhaps you would reconsider the matter?

Yours sincerely,

33 Staff association declines legal enforceability

Dear Mr Brown,

The Officers of our Association have carefully considered your letter but respectfully disagree to your proposal that we should permit our collective agreements in future to have legally binding effect. We consider that it would be potentially disastrous to have any dispute actually or potentially embroiled in the toils of the law. We think that disputes over the interpretation or carrying out of agreements are best dealt with swiftly and as informally as possible—in the future as they have been in the past.

I am instructed by my Committee to say that we would not be prepared under any circumstances to agree to any bargain which did not include a non-enforceability clause.

Yours sincerely,

Chapter 5

Procedure Agreements

PROCEDURE ARRANGEMENTS and procedure agreements must either be contained in a man's contract of employment or in the written particulars supplied thereunder or be reasonably accessible to him (details in Chapter 19).

By all means negotiate an appropriate procedure agreement, with the trade union representatives (letters follow). But if a procedure agreement is either non-existent or defective, application may be made to the Industrial Court to set up the appropriate procedure. As in most cases, the Court will normally refer the matter to the Commission on Industrial Relations for review and report—and then make the appropriate Order.

34 Suggested alteration of procedure agreement

Dear Mr Brown,

I know that your Union wants agreement as much as we do. But the present procedure arrangements are, I think, quite inadequate.

You have often said that you felt that workers' grievances were not dealt with sufficiently speedily. This may be the fault of the procedure—it is certainly not my wish, nor that of any of my colleagues in the management.

In the circumstances, I would be happy to discuss with you potential changes in the procedure arrangements. Would this idea commend itself to you? Obviously, such a meeting would be without any obligation whatsoever on either party. We could simply explore the ground.

Yours sincerely,

35 Attempt to avoid going to the court, to change procedure agreement

Dear Mr Smith,

Section 37 of the Industrial Relations Act would allow us to apply to the Court for our present procedure agreement to be examined and amended. Frankly, this idea appeals to me very little—but it is a possible alternative to the present state of ill will which has grown up—and which I know that you deplore as much as we do.

I would like to make one last attempt at getting things sorted out, without the intervention of the Court—and perhaps you would join me for lunch, next ______, so that we could—quite informally and without any obligations on either party—simply discuss the possibility of some change which might operate to our mutual advantage? Please do let me know.

With best wishes,

Yours sincerely,

36 Procedure agreement needed

Dear Mr Graham,

You were quite right. The present informal grievance procedures are not working properly. There is no proper procedure agreement in operation in our Company, and I think that it is about time that we had one.

In the circumstances, I have pleasure in inviting you and such other colleagues as you may wish to bring from your Union/Association to spend the day at the Company headquarters at ______, to discuss with my colleagues and myself the possibility of coming to such an agreement. Please would you give this suggestion your urgent consideration and let me have your views on it.

With kind regards,

Yours sincerely,

Part Two

Unfair Dismissal

Introduction

Section 22 of the Act says this:

'In every employment to which this Section applies, every employee shall have the right not to be unfairly dismissed by his employer; and accordingly, in any such employment, it shall be an unfair industrial practice for an employer to dismiss an employee unfairly.'

The excluded categories are dealt with at the end of Chapter 6 and also in Chapter 7. There are others—dock workers, share fishermen and teachers in Scotland in particular. But omitting the exclusions, there is enough left to provide considerable help to employees—and major headaches to employers. At best (or at worst—depending on your viewpoint) a dismissed employee may get as much as £4,160—probably tax free.

In practice, the 'unfair dismissal' provisions of the Act are likely to affect the majority of employers more than any other—and certainly no employer can afford to ignore either the rules or the letters which should be written in order to put their position, fairly and accurately, before the employee and later (if necessary) before an Industrial Tribunal. Most of those which you are likely to use are contained in this Part—ready to be adapted to the particular circumstances of the case.

Obviously, if you are yourself 'unfairly dismissed', you can re-adapt the letter for your own use—and in any event two separate chapters for dismissed or wronged executives are included at the end of the book (Chapters 21 and 22). I hope that you will not need to use them.

Chapter 6

Unfair Dismissal

AN EMPLOYEE who is 'unfairly dismissed' may recover as much as £4,160 (that is, two years' pay at £40 per week). Conversely, the executive who dismisses too many people at a cost to his company of several thousand pounds is unlikely to find his own position particularly secure.

It follows that when you dismiss, it is absolutely vital that you write the correct letters.

There is no law, of course, which says that you must dismiss in writing. The *Landlord and Tenant Act, 1954*, says that a business tenant is entitled to stay on until he receives the appropriate six months' notice to quit—in writing and in the prescribed form. But you may dismiss orally, if you wish—and there is no 'prescribed form' for a letter of dismissal.

This chapter starts with letters of dismissal, where notice of pay in lieu is given. Later come letters of summary dismissal. BUT PLEASE NOTE: While 'damages for wrongful dismissal' are only obtainable if you dismiss summarily, without proper cause, 'compensation for unfair dismissal' is payable if the dismissal is 'unfair', and whether or not you dismiss with notice or pay in lieu. Naturally, the compensation is likely to be less if you have already paid an employee on his way out. But in either case, it is essential to have your documents properly in order.

NOTE:

The dismissed employee must present his complaint within 4 weeks of the date when his employment terminates, 'unless the Tribunal is satisfied that in the circumstances it was not practicable for the complaint to be presented before the end of that period'.

37 Take notice—no reason stated

Dear Mr Jones,

Please accept this letter as giving you ____ weeks notice to terminate your employment as from your next pay-day. This notice, of course, is for the period agreed and contained in your contract of service.

Yours sincerely,

NOTE:

(1) *Even now, there is no law which says that you must give your employee any reason for his dismissal. Where an employee is suspected of misconduct and no evidence is available, it is often wise to say nothing. After he leaves, you will probably find other employees saying: 'We didn't like to mention this, while he was still working with us, but did you know that . . .?'*

(2) *On the other hand if you are faced with a claim for compensation for 'unfair dismissal', the burden of proving that the dismissal was 'fair' will rest upon you.*

Section 24 (1):

'In determining for the purposes of this Act whether the dismissal of an employee was fair or unfair, it shall be for the employer to show—

(*a*) *What was the reason (or, if there was more than one, the principal reason) for the dismissal, and*

(*b*) *that it was a reason falling within Section 24 (2) 'or some other substantial reason of a kind such as to justify the dismissal of an employee holding the position which that employee held.'*

(3) *'It shall be for the employer to show what was the reason', says the Act. It does* not *provide that the employee must be told that reason, from the outset. So in each case, you must consider whether or not your silence may prove golden.*

38 Pay in lieu—no reason stated

Dear Mr Brown,

Your employment with the Company will terminate on the ______, expiry of ______ days/weeks/months from your next pay day, the ______. I enclose herewith your appropriate pay in lieu of notice; your accrued holiday entitlement; and your cards.

Yours sincerely,

NOTE:

(1) *As in the past, any employee may be dismissed at any time, if he is given his pay in lieu of notice. If (for example) you suspect an employee of stealing, and even though you are fairly certain of your ground, you cannot prove your case, you may be wise to give him his*

pay in lieu of notice—and hope that within the period concerned he obtains another job. You will then not have him on your premises—and if he obtains other work, he will not get compensation from you even if you cannot prove that the dismissal was 'fair'.

(2) *In circumstances of the above kind, brevity remains the soul of success.*

39 Take notice—with regrets

Dear Mr Smith,

I must regretfully inform you that I am required [by the Board] to give you notice to terminate your employment by the above company. According to your contract, you are entitled to only the minimum periods as laid down by the *Contracts of Employment Act, 1963*, as amended. As you have been with us over three months but less than two years, that entitlement is seven days' notice. But I am pleased to extend that period to fourteen days, in your case.

I wish you every success in the future,

Yours sincerely,

NOTE:

(1) *This letter still gives no reason for the notice. It is best used in cases where there has been no misconduct, but where lack of 'capability' or 'qualification' is relied upon (see later in this Chapter). Of course, if you do rely upon misconduct, it is not wise to send a letter which shows cordiality.*

(2) *The fact that a contract of service provides a period of notice never prevents you from giving more. Good employers often do so—and nowadays generosity of this sort is not entirely altruistic, in any case where the employer may have difficulty in proving that he dismissed 'fairly'. After all, he may have to pay compensation in the long run—and he is meanwhile not only giving both appearance and substance to his statement that he acted 'fairly in all the circumstances', but he is also giving his employee further paid time within which to find alternative employment. And (as we shall see) an employee remains (as before) under an obligation to mitigate his loss, as best he can.*

40 Dismissal—no notice required

Dear Mr Green,

I regret that I am instructed to give you notice, terminating your employment as from the end of this week. You will appreciate that your contract of employment provided that you were entitled to minimum periods of notice as prescribed by the *Contracts of Employments Act*, 1963, as amended. And as you have been with us less than 13 weeks, you are not, strictly speaking, entitled to any notice at all. However, we hope that by giving you the best part of a week, this will enable you to obtain alternative employment.

Yours sincerely,

NOTE:

(1) *An employee is entitled to the notice agreed between his employer and himself; in the absence of agreement, he is entitled to 'reasonable notice'—such notice as is reasonable in all the circumstances, having regard to his status, responsibilities, and length of service, the basis of his pay . . . and all other relevant factors. But such notice cannot be less than the minimum period appropriate to his length of service, as prescribed by the* Contracts of Employment Act, 1963, *as amended by Section 19 of the Act. These minimum periods are as follows:*

1 *Up to thirteen weeks, no minimum.*
2 *From thirteen weeks to two years, seven days.*
3 *From two years to five years, two weeks.*
4 *From five years to ten years, four weeks.*
5 *From ten years to fifteen years, six weeks.*
6 *After fifteen years, eight weeks.*

(2) *The above periods of employment must be 'continuous'. If in doubt as to the meaning of 'continuity' in any particular case, consult your solicitor.*

(3) *Note especially that the Contracts of Employment Act does* not *lay down periods of notice—it only provides* MINIMUM *periods. It is wrong and misleading to say (as vast numbers of employers do) in their contracts of employment or written particulars: 'You are entitled to the periods of notice specified by the Contract of Employment Act, as amended'. Neither the original Act nor the amendments specify such periods. They remain matters for agreement, express or implied.*

41 Letter of warning

Dear Mr Brown,

I must warn you that if you persist in . . . we shall have no alternative other than to give you your notice. I do hope that this will not become necessary.

Yours sincerely,

42 Alternative warning

Dear Mr Green,

We have now warned you on many occasions that we are dissatisfied with. . . . Unless the situation improves, we will have no alternative other than to dismiss you. Please take this warning seriously.

Yours sincerely,

NOTE:

(1) *A warning—or many warnings—may not justify dismissal, either summarily or with notice. The warnings themselves may be unreasonable or insufficient. Everything depends upon the facts of the particular case. However, the more warnings that are given, and the stronger their terms, the more likely it is that the Tribunal would regard the employer's behaviour as 'fair', if he eventually does have to dismiss.*

(2) *As with agreements, so with warnings—there is no law which says that they have to be in writing. But a written warning is admissible in evidence and (obviously) very useful.*

43 Notice of impending dismissal

Dear Mr Green,

As you know, we are affected by the current recession in the trade and are likely to have to cut down our payroll, before long. In the circumstances, we are trying to give our employees the maximum possible warning, in the hope that they may find other jobs in the area. If you find one, then we shall be pleased to provide you with a reference.

We are very sorry that the situation has come to the present pass—but it is not of our making.

With our best wishes to you,

Yours sincerely,

NOTE:

This letter does not amount to a 'dismissal'. If an employee leaves, having been warned of impending dismissal—or, for that matter, that redundancies are on the way—he loses his rights either to redundancy pay or to compensation for unfair dismissal. In the former case, a man has to prove that he was 'dismissed'—at which stage a redundancy will be presumed. In the latter case, he must also show that he was 'dismissed' before his employer has to show that the dismissal was 'fair'. Any employee who jumps the gun does so at his own risk. In case you *meet this situation, I suggest the following letter:*

44 Executive declines to leave prior to 'dismissal'

Dear Mr Green,

I appreciate the warning which you have been good enough to give to me, concerning forthcoming redundancies. However, I am not prepared to resign under any circumstances. You will appreciate, I am sure, that if I were to do so I would jeopardise my right to redundancy pay—accumulated as a result of many years of loyal and enthusiastic service for the Company.

Yours sincerely,

NOTE:

(1) *A former employee cannot get both redundancy pay and compensation for unfair dismissal. Whether one or the other would suit him the better depends on the circumstances—and, often, upon his length of service.*

(2) *Either way, added strength is given to the vital, legal message, which should be inscribed upon the mind of every executive—and, indeed, of every other employee—'Never resign' Well, hardly ever. . . . And at least not unless he gets 'severance pay'—tax-free and in sufficient measure to make up for his loss of other benefits which depend upon the proof of 'dismissal'—or a much better job.*

However, once you have been dismissed, i.e. given your notice, telling you that you will have to go very shortly, you may be able to jump the gun, if you do it properly. As we shall see shortly (in Letter 47).

45 Notice to terminate contract of employment —of executive

Dear Mr Brown,

I regret that I must ask you to treat this letter as notice terminating your employment in accordance with your contract, at the end of the period of three months from ______, your next pay day.

Yours sincerely,

NOTE:

(1) *A variety of letters of dismissal are offered in this book—please see Index. You must consider in each case whether or not to include details of the reasons for the dismissal.*

(2) *From the point of view of the dismissed employee, his rights under the Act—and under the* Redundancy Payments Act, 1965—

all commence only if he is 'dismissed'. And however harshly or kindly that dismissal is effected, if 'the contract under which he is employed by the employer is terminated by the employer, whether it is so terminated by notice or without notice . . . or if under his contract of employment he is employed for a fixed term and that term expires without being renewed under the same contract . . .' he is dismissed (*Section 23*).

(3) *You could probably give notice commencing from the date of the letter. But it is preferable to do so from the next pay day.*

46 Alternative letter of dismissal—with kindness

Dear Roger,

I am very upset indeed that it has become necessary for me to give you notice, in accordance with the terms of your contract. Your contract will therefore terminate on the ______.

I do hope that you will be able to obtain alternative employment, at an early date—and if I can be of help to you in any way, please do not hesitate to let me know.

Yours sincerely,

NOTE:

After a letter like this, it will be very difficult to suggest that the employee was dismissed because of any misconduct.

47 Notice by employee to terminate contract earlier than expiry of notice

Dear Mr Smith,

I hereby give notice in accordance with Section 23 (3) of the Industrial Relations Act, to terminate my contract of employment on the ______, which is a date earlier than the Company's notice to me ______ dated the ______ is due to expire.

With best wishes,

Yours sincerely,

NOTE:

(1) *The relevant sub-section reads as follows:*

'Where an employer gives notice to an employee to terminate his contract of employment and, at a time within the obligatory period of that notice, the employee gives notice in writing *to the employer to terminate the contract of employment on a date earlier than the date*

on which the employer's notice is due to expire, the employee shall for the purposes of this Act be taken to be dismissed by the employer, and the reasons for the dismissal shall be taken to be the reasons for which the employer's notice is given.'

Hence you may jump the gun—and there is no provision in this Act (as there is in the Redundancy Payments Act) for the employer to serve a counter-notice, requiring the employee to stay on until his period of notice expires.

(2) *The 'obligatory period' referred to—in relation to the employer's notice—'means that period which, being equal to the minimum period which . . . is required to be given by the employer to terminate the contract of employment . . . expires at the time when the employer's notice expires. . . .*

'If the actual period of the employer's notice—that is to say, the period beginning at the time when the notice is given and ending at the time when it expires—is equal to the minimum period which (whether by virtue of any enactment or otherwise) is required to be given by the employer to terminate the contract of employment, then the obligatory period, in relation to that notice, means the actual period of the notice'. [*Section 23* (*4*)].

(3) *There is no specific 'prescribed form' for an employee's letter in the above circumstances—any words will do—and, in general, the briefer the letter, the better. But note: if the reason why the employee wishes to leave before his notice expires is that he proposes to take on another job, his loss as a result of the dismissal will be greatly reduced —and if he obtains other work at the same or at a higher rate of pay, it will disappear altogether. He may then have been unfairly dismissed, but he will get no compensation. He must 'mitigate his loss'—as in the case of any other contractual breach. Hence, if he is taking a job at a lower rate of pay, the following letter is suggested:*

48 Employee jumps the gun—to obtain lower paid job

Dear Mr Brown,

I am happy to say that I have obtained another post, and I shall therefore be leaving prior to the expiry of the period of notice which has been given to me by the Company. My new employment starts on the ______, and I shall therefore be leaving on the ______. This notice is given to you in accordance with Section 23 of the Industrial Relations Act.

Unfortunately, I shall not be earning the same salary/receiving the same pay/remuneration/commission/terms, as I was receiving while working for your Company. The above notice is without prejudice to any claim which I may hereafter find it necessary to bring, for compensation for unfair dismissal.

Yours sincerely,

49 Allegation that employee has failed to 'mitigate his loss'

Dear Mr Brown,

I was upset to learn that you had rejected the offer of employment made to you by ——. May I draw your attention to Section 116 (2) of the Industrial Relations Act? Where an employee is dismissed, he is bound to mitigate his loss, if he reasonably can. You have been given the opportunity to keep that loss to the minimum—and if you see fit to carry out your threat and to institute proceedings for 'unfair dismissal' (as, of course, you are fully entitled to do), not only will the Company deny that your dismissal was 'unfair', but it will contend that you have failed to mitigate your loss as you could have done.

Yours sincerely,

50 Employee's reply—alternative job not reasonably comparable

Dear Mr Jones,

I agree that I have been offered a job by ——. But my status, responsibility and pay are not comparable to those which I enjoyed while with the Company. I appreciate that it may be difficult for me to replace my former position with one which is as satisfactory, but I am certainly not prepared to down-grade myself, without at least a very firm effort to re-establish myself at a reasonably comparable level.

Incidentally, if I were to accept a lower paid job without seeking a better one, I suspect that you would then criticise me for not having taken more energetic steps to mitigate my loss.

Yours sincerely,

NOTE:

(1) *While an employee who seeks either damages for wrongful dismissal or compensation for unfair dismissal must do what he can to keep his loss to the minimum, this does not mean that he must take either the first job offered to him or one which would result in a vast*

change in his status. To take an obvious example, a Member of the Board need not accept work as a lift attendant.

(2) *Naturally, the question as to whether a dismissed employee has acted reasonably is one of fact, depending on all the circumstances of the case. If in doubt, consult your solicitor.*

51 Allegation that dismissed employee has brought about his own downfall

Dear Mr Jones,

I fully appreciate how you feel. But the circumstances of which you complain were, in our view, entirely brought about by your own actions. In particular, I would refer to the following:

(a) . . .
(b) . . .
(c) . . .

I am sorry that the situation has reached this unhappy state. It is not of the Company's making.

Yours sincerely,

NOTE:

(1) *Section 116 (3) of the Act reads: 'Where the Industrial Court or Industrial Tribunal finds that the matters to which the complaint relates were to any extent caused or contributed to by any action of the aggrieved party in connection with those matters (whether that action constituted an unfair industrial practice on his part or not), the Court or Tribunal shall reduce its assessment of his loss to such extent as, having regard to that finding, the Court or Tribunal considers just and equitable.'*

(2) *No one knows quite how this Section will be interpreted—it is roughly equivalent to the 'contributory negligence' rules, in negligence cases. Presumably it means that even if the dismissal was unfair, the fact that there was some justification for it may be taken into account. Hence, the dismissed executive who feels that he is not to blame for the circumstances which have led to his dismissal should reply to a letter such as the above, approximately as follows:*

52 Reply to allegation of 'contributory' actions

Dear Mr Brown,

I vehemently deny that the alleged or any actions on my part have caused or contributed to the situation which led to my unfair dismissal by the Company.

The facts are as follows:

(a) . . .
(b) . . .
(c) . . .

Yours sincerely,

NOTE:

(1) *If the employer's letter gives details of the allegations, then the employee's reply should do the same. Conversely, if the employer's letter is brief and unparticularised, a simple denial will do. This would be the same as the above draft, without the second (or the numbered) paragraphs.*

(2) *It must be re-emphasised that when the executive—or any other employee—is attempting to protect his position, the basic rule remains the same: He is not bound to put anything into writing, but if he does so, he will find that a Tribunal is more likely to accept his case. On the other hand, anything he does commit to paper must be thoroughly accurate and carefully thought out.*

(3) *It follows that if a letter is likely to find its way to Court, it is often wise to have it drafted by a solicitor—even if it is signed by the actual or potential litigant. There is no law which says that lawyers' letters must be signed by them. In practice, there are many occasions when they simply advise on the letter which the client should write—or draft that letter for his signature. So if you receive a well-drafted letter—either from the Company or from an employee—you may well suspect (correctly) the hidden hand of the lawyer.*

Chapter 7

Exclusions from Unfair Dismissal Protection

NOT EVERYONE can successfully claim compensation for unfair dismissal, even if he has been 'unfairly dismissed'. This chapter contains letters telling claimants why they come within *excluded* categories.

53 Part-time employees

Dear Mr Brown,

As you work for us under a contract which 'normally involves employment for less than 21 hours weekly', you could not under any circumstances qualify for compensation for unfair dismissal. By all means consult solicitors, as you suggest—and no doubt they will explain to you the meaning of Section 27 (1) (f) of the Act. To assist your solicitors, I enclose herewith a list of the actual hours which you have worked during the past 52 weeks.

Yours sincerely,

NOTE:

(1) *Here is yet another incentive to employ part-timers—for less than a normal 21 hours a week.*

(2) *If a part-timer is employed occasionally—or seasonally—for more than 21 hours a week, provided that his 'normal' working hours are less than this maximum, he will not get compensation for 'unfair dismissal', under any circumstances. Hence:*

54 Part-time—over 21 hours at Christmas

Dear Miss Green,

I agree that during the Christmas season you worked well over 21 hours—but this was an abnormal situation. Your work normally involves employment for less than 21 hours a week. In the circumstances, quite apart from our vehement denial that you were unfairly dismissed, it is our view that you could not conceivably obtain compensation for unfair dismissal against the company.

Yours sincerely,

55 Part-time—special pressures

Dear Mr Brown,

Although you were good enough to put in a full working day during the recent rush job, you were normally employed for less than 21 hours a week. In the circumstances, your claim for compensation for alleged 'unfair dismissal' cannot possibly be accepted.

I would add that in any event your dismissal was because of the manner in which you carried out your job, and was not 'unfair', in any sense of that word.

Yours sincerely,

56 Wives—and husbands

Dear Mary,

I agree that as a result of our unhappy matrimonial disputes it became impossible to employ you any longer in the business, and you were dismissed accordingly. But I am told that where the employer is the husband or wife or a close relative of the employee, no compensation for 'unfair dismissal' could be obtained, even if the dismissal were (as I deny) unfair.

Yours sincerely,

NOTE:

(1) *The above exception applies where you employ your wife—but not where your company does so. It protects the individual and not the corporate employer.*

(2) *'Close relative' is defined as meaning a person's 'father, mother, grandmother, grandfather, step-father, step-mother, son, daughter, grandson, granddaughter, step-son, step-daughter, brother, sister, half-brother or half-sister.'*

57 Small businesses

Dear Elizabeth,

You were not dismissed unfairly. In any event, I am told that Section 27 (1) (a) of the Industrial Relations Act excludes anyone employed in an undertaking in which, immediately before the effective date of the termination of employment, employed less than four people who had been continuously employed for not less than 13 weeks. We have only ever had three people in our business.

Yours sincerely,

NOTE:
The above exception is intended to exclude small businesses. But it matters not whether employees are 'employed at the same place . . . or at different places'. So employees who may actually work in a place with only a couple of colleagues may still be protected by the Act, provided that the business employs, in the aggregate, four or more people.

58 Employees outside Great Britain

Dear Bill,

I appreciate your feelings about your dismissal—although I cannot agree that you have been unfairly treated in any way. In any event, under your contract of employment you ordinarily worked outside Great Britain and in the circumstances there can be no question of a successful claim by you for compensation for unfair dismissal. I am sorry that our relationship should have to end on this note.

Yours sincerely,

NOTE:
The 'unfair dismissal' provisions do not apply 'to any employment where, under his contract of employment, the employee ordinarily works outside Great Britain'. This does not include people who 'ordinarily work' in Great Britain but are required to do jobs abroad—even if they are overseas for some considerable time. There will, of course, be many borderline cases.

If you take on someone who may be such a borderline case, it may be well to include a term in his contract of employment indicating that he is ordinarily to work outside Great Britain. If that is what his contract of employment provides, even if a court might otherwise consider that he 'ordinarily worked' inside Great Britain, he may still be outside the protection given by the Act. In other words, this would appear to be a curiously drafted section, likely to be interpreted to the employer's advantage.

59 On board ship

Dear Mr Jones,

I appreciate that you were employed to work on board a ship registered in the UK. But Section 27 (3) of the Act says that where the employment is wholly outside Great Britain or the claimant is not ordinarily resident in Great Britain, he is to be regarded as a person who under his contract of employment 'ordinarily works' outside Great Britain. You have not only been employed wholly outside Great Britain but are ordinarily resident, I understand, in ——. In the circumstances, even if (which is denied) you would otherwise be entitled to compensation for unfair dismissal, you come within one of the exclusions provided by the Act.

Yours sincerely,

60 Under two years' employment

Dear Mr Jones,

You could not possibly qualify for compensation for 'unfair dismissal' by the company, because you have not been continuously employed for two years, prior to the date of the termination of your employment.

Yours sincerely,

NOTE:

The minimum two-year period does NOT apply where you dismiss an employee because he has exercised or has indicated his intention to exercise any of the rights conferred on him by Section 5 (1) of the Act—that is, to join or not to join a trade union (see Chapter 13). If, for instance, there is no agency shop agreement in force; you take a man into your employment, and then—perhaps as a result of pressure from an unregistered trade union—you decide to dismiss him—he may claim his compensation for unfair dismissal, even though he has not been with you for the two-year period.

61 Above retiring age—man

Dear Mr Green,

You were dismissed after reaching the age of 65 and in the circumstances there is no possible question of compensation for 'unfair dismissal'. We would like to point out, in any event, that we kept you on beyond retiring age because of our high regard for you—and we feel that we have acted more than fairly in your case. And we hope that on reflection you may agree.

Yours sincerely,

62 Above retiring age—woman

Dear Mrs Brown,

Once a woman attains the age of 60, she is no longer protected against 'unfair dismissal'. So as you yourself were beyond retirement age when you were dismissed, the Industrial Relations Act cannot help you.

In any event, I cannot agree that you were dealt with unfairly. We in fact kept you on as long as we possibly could. And you were given more than the required period of notice when we decided that you would have to leave us.

I am sorry that I cannot be of help to you.

Yours sincerely,

NOTE:

The upper ages are the normal retiring ages applicable in the business, or 65 for men, 60 for women. There is no lower age limit (for redundancy pay, you have to be at least 20—having continuously served for two years after reaching your eighteenth birthday). The absence of a lower age limit is particularly relevant when considering the rights of apprentices.

Chapter 8

'Fair' Dismissal—With Notice

IN THE PAST, an employee's only protection against the miseries of dismissal has been the length of his period of notice. He now has two cushions—redundancy pay—and compensation for 'unfair dismissal', which he can get whether or not he has been given his notice.

It follows that (as we have seen in Chapter 6) there may be many occasions when it is still advisable to give no reasons in your letter of dismissal, it is often wise now to be specific—and to indicate your reasons, so that if your employee does make a complaint to an Industrial Tribunal, you will be able to show both reason and consistency.

Naturally, if you dismiss an employee summarily you will not say to him: 'If you sue me for damages, this letter indicates the defences which I will raise'. Equally, if he is dismissed with notice, you will not say to him: 'If you see fit to claim for compensation, these are the defences we shall raise'. But you should still make those reasons plain in your letter, where possible.

There are circumstances in which you have been told by an employee—or by his union representative—that if you do give notice, you will be taken to the Tribunal. In that case, it becomes all the more important for you to express yourself clearly, concisely and firmly in your letter. This will be taken before the Tribunal—unless, of course, the case is settled before reaching that stage (see Chapter 5). So take care.

63 Lack of 'capability'—insufficient 'skill'

Dear Mr White,

Unfortunately, the series of unhappy accidents in which you have recently been involved have made it plain that you no longer possess the skill necessary for the carrying out of your work. It is therefore with the greatest regret that I must ask you to treat this letter as giving you notice, to terminate your employment on the

______. You will appreciate that you are entitled under your contract of employment to ______ weeks notice.

I would only add that were it possible to find other work for you within our business, we would have been happy to do so. Unfortunately, no such work is available.

We wish you success in the future,

Yours sincerely,

NOTE:

(1) *If an employer wishes to show that dismissal was 'fair' he must show one of the specified reasons, or some other 'substantial reason'. The first such reason given* [*in Section 24* (*2*) (*a*)] *is one which 'relates to the capability . . . of the employee for performing work of the kind which he was employed by the employer to do'.*

(2) *'Capability' is defined as meaning 'capability as assessed by reference to skill, aptitude, health or any other physical or mental quality'.*

(3) *When a man is dismissed because he does not possess the requisite skill, this is very often in no way his fault.*

(4) *Even if you can prove one of the specified reasons, you will still have to pay compensation, if the employee suffers loss as a result of his dismissal, unless you can show that the dismissal was 'fair'. And Section 24* (*6*) *says that the Tribunal will consider whether 'in the circumstances the employer acted reasonably or unreasonably as treating that reason as a sufficient one for dismissing the employee; and that question shall be determined in accordance with equity and the substantial merits of the case'.*

(5) *In other words, a Tribunal will ask: Was the dismissal fair in all the circumstances? Did the employer act 'reasonably'?*

If you dismiss a man because he did not possess the requisite skill, then it may be unreasonable to do so if there is other work available for him—so it is wise in the letter to indicate that such work could not be provided. And in all such cases (*as in the ones now following*) *I advise the maximum possible generosity in the periods of notice actually given—which, in my opinion, should* (*out of both kindness and for tactical reasons*) *exceed the minimum required in the circumstances.*

64 Lack of 'qualifications'

Dear Mr Redd,

Unfortunately, due to the introduction of the new machinery/equipment, you are no longer qualified to carry out your duties. We have offered you the opportunity to undergo a training course, at our expense, so as to equip you to do your work in the new circumstances, but you have declined to undergo such training.

In the circumstances, please treat this letter as notice to terminate your contract of employment as at the ______. By giving you ______ weeks notice—instead of the ______ weeks, as required by your contract of employment—we hope that this will enable you to obtain other work, for which you remain qualified. And we thank you for your co-operation during the time that you have been with us.

Yours sincerely,

NOTE:

(1) *Lack of 'qualifications' may be a good reason for 'fair' dismissal—normally with notice. 'Qualifications' are defined as meaning 'any degree, diploma or other academic, technical or professional qualification relevant to the position which the employee held'.*

(2) *In industries in which there are frequent technological changes—and even in offices or businesses where computers are introduced—this ground of dismissal is fairly common. In my view, it is unlikely that a Tribunal would regard lack of qualifications as forming a reasonable ground for dismissal unless the employee has (where possible) been given the opportunity of acquiring the qualifications he needs. The longer his service with the company, the more important it becomes to allow him to obtain the necessary training—or at least, in the letter of dismissal, to indicate why such training was not undergone.*

65 'Capability' and 'qualifications' combined

Dear Mr Black,

As discussed with you, when you called on me this morning, I regret very much that your health, combined with your lack of technical qualification, have forced us to terminate your services. In the circumstances, please treat this letter as notice, terminating on ______.

Yours sincerely,

NOTE:

(1) *If there has been an oral discussion, then by all means refer to it. It shows that you have at least taken the trouble to see the employee—and this sort of opening may be used in all similar circumstances.*

(2) *If you have more than one reason for the dismissal, say so. If you come before a Tribunal and wish to add reasons which were not set out in your original letter, you may find your case disbelieved.*

66 Lack of 'aptitude'

Dear Mr Pink,

I am sorry that you have proved unable to cope with the tasks allocated to you. I hope that you will be successful in finding other work elsewhere, more in your line. As I told you this morning, the company will not require your services after the ______ of this month.

Yours sincerely,

NOTE:
You do not need to go into details—but if there are specific, vital tasks with which your employee could not cope, then you may wish to say so in your letter.

67 'Physical or mental quality'

Dear Harry,

We had all hoped that you would manage to cope with your job—but this has proved impossible. So I must give you notice terminating your employment on ______. If you would like to discuss this or any other matter with me, please do not hesitate to call on me in my office.

Yours sincerely,

NOTE:
It is sometimes kind to say little—and most Tribunals will accept this as a reason for putting little into a letter. You may not wish to tell an employee that he is 'getting beyond it'—or that some physical or mental incapacity prevents him from doing his work properly. Still less may you wish to put this into writing. But in those circumstances I strongly advise you to keep a note on your file, attached to the letter. This could be merely a memo, for yourself—or those who succeed you. It could be a note addressed to your superior. Thus:

68 Note of reasons, to superior

Dear Bill,

I enclose herewith a copy of a letter which I have today handed to Harry Smith. The unfortunate chap is still suffering from ______. He simply cannot do his job properly. Indeed, his lack of concentration is proving a danger to other employees. But I have thought it best not to say too much in his letter. I do not want to upset him—he is a good man.

I hope that you will also approve of my having given him a good deal longer notice than is strictly required.

Yours sincerely,

NOTE:
Be sure to keep a copy of all letters, notes and memoranda. Careful filing now can save both money and worry at a later stage. Documents win cases.

69 Misconduct

Dear Mr Blue,

I have now had to warn you on at least ______ occasions, of your carelessness. This not only causes danger to yourself but also to fellow employees. In the circumstances, I feel that I have no alternative other than to terminate your employment forthwith. I enclose herewith your pay in lieu of notice—although I think it right to point out that having regard to the persistent and habitual nature of your misconduct, I take the view that the company would have been entitled to dismiss you summarily. However, it is appreciated that there are mitigating circumstances in your case, and we do in particular know that you have not been in good health. So, without prejudice to the company's rights, I am pleased to be able to enclose a cheque herewith in the sum of £______, details of which are contained in the attached slip. You will appreciate that this also includes your accrued holiday pay as at the date when your notice terminates.

Yours sincerely,

NOTE:
(1) *It is vital to appreciate that where you give notice or pay in lieu, in circumstances in which you would have been entitled to dismiss summarily, this should be stated in your letter—for your own protection.*

(2) *By all means give details of the misconduct, at greater length, if you wish. The letters which now follow briefly indicate the sort of minor misconduct which would have led, before the Act, to dismissal with notice—and which you must now hope would be sufficiently 'habitual' or 'persistent' to enable you to satisfy a Tribunal, if necessary, that it was 'fair'.*

Section 24 (b) says that one reason which may warrant 'fair' dismissal 'relates to the conduct of the employee'. This will not mean just any 'misconduct'—we are all capable of having an occasional 'off day'—and any employee may be guilty of a momentary slip or an occasional misdemeanour. As you will see (in Chapter 9), to warrant 'summary dismissal'—with neither notice nor pay in lieu—misconduct must be sufficiently serious as to amount to a 'repudiation by the employee of his contract of service'. I think that a Tribunal is likely to regard a reason 'relating to the conduct of the employee' as warranting dismissal with notice, when it is somewhat less serious than that which warrants summary dismissal—but not much less. You must prepare your letter of dismissal accordingly.

70 Poor timekeeping

Dear Mr White,

I have now warned you on at least six occasions that your failure to arrive at work on time was disrupting our production. I have also told you that if this continued, I would have to give you your notice. I must now do so. Your employment with the company will terminate on ______.

I would only add that we do fully appreciate your difficulties, as you live so far from the plant. It is for this reason that we have been exceptionally patient in your case.

Yours sincerely,

71 Alternative—extended lunches

Dear Miss Jones,

Despite frequent warnings, you have seen fit to return late from lunch—culminating this week with your being over one hour late, on three days. In the circumstances, I enclose herewith your pay in lieu of notice. We shall no longer be requiring your services.

Yours sincerely,

NOTE:

(1) *Warnings may not of themselves be enough to warrant dismissal. But if you have warned, then say so.*

(2) *Compensation for 'unfair dismissal' is only available to compensate ex-employees for financial loss suffered. If your secretary finds other work during the period of notice represented by her pay in lieu—or, of course, by such period of notice as you see fit to give her—then*

she will no more get compensation than she would otherwise obtain damages for summary dismissal.

72 Redundancy

Dear Martin,

As we indicated to you some time ago, it has become inevitable that your department must be closed. You will therefore be dismissed and made redundant as from ______. I enclose herewith a calculation of the redundancy pay to which you will become entitled.

We all greatly regret this end to our long and happy association—and I wish you good luck in the future.

Yours sincerely,

NOTE:

(1) *An employee cannot get both redundancy pay and compensation for unfair dismissal. Where there is a choice between the two, the following situations arise:*

1 *50 per cent of any redundancy payment comes from the Revenue.*
2 *The Department of Employment will doubtless be doubly careful to ensure that the cases where there is really an 'unfair dismissal', the redundancy fund does not get milked. And 'redundancy' must not be used as an excuse to sack unwanted employees.*
3 *Compensation for unfair dismissal may be as much as £4,160—from the company's account. Redundancy pay will probably be much less—and only 50 per cent of it from the company.*
4 *Sometimes even 50 per cent may be higher than the compensation for unfair dismissal. Where an employee is 'dismissed as redundant', he gets his redundancy money even if he obtains another (and better) job the next day—assuming, that is, that he has been employed for the minimum two year period and complies with the other necessary qualifications. An employee who is dismissed—however unfairly—will only be compensated for his actual loss. If he loses nothing, he gets no compensation. So do help your ex-employee to get other work, where you properly can.*

So consider carefully, in each case where redundancy is a possibility. Is it genuine? If so, then

1 *Whether—applying the above principals—you would like to prove redundancy, if you could.*
2 *If so, then how you could best set out the reasons for the redundancy, in your letter of dismissal.*

73 Illegality

Dear John,

I am very sorry that we have been unable to obtain the necessary clearance for you—and in view of the top secret work which we are now carrying out, I regret that I have no alternative other than to forthwith give you your severance pay, equivalent to the period of notice prescribed in your contract of service. The company cheque herewith also includes accrued holiday money. Details as to the manner in which the sum is arrived at are attached hereto.

Please return the company's car to our transport depot at ______, not later than ______, being the date when your notice would otherwise have expired.

I would like to add my personal regrets—but you will appreciate that this is a matter entirely beyond my control, or, indeed, that of the company. Were you to continue to work in the position which you have held, there would be a contravention on the part of the company of a restriction imposed by the Industrial Relations Act.

Yours sincerely,

NOTE:

(1) *Dismissal will normally be fair if 'the employee could not continue to work in the position which he held without contravention (either on his part or on that of his employer) of a duty or restriction imposed by or under an enactment' [Section 24 (2) (d)].*

(2) *Apart from security problems, this ground will probably apply most often where you employ foreigners, whose work permits expire.*

(3) *You should, of course, consider whether you would not have other work in your concern, suitable for the employee in question, and in which his employment would not be 'in contravention of a duty or restriction' imposed on you. You will still have to prove that—'in accordance with equity and the substantial merits of the case'—you acted reasonably in dismissing the employee [Section 24 (6)].*

74 Denial that dismissal is because employee intends to join union

Dear Mr Rogers,

Thank you for your letter. It is not correct that you were dismissed because of your intention to join the ______ Union. The reasons for your dismissal are set out in my letter to you of the ———. Any employee of this company is fully entitled to join or not to join a union, as he sees fit, in accordance with Section 5 of the Industrial Relations Act. Your dismissal was completely irrespective of your intentions regarding union membership.

Yours sincerely,

NOTE:

(1) *'For the purposes of this Act, the dismissal of an employee by an employer shall be regarded as having been unfair if for the reason for it (or, if more than one, the principal reason) was that the employee had exercised, or had indicated his intention to exercise, any of the rights conferred on the employee by Section 5 (1) of this Act'.*

Section 5 (1) is dealt with in full in Chapter 13—briefly, it confers on a worker the right to join or not to join a registered trade union. And if an agency shop agreement is in force, he may still refuse to join, if he pays the 'appropriate contribution' to the union (or one of the unions) concerned—or, in the case of 'conscientious objection', if he pays the money to a charity.

(2) *If an employee alleges that his dismissal is because of his intention to exercise his Section 5 rights, and you deny that allegation, say so—in writing, and in the clearest terms.*

75 Redundancy—other employees kept on

Dear Mr Brown,

I agree that there is a redundancy situation in the plant and that other employees who could have been dismissed have in fact been kept on. But this does not mean that you were dismissed 'unfairly', within the meaning of Section 24 (5) of the Act. I suggest that you consult your union representative.

As you know, we are doing our best to cope with a substantial decrease in trade, and I am only sorry that it has been necessary to dismiss a portion of our work force. I do hope that you will succeed in obtaining other work, at an early date.

Yours sincerely,

NOTE:

(1) *Section 24 (5) applies in cases where 'the reason or principal reason for the dismissal of the employee was that he was redundant'. If it is shown that 'the circumstances constituting the redundancy applied equally to one or more other employees in the same undertaking who held positions similar to that held by the dismissed employee, and*

who have not been dismissed by the employer', then the dismissal may be regarded as 'unfair', even if the man was redundant. That can apply only in one of two circumstances:

'1 *If the reason (or, if more than one, the principal reason) for which the dismissed employee was selected for dismissal was that he had exercised, or had indicated his intention to exercise, any of the rights conferred on him by Section 5 (1) of the Act'; or*

'2 *If the employee was selected for dismissal in contravention of a customary arrangement or agreed procedure relating to redundancy and there were no special reasons justifying a departure from that arrangement or procedure in his case'.*

(2) *If your employee is dismissed as redundant after only a comparatively brief period (perhaps two and a half years)—so that his redundancy pay is comparatively small—and is then out of work for (perhaps) two years—he would obviously be very much better off if he could obtain compensation for unfair dismissal.*

(3) *But even if other employees are kept on when he is not, the man dismissed as redundant will only get compensation for unfair dismissal if he can show that he was dismissed because he (probably unlike the others) sought to exercise his rights under Section 5 to join a union—or that the procedure rules were ignored, because the employers (for whatever reason) wanted to get rid of him, before his colleagues.*

(4) *If you consider that an employee ought to be independently advised, refer him to his union. (If he is not a union member suggest that he consult his solicitor.) It is not clever to attempt to keep your employees at a disadvantage. Conversely, a Tribunal would certainly commend your action in referring an employee to someone who can give him independent advice, if you feel that he is insufficiently informed —or misinformed—as to his rights under the Act.*

76 Re-engagement after lock-out

Dear Mr Jones,

Work at our ______ plant will be resumed as from next Monday, the ______. I hereby offer you re-engagement as from that date. Please do not trouble to reply to this letter. Your presence at work on Monday will be taken to constitute acceptance of this offer.

Yours sincerely,

NOTE:

(1) *'The dismissal of an employee by way of a lock-out . . . shall not be regarded as unfair if the employee is offered re-engagement as from the date of resumption of work'* [*Section 25 (1)*].

(2) *If an employee is dismissed 'by way of a lock-out' and not offered re-engagement, then an employer may still manage to show that the dismissal was 'fair', if he proves an appropriate 'substantial reason', plus 'reasonableness'. I repeat: 'Reason' and 'reasonableness' are necessary in all 'unfair dismissal' cases—and the burden of proving both rests upon the employer.*

77 Dismissal for taking part in a strike

Dear Mr Brown,

I deny that your dismissal was unfair. You were, as you know, dismissed because you took part in the recent strike—and all other employees who did so were dismissed in the same way as yourself. None of them have been offered re-engagement. In the circumstances, your claim is rejected.

Yours sincerely,

NOTE:

(1) *If a man is dismissed when, on the date of dismissal, he was taking part 'in a strike or any irregular industrial action short of a strike', then his dismissal may be 'unfair'. (But note that 'an irregular industrial action short of a strike' does not include a genuine 'work to rule'—which, by definition, is not 'irregular' because the man is merely complying with the letter of the rules.)*

Dismissal for taking part in the strike will be 'unfair' if 'one or more employees of the same employer . . . who also took part in that action, were not dismissed for taking part in it' or if 'one or more such employees, who were dismissed for taking part in it, were offered re-engagement on the termination of the industrial action and the claimant was not offered such re-engagement'.

(2) *But note: 'Re-engagement' is not the same as 'reinstatement'. I think it likely that the employee who is 're-engaged' starts a new period of employment, from the viewpoint of both the Redundancy Payments Act and this Act. Similar observations apply to a Tribunal's recommendation that a dismissed employee be 're-engaged' (see Chapter 12).*

Chapter 9

'Fair' Dismissal—Without Notice

AS WE HAVE seen (in Chapter 8), one of the reasons which an employer may give for 'fair dismissal' relates to the employee's 'conduct'. But equally, the employer has to show that 'in the circumstances he acted reasonably' in treating the conduct (or, to be precise, the misconduct) concerned as 'a sufficient reason for dismissing the employee'. The Industrial Tribunal will look at all the facts, and determine the case 'in accordance with equity and the substantial merits of the case' (to use the ringing legal phrase—which means nothing more or less than this: The Tribunal will consider whether the dismissal was or was not 'fair').

Anyway, a Tribunal will certainly look at any relevant documents—and in particular, any letters passing between the parties—when deciding whether dismissal for misconduct was 'fair'. And once you have put your complaints into writing, they are there forever. So mind your pen. If it slips, it may cost the company up to £4,160—and you your job.

In any event, if you are dealing with a borderline case—the sort of employee whom you would previously have given his notice or pay in lieu, rather than sacking summarily—do please consult the company solicitor (or at least, your own superior, if you have one) before making the decision.

If in doubt, I still recommend that you give notice or pay in lieu—but strictly on the basis that you do so 'without prejudice' to your rights.

78 Severance pay—'without prejudice'

Dear Mr Green,

Your conduct has been such as to render you liable to summary dismissal. I would refer in particular to the following matters:—

(1) . . .
(2) . . .

(3) . . .

However, without prejudice to the foregoing, I am instructed to send you herewith your normal pay in lieu of notice, in the sum of £——, plus your accrued holiday money. Details as to how this sum is arrived at are contained in the salary slip herewith. I would emphasise that, in my view, you are not entitled to this payment; your conduct has been a great disappointment to us all; but, having regard to your long association with the company, it is the wish of the Board that you should leave with the minimum ill-feeling, and the maximum time to find other work.

Yours sincerely,

NOTE:

You are not bound to set out the misconduct relied upon (see Chapter 8). But it is wise to do so—and no less wise because you are giving pay in lieu of notice. Indeed, I think it even more important. If you were simply to pay a man his money, he could say (with some justification): 'My misconduct could not have been that serious or you would not have paid me'—and hence, it was 'unreasonable' (and thus 'unfair') for you to dismiss him as you did. If you have made it quite plain that you consider that you were entitled to regard his conduct as sufficiently serious to amount to a repudiation of the entire agreement, you are on safe ground.

79 Dismissal for theft

Dear Miss White,

You admitted to me, in the presence of Mr Jones, that you have been stealing from the company. You may consider yourself extremely lucky that we have decided not to institute a prosecution against you or to report the matter to the police. However, we cannot possibly go back on our decision that you be dismissed instantly. I therefore enclose herewith your wages earned to date; your accrued holiday pay, and your cards.

Yours sincerely,

NOTE:

(1) *One single act of really serious misconduct will warrant summary dismissal—and, I think, would be regarded by any Tribunal as sufficient to make a dismissal 'fair'. It would be quite wrong for an employer to be forced to retain in his service an employee who steals.*

(2) *Even though the dismissal was oral, it is wise to confirm it in*

writing—including confirmation of the fact that the employee confessed to a criminal offence in the presence of another person.

(3) *The old crime of 'misprision of felony' having been abolished, you are no longer bound to inform the police if you catch a culprit. Provided only that you do not demand more back from that culprit than he has taken from you, the law will not interfere if you decide to let the matter rest.*

80 Dismissal for bribery

Dear Mr Young,

As discussed with you this morning, having discovered that you have accepted a bribe in your capacity as a buyer for this company, you are hereby dismissed from its service. All money due to you from the company will be forwarded as soon as possible. Will you please return the company car to the transport depot, forthwith.

Yours faithfully,

NOTE:

A present is one thing; a bribe—given and received 'corruptly'—is quite another. A Tribunal would be unlikely to say that the corrupt giver or recipient of a bribe had been 'unfairly dismissed'.

81 Dismissal—for giving away your secrets

Dear Mr Smith,

As a research chemist, you knew perfectly well that the information with which you were dealing was entirely confidential. You say fit to enable ______ Limited, to obtain copies of numerous formulae, thus causing our company to suffer grave and permanent loss. You are hereby dismissed from its service. All money due to you will be remitted by post.

Yours faithfully,

NOTE:

Industrial espionage is not, as such, an offence against the criminal law. But just as it warrants 'summary dismissal', so it is likely to suffice to justify 'fair dismissal'.

82 Persistent minor acts—of negligence, discourtesy, disobedience, poor timekeeping . . .

Dear Miss Yellow,

I have had to warn you on numerous occasions concerning your conduct. Complaints have included the following:

(1) . . .
(2) . . .
(3) . . .

In the circumstances, I have decided that the company can no longer put up with this sort of misconduct and you are therefore dismissed summarily and forthwith. I enclose herewith your cards, together with all money to which you are properly entitled.

Yours truly,

NOTE:

(1) *Many minor acts of misbehaviour add up to a major breach of contract—and hence a 'repudiation'. When you accept that repudiation, you are not yourself destroying the contract of service—the employee has done that for you.*

(2) *Once the misconduct was sufficiently serious to destroy the contract, I think it most unlikely that any Tribunal would say that you should have kept it alive, to be 'fair'.*

(3) *Conversely, you must still put up with minor misconduct—and, indeed, the Act ensures that employers should think very carefully, before they dismiss.*

To protect the employee's position, even a settlement will only be binding on the employee if it has the blessing of a conciliation officer. As we shall soon see.

Chapter 10

Apprenticeships—and Other Fixed-Term Contracts

IN SOME CASES, employees on fixed-term contracts are automatically excluded from the operation of the Act. In others (including apprenticeship agreements made before the Act came into force), the rules apply—unless the employee contracts out of his rights.

When dealing with executives, you may reasonably expect that they will know what they are doing if they decide that—in return for a fixed term contract of two years of more—they agree that when the contract comes to an end, they will not claim compensation for unfair dismissal if you do not offer them further employment. But apprentices are unlikely to understand. To avoid unfair treatment (by whatever definition)—and inevitable unpleasantness and dispute—I advise that apprentices whose contracts are to be varied should be referred to their unions. Or at least their parents should be told what is happening.

When it comes to making new contracts of apprenticeship, though, employers who understand Section 30 of the Act will undoubtedly include a term, freeing them from liability if they do not wish to keep the former apprentice on their books. And—especially in those industries where the journeyman principle applies—apprentices may be only too willing to go to work for employers other than those with whom they served their term.

Section 30 says that Section 22 of the Act (which gives a right, in appropriate cases, to damages for 'unfair dismissal') does *not* apply:—

'(a) To dismissal from employment under a contract for a fixed term of two years or more, where the contract was made before the commencement of this Act and is *not* a contract of apprenticeship, and the dismissal consists only of the expiry of that term without its being renewed.'

In ordinary English, the section says that where there is a contract for a fixed term of two years or more which was made before this part of the Act came into force (28 February 1972), the employee will not get damages for 'unfair dismissal', if his employers decline to grant him a further period of employment when the fixed term expires. But this exception does not apply to apprentices. They are protected, whenever their contracts of apprenticeship were made—whether before or after the Act.

Section 22 also does *not* apply:—

> '(b) To dismissal from employment under a contract for a fixed term of two years or more, where the dismissal consists only of the expiry of that term without its being renewed, if before the term so expires the employee has agreed in writing to exclude any claim in respect of rights under that Section in relation to that contract.'

So an employee—whether he is a callow apprentice or a mighty executive—will be entitled to further employment, when his fixed term comes to an end—or may have a good claim for compensation for 'unfair dismissal'—unless he contracts out of his protection. And where, as in most cases, contracting out is not permitted, this is an extremely important exception.

83 Fixed-term contract made before commencement of the Act—expires

Dear Mr Green,

I would remind you that your contract of service expires on ______. I regret that the company will not be able to offer you further employment. However, you may be sure that if we can be of any assistance to you in your efforts to obtain alternative work, we shall be only too pleased.

Thank you for your efforts on the company's behalf, during the past ______ years. Were it not for the current recession in the trade/our reorganisation scheme/the change in the nature of our business, we would certainly have been pleased to keep you with us

Yours sincerely,

84 Executive—fixed-term contracts made after Act commences

Dear Mr Bright,

Your contract of services expires on the ______. I regret that I am unable to offer you further employment with the company, for the following reasons:

Yours sincerely,

NOTE:
The employee whose term is not renewed or extended is in precisely the same position as any other employee, dismissed with or without notice. He may claim compensation for 'unfair dismissal'. You should therefore consult Chapter 6, and adapt the appropriate letter to your needs.

85 To apprentice—who has not contracted out

Dear Smith,

I write to remind you that you will have completed your apprenticeship with this company on the ______. As you know, the journeyman principle applies in this industry and it is not normal for apprentices to stay on with the company with whom they served their apprenticeship. In the circumstances, it is presumed that you would wish to seek employment elsewhere. Please let us know if you have any difficulty in finding a place and we will do whatever we can to help you. [We would also be prepared to consider an application for further employment with the company.]

Yours sincerely,

NOTE:

(1) *This letter leaves the door open for the apprentice to ask for further employment. If you receive such a request, you turn it down at your risk.*

(2) *On the other hand, if there is other work available for the apprentice, he (like any other employee) must 'mitigate his loss'. He must keep it to the minimum (see Chapter 6, for the principles on which compensation is assessed). So if other work is available, even if the dismissal is technically 'unfair', it will not give the apprentice any rights against you.*

86 Offer of fixed-term to executive—provided he contracts out

Dear Mr Plant,

We appreciate that you would like a lengthy period of security, if you are to pull up your roots and to join the company in London. In the circumstances, we are prepared to offer you a two-year contract. But you will appreciate that any continuation of your service when that contract concludes would have to depend upon the current facts which cannot be anticipated at the present time. In the circumstances, will you please confirm that you are prepared to accept an engagement on the above basis, and in particular that you are agreeable that Section 22 of the Industrial Relations Act, 1971, which would otherwise give you a right to claim unfair dismissal if we did not renew your term, shall be excluded.

As to the remaining terms of your employment, these are as contained in my previous letter dated ______.

I look forward to hearing from you.

Yours sincerely,

87 Informing an executive of Section 30 exclusion

Dear Mr Brown,

I am in receipt of your letter claiming compensation for unfair dismissal. It is appreciated that under the Industrial Relations Act, not to renew a fixed term contract would generally amount to a 'dismissal'—but in your case, as your contract was made before the commencement of the Act, Section 30 (a) applies. In the circumstances, I understand that you are not in any circumstances able to claim compensation under Section 22 of the Act. However, you might like to confirm that with your own solicitor.

I wish to add that, in any event and without prejudice to the above, it is denied that your dismissal was 'unfair'. As you well know, circumstances were such that it was not possible to re-engage you.

Yours sincerely,

88 Offer of apprenticeship—term excluding Section 22 rights to be included

Dear White,

I have considered your application for an apprenticeship with our company, and am pleased to say that we are prepared to take you on. I enclose herewith the proposed indenture. Would you please read it through very carefully; discuss it with your parents—and if there are any points you would like to raise with me, please do so. If you and your parents are satisfied with the proposed arrangement, would you and they please sign, where indicated.

As you know, this agreement will last for four/five years—and we all hope that you will have a very happy time here. If at the end of your apprenticeship we have a place for you and you are satisfied in every way with your work, we shall be pleased to offer you further engagement. However, the contract contains our usual term [as referred to in Section 30 (b) of the Industrial Relations Act, 1971] excluding any claim in respect of rights which you might otherwise have, if it is decided not to offer you further employment after your apprenticeship terminates.

I look forward to hearing from you.

Yours sincerely,

NOTE:

(1) *In my view, it is sensible to draw the attention of the proposed apprentice to the 'contracting out' clause. It is also fair. But the law would not require you to do so. If he signs the agreement, all is well.*

(2) *There is no law which says that parents must guarantee that the apprentice will carry out his duties—and, in practice, it is very rare that such an agreement is enforced against a parent. However, it is as well to let the parents feel that they do owe you some responsibility—they may well, in the circumstances, feel it right to induce their son to carry out his obligations under his agreement. But that, of course, is entirely a matter for you.*

89 Variation of executive's contract, subject to contracting out clause

Dear Mr Black,

I am pleased to inform you that we are prepared to increase your pay from £______, to £______ per week/month. However, this is conditional upon your agreeing that in the (I hope, unlikely) event of the company not wishing to renew your contract after the present term expires, your contract will contain a clause excluding any claim in respect of rights under Section 22 of the *Industrial Relations Act, 1971*, that is for compensation for 'unfair dismissal'.

I look forward to hearing from you.

Yours sincerely,

NOTE:

(1) *You cannot force any employee, of whatever status, to vary his contract of service so as to include a contracting out clause—which, after all, is against his interest.*

(2) *On the other hand, any contract of service may be varied, by agreement between the parties. You are fully entitled to invite your employee to accept a variation.*

(3) *Employees are far more likely to agree willingly to variations, if you put the matter to them at the time when you are increasing their*

pay. Hence the above letter. You may even want to serve written particulars, complying with the Industrial Relations Act (see Chapter 19)—and to revamp many of the employee's terms (including, for example, restraint clauses). By all means do so in one go—which includes contracting out.

If the employee is not prepared to contract out, then you certainly have no right to dismiss him for that reason, however early or late in his 'fixed term' it may be.

If you *are asked to contract out of a possible right to compensation for unfair dismissal, think carefully before you agree. You are giving up a potentially extremely important claim. And before you invite your employees to do so, you may well wish to refer them to their unions—or at least to include the arrangement as part of a package deal which, when looked at as a whole, will be to the employee's considerable benefit.*

90 Invitation to apprentice to vary

Dear Black,

I enclose herewith a form prepared in accordance with Section 30 (b) of the *Industrial Relations Act, 1971.* Its effect would be to exclude any claim in respect of 'unfair dismissal', if the company were to decide not to offer you employment at the end of your apprenticeship.

You will appreciate that in our industry it is not normal for employment to be offered to apprentices, in the same firm in which they served their apprenticeship. But by all means consider the matter carefully and with your parents.

Please let me know your decision.

With best wishes,

Yours sincerely,

NOTE:

(1) *In practice, it is the borderline apprentice—whom one would not really want to keep on after his term—that will provide the worry. And he is very unlikely to agree in writing to give up his rights—particularly if he is well advised. Still, the Act says that he may do so, if he wishes—and there is no harm in asking.*

(2) *But it is important, I think, to tell the apprentice to consult (at least) his parents, before he signs.*

(3) *If the apprentice is an 'infant'—under the age of 18—then the contracting out agreement may be a nullity.*

91 If no 'consideration', apprentice's agreement not to invoke Act is a nullity

Dear Jones,

As discussed with you, I enclose herewith a form for your consideration. It excludes potential liability on the part of the Company in the event of your not being re-employed, when your current apprenticeship comes to an end. On the basis of your signing this, we are prepared to increase your pay, as follows:

. . . .

We would add that, in practice, we think it highly unlikely that your agreement to the above would affect your position. If you serve out your term in a satisfactory way, we shall do our best to find a position for you. (Alternatively: As you know, it is not customary in this Company for us to employ ex-apprentices—we think it much better for them to start their career with another Company.)

With best wishes,

Yours sincerely,

92 Effort to obtain another job for apprentice

Dear Mr Brown,

George Smith has been apprenticed to this Company for ______ years, and on the ______, his apprenticeship will come to an end. In this Company, we feel strongly that it is best for apprentices to move on and not to serve their entire time with the same outfit—and we understand that you agree. In the circumstances, I was wondering whether you would have a vacancy for George? He is an excellent young man—and I am sure would be useful to your Company.

For our own part, if there are apprentices whom you would recommend, we would be pleased to consider taking them on to our books, when their training by and with you terminates.

With best wishes,

Yours sincerely,

NOTE:

If you dismiss your apprentice by not re-employing him, then the dismissal is (as we have seen) likely to be 'unfair'. But if he immediately obtains other work, he will have suffered no loss as a result of his dismissal and will therefore obtain no compensation under the Act. Hence it is now not only an act of kindness to your apprentice but also of good sense and even necessity from the company's viewpoint, to use your best endeavours to obtain other work for him. There are, however, occasions when you have to provide an unhappy reference, this:

93 Poor reference for ex-apprentice

Dear Mr Green,

I note that George Smith has applied for a post with your Company, upon the termination of his apprenticeship with us. You ask for a reference.

If you would care to speak to me by telephone, I will be pleased to discuss Mr Smith with you.

Yours sincerely,

NOTE:

(1) *You are not bound to give a reference. If you give a bad one, then it is defamatory. Put it into writing, and it is a libel. Say it orally and it is a slander.*

(2) *Slanders are much more difficult to prove than libels—hence if you feel bound to give a poor reference, it is normally best to do so by telephone. But in practice you have little to worry about because the honest givers of even poor references are protected by law. Apart from 'justification'—the defence that the statement made was substantially true—you would plead that the occasion was one of 'qualified privilege'. You were under a moral obligation to give the reference and the recipient had a direct interest in its contents.*

(3) *Note that no 'disclaimer' will assist you. But in case you give a good reference to the wrong person—and this does happen—particularly in large outfits—you should in fact disclaim—as in the next letter.*

94 Satisfactory reference for ex-apprentice

Dear Mr Green,

I am pleased to say that George Smith has proved a very good apprentice. He is reliable and hard working and I am sure would be a credit to your company.

While we are pleased to supply references for ex-employees, this is done on the basis that no legal responsibility therefor is accepted by the Company or any of the employees.

With best wishes,

Yours sincerely,

NOTE:
There are many other angles to references, which cannot be dealt with fully in this book. They will be found in my companion book, Letters of the Law.

Chapter 11

Conciliation Officers—Contracting Out—and Settling Claims for Compensation

IN GENERAL, neither employers nor employees can contract out of the Act. Section 161 says that, with certain exceptions:—

'*Any* provision in an agreement (whether a contract of employment or not) shall be *void*, insofar as it purports—

(a) to exclude or limit the operation of any enactment contained in this Act; or

(b) to preclude any person from presenting a complaint to or bringing of proceedings before the Industrial Court or an Industrial Tribunal under this Act.'

Certain forms of contracting out we shall consider later:

1 The agency shop agreement or approved closed shop agreement, under which an employee is no longer left with his complete right not to join a trade union, if he wishes to remain apart; (Chapter 14)
2 provisions in a collective agreement, indicating that the parties do not intend that agreement to have legally binding effect'. (Chapter 15)

In addition, we have already considered contracting out under Section 30 (b), i.e. agreements by apprentices and other employees with fixed terms of two years or more, under which they agree to exclude their potential right to claim compensation for unfair dismissal, if they are not offered new contracts.

But the more important form of contracting out, when it comes to unfair dismissal, is provided by Section 161 (2), which says that the rule against contracting out shall not apply to any agreement to refrain from presenting a complaint nor from proceeding with a complaint in respect of unfair dismissal, 'where a conciliation officer has taken action' in accordance with his powers.

It follows that if you wish an employee to be bound by his agreement not to proceed with a complaint against your company, claiming compensation for unfair dismissal, you must bring in the conciliation officer. Here are drafts of the sort of letters you will need.

95 Letter to employee, suggesting compromise

Dear Mr Jones,

Without prejudice

Without prejudice to the company's contention that you are not entitled to any compensation whatsoever in respect of your dismissal—which, as I pointed out in my letter of ——— was entirely 'fair' and reasonable in all the circumstances—I am instructed to offer you the sum of £100 in full and final settlement of your claim. As your claim, has in our view, nuisance value only, I regard this offer as generous. If you wish to accept it, please let me know and I will ask a conciliation officer to consider it and to sanction the compromise, in accordance with Section 161 (2) (d) and (e) of the Industrial Relations Act.

Yours faithfully,

NOTE:

(1) *The magic words 'without prejudice' protect you, in case no deal is done. Your letter will not find its way before the Tribunal.*

(2) *If your offer is accepted, then the situation changes dramatically. The correspondence ceases to be 'without prejudice'—and may be produced to the Tribunal by either side.*

96 After acceptance of compromise

Dear Mr White,

I was pleased to learn that you are willing to accept the sum of £100 in full settlement of your claim for compensation for alleged 'unfair dismissal'—this being on the basis, so far as the company is concerned, that your claim was without merit.

I am now asking a conciliation officer to sanction this arrangement.

Yours sincerely,

97 Unfair dismissal denied—then compromise suggested

Dear Miss Redd,

I acknowledge receipt of your letter of the ———. It is denied that you were unfairly dismissed, as alleged or at all. The reasons for your dismissal were fully set out in my letter to you of the ———. In the circumstances, your claim for compensation for unfair dismissal is rejected. You must take such steps as you may be advised in that regard.

Without prejudice

While not conceding for a moment that your claim has any merit, I am instructed by the Board to offer you the sum of £100, in full and final settlement of your claim. If you wish to accept this offer—which will remain open for seven days only—kindly inform me. I will then ask the conciliation officer to approve of the arrangement.

Yours sincerely,

NOTE:

It is generally better to have two letters—one 'without prejudice' and one open. But they may be combined, as above, if desired.

98 Request to conciliation by employer and employee

Dear Sir,

I write on behalf of the company to request that you exercise your powers under Section 146 (2) (a) of the *Industrial Relations Act, 1971*, and endeavour to promote a settlement of the complaint which Mr James Jones of ______ has made against the company, in respect of alleged unfair dismissal.

I shall be pleased to hear from you,

Yours sincerely,

NOTE:

This precedent is for use where a complaint has been presented to a Tribunal.

99 Request to conciliation officer—by employer alone

Dear Sir,

Richard Jones

The above named has ceased to be employed by my company and alleges that he was unfairly dismissed. He has not yet brought a complaint under Section 106 of the Act. Will you kindly make your services available to the company and to Mr Jones, in an attempt to promote a settlement of the complaint.

I would appreciate a swift reply.

Yours faithfully,

NOTE:
This precedent may be used before a complaint has actually been made. Where a complaint has actually been presented, the conciliation officer may only investigate if he is requested to do so by the employee who presented the complaint and *by the employer against whom it was presented,* or *'if, in the absence of any such request, the conciliation officer considers that he could act . . . with a reasonable prospect of success, to endeavour to promote a settlement of the complaint without its being determined by an Industrial Tribunal'.*

In other words, once a complaint has actually been placed before the Court, the employer on his own cannot (in theory at least) bring in the conciliation officer. However, presumably the suggestion that the conciliation officer could act 'with the reasonable prospect of success' might be brought to his attention by an alert employer.

100 Application to conciliation officer to approve agreement

Dear Sir,

Richard Jones

The above-named employee notified my company of his intention to present a complaint for alleged 'unfair dismissal'. This man was in fact dismissed, with notice, due to his inability or unwillingness to do his job in a proper manner. It was therefore denied that the dismissal was in any way 'unfair'.

In any event, I am happy to say that the company has come to terms with Mr Jones, and has agreed to pay him the sum of £______, in full settlement of his alleged claim.

In the circumstances, I would be glad if you would exercise your powers to promote a settlement of the complaint. It is hoped that you will regard the above compromise as a fair one and that you will give it your approval, at your early convenience.

Yours faithfully,

NOTE:

(1) *The Act does not specifically say that the conciliation officer may be called in to approve settlements, as such—but this appears to me to be the likely inference of the Section, as drafted.*

(2) *The object, of course, is to protect the employee—who is unlikely to be as well advised in law as his employer. Indeed, unless he has the help of a union, he may well be completely unadvised. Hence the conciliation officer should be able to provide him with considerable protection, if the employer seeks to take advantage of his lack of legal*

knowledge or experience—or, indeed, of his inability to negotiate satisfactorily on his own behalf.

(3) *If the above interpretation of the role of the conciliation officer is correct, hundreds will be needed. So some experts think that their job will largely be limited to conciliation between union and employer. We shall see.*

Chapter 12

Compensation for Unfair Dismissal

SOME YEARS ago now, a Mr Addis was dismissed from his executive post by his employers, the Gramophone Company. He claimed damages for wrongful dismissal—he had received neither notice nor pay in lieu. He won his case—but his damages were limited to the remuneration which he should have received during his period of notice. He had earned no money during that period, and had been unable to 'mitigate his loss'.

Unfortunately, the case took some five years before it reached the House of Lords—which, incidentally, indicates one reason why many industrialists and trade unionists alike would rather settle matters without having to get in the toils of the law. Anyway, Mr Addis could not get other work—and had lost a great deal of money.

The House of Lords held that the unfortunately ex-executive could not be put in a better position if he were wrongfully dismissed than he would have been in, had he received his proper notice or pay in lieu. He got nothing for his loss of status.

Ever since, an executive's entire security lay in the length of notice which he was able to extract from his employers. Indeed, this applied to every employee—with the possible exception of apprentices, who (thanks to a recent Court of Appeal ruling) became entitled to damages if they were prevented from completing their apprenticeship and from obtaining their qualification.

All this has changed, thanks to the new rules on unfair dismissal—as set out in the previous chapters. Now the basis of compensation is laid down in Section 116 of the Act. The aggrieved party shall be paid 'such amount as the . . . Tribunal considers just and equitable in all the circumstances, having regard to the loss he has sustained, or in consequence of the matters to which the complaint relates, insofar as that loss was attributable to action taken by or on behalf of the party in default'. He is entitled to claim 'any expenses reasonably incurred by him in consequence of the matters to which the complaint relates', together with 'loss of any benefits which he might reasonably be expected to have had but for those matters'.

However, he is under the same duty 'to mitigate his loss' as applies in an ordinary breach of contract action. He cannot just sit back and do nothing—he must try to get other work.

Again, where a Tribunal finds that the complainant was guilty of conduct which 'caused or contributed to' his loss, his compensation will be reduced accordingly.

Above all, where there is a complaint for unfair dismissal, the Tribunal is given a substantial new power. If it considers that the complaint has been proved and that it would be practicable 'and in accordance with equity for the complainant to be re-engaged by the employer, or to be engaged by a successor of the employer or by an associate of the employer', then it 'shall make a recommendation to that effect, stating the terms on which it considers that it would be reasonable for the complainant to be so re-engaged or engaged'.

If a recommendation is made and is not complied with, then the Tribunal will consider why its recommendation was ignored. If it finds that the employers could and should have re-engaged the complainant, but failed to do so, then the damages will go up. Conversely, if the complainant is offered re-engagement but unreasonably turns it down, his compensation will fall.

In any event, Section 118 lays down maximum compensation payable—104 weeks pay or £4,160 (that is to say, 104 x £40), whichever is the less.

To round off this Part of the book, then, here are some draft letters affecting compensation.

101 Offer of re-engagement

Dear Mr Brown,

In accordance with the recommendation made by the Industrial Tribunal, I am pleased to offer you re-engagement by the company, in the capacity of ______ at a salary of £______, i.e. on terms recommended by the Tribunal.

Kindly let me know at your earliest convenience whether this offer is acceptable to you.

Yours sincerely,

102 Acceptance of re-engagement

Dear Mr Jones,

Thank you for your letter offering me re-engagement on the terms set out therein. Your offer is accepted and I shall be pleased to attend for work on ______.

Yours sincerely,

103 Refusal of re-engagement

Dear Mr Jones,

Thank you for your letter offering me re-engagement by your company. First, the terms set out are not those recommended by the Tribunal. They differ in the following respects:

(a) . . .
(b) . . .

[In any event, having regard to the thoroughly unpleasant manner in which I have been treated by ______, I do not feel that it would be possible for me to return to working in the same department/under the supervision of Mr ______. If you are able to offer some alternative arrangement, then I will of course be only too pleased to consider it. Meanwhile, you may be sure that I am continuing my efforts to obtain alternative employment and hence to mitigate the loss caused to me by your unfair dismissal.]

Yours sincerely,

NOTE:
It is vital in a letter of this sort to say why you are not prepared to accept the offer of re-engagement—particularly if you can show that the offer does not accord with the terms recommended by the Tribunal. It is also important to show that you are attempting to keep your loss to the minimum.

104 Denial that employee has mitigated loss

Dear Mr Pink,

I note your claim—which is disputed, in its entirety. In any event, my enquiries in the trade reveal that you have made no efforts to obtain alternative employment, and hence to mitigate your loss.

In my view, any loss which you may have suffered has been due not only to your own conduct while you were in the company's employment, but to your own inactivity thereafter. In the circumstances, any claim for compensation or damages will be contested.

Yours faithfully,

NOTE:
There remains a difference between a claim for damages for wrongful dismissal and for compensation for unfair dismissal. But presumably—as so much more money can be obtained in a claim for compensation—under the Act—claims for damages will disappear as such, becoming

incorporated into unfair dismissal proceedings before Industrial Tribunals.

105 Claim for compensation—with details of loss

Dear Mr Green,

Thank you for your letter, specifying alleged grounds for my dismissal. These I do not accept. I was unfairly dismissed. Even if (which I deny) I was guilty of the alleged failure to obey instructions, it was certainly not reasonable to treat such failure (which, I repeat, I deny) as sufficient grounds for terminating my employment. You appear to forget that I have been with the company for ______ years.

In the circumstances, unless I receive a substantial offer from you, I shall bring a claim before the Industrial Tribunal, to compensate me for the very considerable loss I have suffered. This comes within the following categories:

1 Loss of salary/wage—at £______ per week, and continuing.
2 Loss of the following fringe benefits:
  a subsidised meals;
  b use of company car;
  c health insurance;
  d share option scheme;
  e pension rights;
  f . . .

In addition, I have had to move to London. The costs involved have been as follows:

1 . . .
2 . . .

I have thought it best to place these facts on record, at the earliest possible opportunity. I shall be pleased to hear from you within the next seven days, failing which I shall place the matter in the hands of my solicitors.

This is indeed a very unhappy ending to a long and loyal period of service to the company.

Yours faithfully,

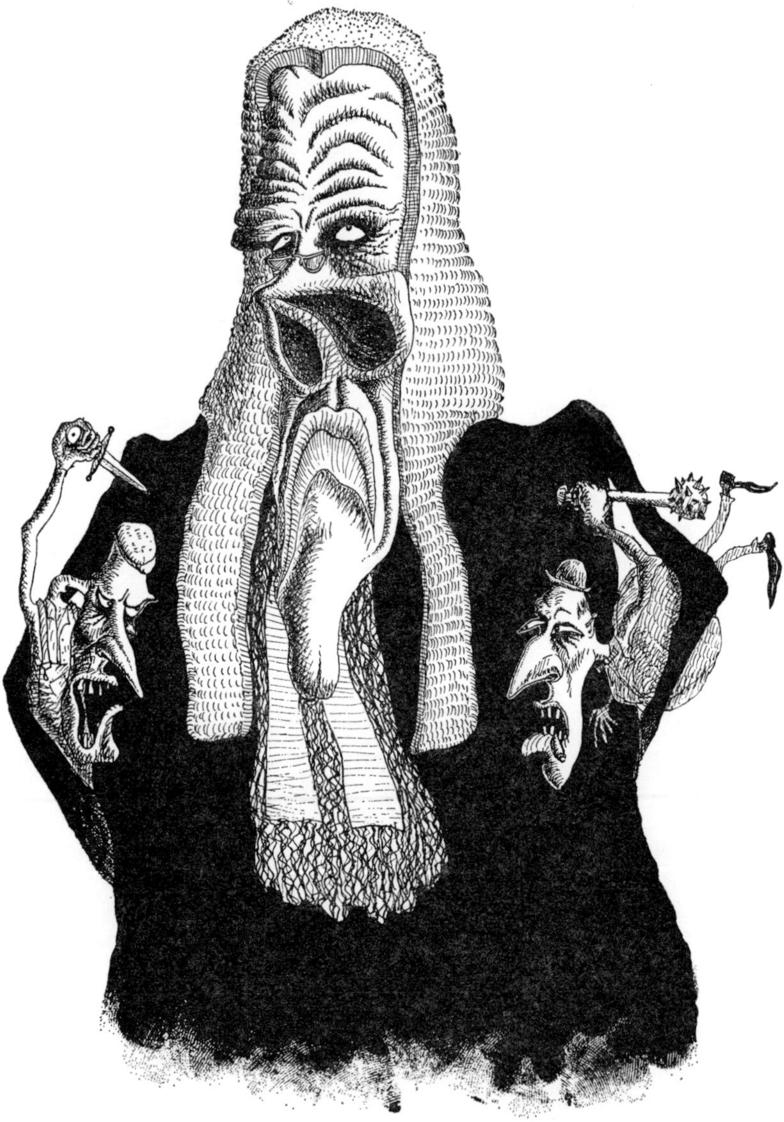

Part Three

Agency Shops, Bargaining Agreements and Workers' Rights

Chapter 13

A Worker's Rights

SECTION 5 of the Act gives every worker the right—as between himself and his employers—to be a member of such trade union as he may choose. Subject to agency shop agreements and approved closed shop agreements (actors and seamen in particular), he also has the right if he so desires 'to be a member of no trade union or other organisation of workers or to refuse to be a member of any particular trade union or other organisation of workers'.

Equally, once he is a member of a trade union, he has the right 'at any appropriate time, to take part in the activities of the trade union (including any activities as, or with a view to becoming, an official of the trade union) and the right to seek or accept appointment or election, and (if appointed or elected) to hold office, as such an official'.

Sections (a) and (b) affect employers directly; (c) you will probably prefer to leave to the unions to sort out for themselves—employers who get involved in the internal affairs of unions are liable to get their fingers burned.

Some of the letters you will need in connection with Section 5 are contained in Chapter 8, because the worker's rights in this connection have to be set out either in his contract of service or in the written particulars thereunder. Other letters now follow. Meanwhile, please note: whereas the words 'trade union' appear in the Act, they mean REGISTERED trade union. The rest are mere 'organisations of workers'.

106 Confirmation of right to join union

Dear Mr Jones,

I confirm that there is no objection whatsoever to your joining the Union of ——, insofar as the management are concerned. Indeed, such membership is welcomed by the company.

Yours sincerely,

107 To union representative or shop steward, confirming management co-operation

Dear Mr White,

I am happy to confirm that the management have no objection whatsoever to any employee joining your Union, if he so chooses. Indeed, union membership is welcomed by the company.

Yours sincerely,

108 Confirmation of right not to join union

Dear Mr Green,

Section 5 (1) (a) of the Industrial Relations Act provides that an employee has the right, if he so desires, not to join a trade union. Indeed, in the absence of an agency shop agreement or an approved closed shop agreement (neither of which apply to your employment) it is an unfair industrial practice for an employer to dismiss, penalise or otherwise discriminate against a worker because he exercises the right given to him under Section 5 (1) (b) of the Act.

In the circumstances, I confirm that no steps will be taken against you, by the management, as a result of your refusal to join the ______ Union.

On the other hand, I would not like it to be thought that the management is in any way encouraging you in the attitude which you have seen fit to take in this regard. I am sending a copy of this letter to Mr ______, who is shop convener/local area representative——of the Union concerned.

Yours sincerely,

109 Letter to union representative, enclosing above

Dear Mr Jackson,

I fully understand and appreciate your views concerning the refusal of Mr Green to join your Union. However, Section 5 (1) (b) of the Industrial Relations Act—combined with Section 5 (2) of the Act—which makes it an unfair industrial practice for us to 'dismiss, penalise or otherwise discriminate against a worker' because he refuses to join a union—ties our hands completely.

In the circumstances, I enclose herewith a copy of a letter which I have today sent to Mr Green.

It may be helpful, though, if we were to meet to discuss the present situation. By all means contact me, if you wish.

Yours sincerely,

NOTE:

(1) *By all means quote from the Act, verbatim, when it prevents you from complying with the wishes of a Union—or causes you to act contrary to the Union's interests. Section 5 of the Act is set out in full in the Appendix to this book. It is worth careful reading and thought.*

(2) *In the case of allegations of unfair dismissal (Section 22 of the Act—Part 1 of this book), complaints under Section 5 are dealt with by an Industrial Tribunal, and not by the Industrial Court. If you act in breach of Section 5, then your company may be brought before a Tribunal and it may be fined. You must consider carefully, e.g. in connection with attempts of unregistered trade unions to make closed shop arrangements with you (see Chapter 14), whether, on occasion, you may not prefer to risk being fined, to falling out with the union—and hence having your production halted. And problems of this sort may well arise in connection with Section 5. They should be considered in depth—with the company's legal advisers. Letters in this connection are probably best avoided.*

110 Protest by staff member, alleging interference with right to join union

Dear Mr Black,

I protest most strenuously at the efforts being made to prevent me from joining the ______ Union. In particular, since I have started my attempts to organise a Branch of the Union amongst the staff in this company, I have been discriminated against in the following ways:

(a) . . .
(b) . . .
(c) . . .

I would respectfully draw your attention to Section 5 (1) of the Industrial Relations Act—which gives every worker the right to join a trade union of his choice; and also to Section 5 (2), which makes it an unfair industrial practice for any employer, or for any person acting on behalf of an employer, to deter a worker from exercising any of these rights or to penalise or otherwise discriminate against him by reason of his exercising any such right.

Members of staff are also 'workers' in this context, and fully entitled to organise. I am sure, on reflection, that you will agree.

My colleague, Mr Jones, and I will be pleased to meet you, if you wish, to discuss the problems.

I shall be pleased to have your assurance that the company will no longer behave in the manner complained of.

Yours sincerely,

111 Threat by employee to take company to tribunal

Dear Mr White,

I regret that the discrimination against myself because of my wish to organise a Branch of the ——— Union in our office, continues unabated. Unless this matter is rectified forthwith, I regret that you will leave me with no alternative other than to lay a complaint against the company, before the Industrial Tribunal. I do hope that this will not prove necessary.

I reiterate my willingness to meet you, in order to discuss this dispute.

Yours sincerely,

112 Complaint by employees' representative of improper 'benefits' to non-joiners

Dear Mr Green,

The Company has seen fit to offer and to grant a bonus to those employees who have failed to exercise the right given to them by the Industrial Relations Act, to join the trade union of their choice—in this instance, the Union of ———. The Company has withheld the bonus from those of my workmates who, like myself, have failed to accept such improper pressure.

I am informed by my Union that the Company has thereby unlawfully discriminated against my colleagues and myself and is guilty of an unfair industrial practice.

In the circumstances, I trust that this matter will be given full consideration—and that we will receive the bonus without further delay. If the money is not forthcoming within the next fourteen days, then a complaint will be laid against the Company before the Industrial Tribunal. So far as I can see, the Company would have no defence.

I would only add that this sort of behaviour is, in my view, creating quite unnecessary ill will among your employees. If you would care to discuss this entire situation with the Union representatives, this could be arranged at very short notice. Please would you let me know?

Yours sincerely,

NOTE:

I hope that you will receive none of these letters—but if you do, I trust that you can put your hand on your heart and (honestly) make the following reply:

113 Denial of allegation of unfair discrimination

Dear Mr Green,

Thank you for your letter of the ——. The reason why you and your colleagues did not receive the bonuses is. . . .

In the circumstances, I deny that the Company has acted improperly in any way.

On the other hand, obviously we have no wish for any ill-will whatsoever and will be pleased to meet with your Union representative and yourself. Would you please contact me, to arrange a mutually convenient appointment?

Yours sincerely,

114 Employee informed of agency shop agreement —hence he must join union

Dear Mr Brown,

Thank you for your letter, stating that you do not wish to join the —— Union. You are, in general, correct in saying that the Industrial Relations Act gives an employee the right to refuse to join a union. But this right is modified where there is an agency shop agreement in force—as is the case, in the office/shop/workshop in respect of your category of work.

In the circumstances, I regret that if you wish to stay with the company, you have the choice between joining the —— Union, or making an appropriate contribution to its funds. Only if you can prove a 'conscientious objection' to joining will you be able to pay an equivalent sum to a charity. I gather however that your objection is not one based on grounds of conscience.

Please let me know your decision within the course of the next few days.

Yours sincerely,

NOTE:

(1) *Section 6 deals with modification of a worker's rights as a result of an agency shop agreement—details of such agreements in Chapter 14.*

(2) *Section 8 regulates 'appropriate contributions to trade union in lieu of membership'. Hence:*

115 Employee opts 'to make appropriate contributions' instead of joining union

Dear Mr White,

I do not wish to join the ______ Union, or any other. I am willing, however, for the appropriate contribution to be deducted from my salary/wages. I appreciate that you have no alternative other than to insist upon my so doing, because of the agency shop agreement which is at present in force. I pay, nonetheless, under protest.

Yours sincerely,

NOTE:

(1) *The employee is, after all, going to get the benefit of pay and conditions negotiated by the union concerned.*

(2) *If the employee wishes to make payments to the union, without getting other potential benefits from it (widows and orphans funds, etc.), that is a matter for him. There is no accounting for tastes and prejudices, is there?*

116 Acknowledgement of employee's letter, indicating wish to make 'appropriate contributions'

Dear Mr Smith,

I note that you are unwilling to join the ______ Union and have decided that you wish to make the appropriate contribution to its funds without having the normal benefits of membership. That, of course, is entirely a matter for you. I note, too, that you wish us to deduct this contribution from your pay, and I will arrange for this to be done.

Yours sincerely,

NOTE:

Section 6 (3) gives you the right to make these deductions from pay—and once you have agreed to a request to deduct, if you fail to comply with that request this will not be regarded as a failure on the part of the worker to pay his contribution.

117 Proposal by worker to union to pay contribution to charity

Dear Mr Jones,

I have great respect for both you and your organisation, but as a Jehovah's Witness, it is contrary to my religious beliefs either to belong to or to pay money to a trade union. I do hope you will understand.

In the circumstances, I propose that I should pay the appropriate contribution to the following charity:

. . . .

I trust that the above suggestion will commend itself to you.

Yours sincerely,

NOTE:

(1) *Section 8 defines 'appropriate contribution', as used throughout this Chapter. In general, it means ordinary contributions and initial membership fee, payable by a trade union member. The man who does not join will have to lay out the same amount of money, either payable to the union or to a charity.*

(2) *To pay to a charity, you have to show objection 'on grounds of conscience'. This would certainly cover religious scruples. But it remains to be interpreted in other senses. The fact that you do not like trade unions will not be a 'ground of conscience'. And even though it is denied that politicians lack a conscience, 'grounds of conscience' are most unlikely to be equated in any case with 'political belief'.*

118 Trade union agrees to charity

Dear Mr White,

Thank you for your letter. Your reasons are understood, although deeply regretted. The charity you name will be satisfactory to us.

Yours sincerely,

119 Trade union objects to charity

Dear Mr Black,

Thank you for your letter. We do not accept that your reason for refusing to join our ranks or to pay us the appropriate contribution is a proper 'ground of conscience'—nor do we, in any event, approve of the charity which you have chosen. If you persist in your refusal to associate—either personally or financially—with us, we shall feel bound to refer the matter to the Tribunal in accordance with Section 10 of the Industrial Relations Act.

Yours sincerely,

NOTE:

(1) *A Tribunal may decide whether objections are 'genuinely objections on grounds of conscience'; to which charity contributions should be payable; or what contributions to a charity would be 'equivalent to appropriate contributions to the trade union'.*

(2) *It is unlikely that many workers will take refuge in Section 9 contributions to charity. If you run into this situation, you should do everything possible to achieve a peaceful and quiet solution—and not to have work disrupted because one man insists upon what unions regard as the utterly unfair right to benefit from all the unions' work and activities and not even to contribute to its funds.*

120 To union—alleging improper pressure

Dear Mr Jones,

May I remind you of Section 33 of the Industrial Relations Act? It is an unfair industrial practice for any trade union or other organisation of workers or any official of a trade union or of such an organisation to apply pressure by threats to strike—or threats of irregular industrial action short of a strike—in order to induce employers not to grant to any employee his rights under Section 5 of the Act.

In the circumstances, may I suggest that the sooner that you and I meet, the better? Would you care to join me for lunch, perhaps tomorrow at 1 pm?

Yours sincerely,

PS: I am sending this letter by hand.

NOTE:

Please see Section 33 in Appendix. But note: 'irregular industrial action short of a strike' [*defined by Section 33* (*4*)] *does not include a work to rule—which, by definition, is not 'irregular'. It cannot be improper for an employee to say that he will strictly abide by the rules which you have been prepared to lay down for him or to agree with him.*

Chapter 14

Agency Shop Agreements

THE DEFINITION of 'agency shop agreement' contained in Section 11 of the Act, may be broken down as follows:

1 It is an agreement. As we shall see, if the parties do not voluntarily agree, then they may have agreement thrust upon them.

2 It is an agreement 'between one or more employers and one or more trade unions or between an employers' association and one or more trade unions'. The word 'trade union' is throughout the Act used to mean trade unions registered under the Act. And an agency shop agreement, then, may be made with one or more employers —probably associated companies. More important, such an agreement may be made with more than one union. If all the unions with whom you work are registered and they can agree on sharing the benefits of an agency shop—then the problem is greatly simplified.

3 The agreement will be 'in respect of workers of one or more descriptions specified in the agreement'. The word 'shop' is not defined in the Act. So an 'agency shop' may include the people in one office, shop, plant, workshop, transport depot, etc.—or in many. It may also include workers of a particular description—office workers, engineers, maintenance engineers, bricklayers or what have you—who work for the employers concerned, possibly in various places.*

4 The agreement is one which requires that the terms and conditions of employment of each such worker 'shall include a condition that every such worker must either—

(a) be or become a member of that trade union or one of those trade unions, as the case may be, *or*
(b) agree to pay appropriate contributions to that trade union, or (as the case may be) to one of those trade unions, in lieu of membership or (where permitted to do so . . .) agree to pay equivalent contributions to a charity.'

* Compare definition of 'bargaining unit' (page 103). Can *you* see any practical difference between the two?

But clearly, most of the negotiating for agency shop agreements will—and must—be carried on orally. But there are still many letters which will have to be written. Some precedents are in the previous chapters—others now follow.

If negotiations break down, then application will be made to the Industrial Court, doubtless on the appropriate forms. An employer may only make such application if one or more of the trade unions wish there to be an agency shop agreement and he (the employer) is unwilling to agree. But if there is a question in dispute in respect of which application has been or could be made to the Court for the establishment of sole bargaining rights (Chapter 15), the Commission on Industrial Relations—to whom the Court will refer the matter—may recommend that the application 'shall not proceed further'.

If there is no such dispute over bargaining rights, then the Commission will set up the appropriate ballot. If two-thirds of those who vote—or a simple majority of those eligible to vote—are in favour of the agreement concerned, it will be made—whether the employer likes it or not.

So however fiercely you may object to having one or more agency shop agreements in your business, you may have this forced upon you—and if you wish your business to be properly organised, it is as well to negotiate—and, if necessary, to give way—gracefully. Industrial peace is worth paying for.

121 From union—requesting agency shop agreement

Dear Mr Brown,

On behalf of the Union of ———, I am asked to suggest that an agency shop agreement be established in respect of the following workers, namely . . .

Alternatively, you may prefer an agreement in respect of all workers of the following descriptions, namely . . .

I look forward to hearing from you.

Yours sincerely,

122 Reply to union's request for agency shop agreement—consenting

Dear Mr Green,

On behalf of my Company, I am instructed to agree to your proposal for an agency shop agreement, in respect of workers of the following descriptions, namely . . .

The agreement is to be made with the following Unions: . . .

I look forward to seeing you, together with the appropriate representatives of the other Unions concerned, in order that details may be arranged.

Yours sincerely,

123 Reply to union request for agency shop agreement—refusing

Dear Mr Black,

I regret that I am unable to consent to the suggestion contained in your letter, concerning an agency shop agreement, for the workers in ——. This would cut right across our plans for a bargaining unit incorporating the entire plant. Please would you call on me so that we could discuss possible alternatives?

Yours sincerely,

NOTE:
If there is a dispute—or a potential dispute—over bargaining rights, it is vital to insert this in a letter of refusal. In the absence of such a dispute, it seems likely that the Commission will be unable to avoid setting up a ballot.

124 A similar refusal—craft unions ignored

Dear Mr George,

The Company is unable to accept your suggestion concerning an agency shop agreement to be made with your Union only. It is felt that this would create grave difficulties with the Union of —— and the Union of ——.

In the circumstances, I was wondering whether you would care to meet me, together with the representatives of the other Unions, to see what could be sorted out?

With best wishes,

Yours sincerely,

NOTE:
(1) *Disputes between employers and employees are difficult to sort out—but where you have inter-union rivalry, these may create even greater havoc for industry. Demarcation disputes have, in the past, caused great trouble. And unions fear that the introduction of the agency shop agreement procedures will bring about highly dangerous inter-union rivalries. All employers must take care not only to create*

(or to keep) goodwill between themselves and their employees and employees' representatives, but also between various trade unions and organisations of workers.

(2) *For the above purpose, cool, calm, courteous and friendly correspondence is essential.*

125 Refusal of agreement—offer of reference to court

Dear Mr Smith,

I am sorry, but I cannot agree to your suggestion for an agency shop agreement applying only to the workers to whom you refer. When our entire plant is unionised—and both of us will be pleased to see this happen—it is essential that we do not have agency shop agreements cutting across various sections of our work force. Either we must have agreements which apply to the physical places within which people work—each of which at present has a shop steward. Or we must define workers by their job functions, so that we do not get duplication of agreements.

I appreciate that duplication is not disastrous, provided that all the unions in the plant are parties to the various agency shop agreements. But I am sure that you will agree that the simpler we can keep the arrangements, the better—particularly so as to facilitate sensible bargaining arrangements.

I suggest that we meet and discuss all this, as soon as possible. Please would you contact me?

Yours sincerely,

NOTE:

This letter sums up some of the difficulties faced by industrial and commercial managers of men, when putting the Act into effect. Adapt the letter to your own circumstances and it covers most of the genuine problems among those who are happy to work with trade unions—and to have post-entry closed shops—provided that the arrangement is one which may prove workable in practice.

126 Refusal of pre-entry closed shop—but suggesting agency shop

Dear Mr Jones,

I fear that the arrangement you suggest would amount to a pre-entry closed shop, which is rendered illegal by Section 7 of the

Industrial Relations Act. We cannot agree with you that we will only take on people who are already members of your Union.

On the other hand, we are quite prepared to discuss with you the possibility of establishing one or more agency shop agreements within our plant. This would certainly be best done by a meeting between us. Would you kindly telephone to arrange a convenient time with Mr White (who is on Extension ______)?

Yours sincerely,

NOTE:

(1) *Section 7 make pre-entry closed shop agreements void. There are exceptions in Section 17 and 18—and in the First Schedule. These, it is anticipated, will apply mainly to members of the National Union of Seamen, of Equity and of the Musicians' Union.*

(2) *Although a union will still be able to refuse membership to someone whom you wish to employ, where an agency shop agreement is in force, it shall not 'by way of any arbitrary or unreasonable discrimination' exclude such person. Section 65 (guiding principles for organisations of workers) applies—and may cause nasty disputes.*

127 Allegation of pressure to anticipate result of ballot

Dear Mr White,

Section 16 of the Industrial Relations Act makes it an unfair industrial practice for a trade union to threaten to strike in order to attempt to induce an employer to enter into an agency shop agreement in respect of the workers of any description after an application relating to workers of that description has been made under Section 11 of this Act.

Such an application has been made—as has the threat of industrial action.

I know that neither of us wants to get embroiled with the law, so by all means let us meet and see whether we can reach some agreement. I am available to you at any time.

Yours sincerely,

NOTE:

Section 16 provides a series of 'unfair industrial practices', which may be committed by employers or employees alike. It is included in Appendix 1.

128 Suggestion for discontinuation of agency shop agreement

Dear Mr Jones,

I understand that you have in your possession a document signed by one-fifth of the people covered by the agency shop agreement at present in operation in respect of workers in the ——/ of the following description, namely ——. I appreciate that in such circumstances application may be made to the Industrial Court for a discontinuance—but before you take this step, I would like to discuss with you various alternatives.

Yours sincerely,

NOTE:

(1) *If the original agency shop agreement was made pursuant to a ballot held after an application to the Court, there is a two-year period within which no further application can be made. Otherwise, there is no time limit.*

(2) *There is no reason why an agency shop agreement should not be cancelled or varied, by the consent of the parties. Thus:*

129 Suggested variation

Dear Mr Williams,

Do you not think that the present agency shop agreement would work better—for yourselves as well as the Company—if it were extended to the following workers . . . ? Please let me know.

Yours sincerely,

130 Suggested reconstruction of system

Dear Mr Williams,

Do you and your colleagues think that perhaps the present agency shop arrangements are causing some disruption in your own organisations, as well as in ours? If so, would you care to meet with my colleagues and myself, to discuss whether we could not come to a more satisfactory arrangement? I am particularly anxious that if we are going to do this, it should be accomplished at the same time as a reconsideration of the bargaining unit—which might also benefit from careful reconsideration.

With my best wishes,

Yours sincerely,

Chapter 15

Bargaining Arrangements

THE ACT in theory changes the entire structure of bargaining arrangements. These will now be organised according to 'bargaining units'.

A 'bargaining unit' (says Section 44) means 'those employees or descriptions of employees of an employer or of two or more associated employers, in relation to whom collective bargaining, in respect of such matters as are not dealt with under more extensive bargaining arrangements, is, or could appropriately be, carried on by an organisation of workers or a joint negotiating panel, or partly by an organisation of workers and partly by a joint negotiating panel'.

That monstrous sentence means, in brief, that a *bargaining unit can comprise any category of employees in relation to whom collective bargaining can appropriately be carried on.**

Once you have a bargaining unit, you will want a 'sole bargaining agent'. This means 'the organisation of workers or joint negotiating panel having negotiating rights in respect of that unit to the exclusion of all other organisations of workers and joint negotiating panels, except in respect of matters which are dealt with under more extensive bargaining arrangements'.

Note, first, that while an unregistered trade union cannot make an agency shop agreement, it may become a 'sole bargaining agent'. It may also form part of a 'joint negotiating panel'—'a body consisting of representatives of two or more organisations of workers which is established for purposes of collective bargaining and is authorised by or on behalf of those organisations to enter into collective agreements on their behalf.'

You must now apply your mind (if you have not already done so) to establishing a bargaining unit for your business—or, perhaps, a series of such units. These will have to dovetail into 'agency shops', where appropriate.

Whether you would prefer an enormous bargaining unit with a sole bargaining agent consisting probably of a joint negotiating panel—or whether you would prefer to leave your smaller units with

* Compare meaning of 'shop' (page 97), which comes to practically the same.

their own bargaining arrangements—is entirely a matter for you.

In any event, here are drafts of some of the letters which you may need to write.

131 Notice to other executive of meeting to discuss bargaining arrangements

Dear Roger,

I am writing to you and to all other Board members/executives/personnel managers/works managers in connection with the bargaining arrangements which we should put into operation in the Company.

In my opinion, it is now essential that we establish proper 'bargaining units'—and, if possible, agree with the organisations of workers and the unions within our works upon the formation of a joint negotiating panel, to be recognised as sole bargaining agent.

I am asking the Company Solicitor to be in the Board Room from 10 am onwards on ______. Would you please join us? Please let me know.

Yours sincerely,

132 Suggestion to union

Dear Mr Green,

The Board has given very careful consideration to your suggestion that each factory within the organisation should operate as a separate bargaining unit. But we think that this would create a very unwieldy situation and on the whole we would much prefer to agree to a sole bargaining agency being granted to all the unions concerned in respect of the entire organisation.

Please would you give this matter your consideration—and if you would like to discuss the situation with us, then we shall be delighted to arrange the appropriate meeting.

Yours sincerely,

133 Notification of intention to apply to Industrial Court for recognition of sole bargaining agent

Dear Mr Tree,

As we cannot reach any agreement upon the recognition of a sole bargaining agent, I am instructed by the Board to inform you that the Company intends to apply to the Industrial Court under Section 45 of the Industrial Relations Act, for reference to the

Commission on Industrial Relations, for consideration as to the nature of the bargaining unit which should be recognised and as to the sole bargaining agency most appropriate in our circumstances.

We still hope that we can achieve results by agreement—and would be happy to meet with you again, for reconsideration of this entire matter. I will be very grateful if you will let me know within the next seven days.

With best wishes,

Yours sincerely,

NOTE:
The above application may be made by an employer or one or more trade unions—or an application may be made jointly, thus:

134 Agreement to joint application to Court

Dear Mr Johnson,

I am pleased to confirm that you agree to our suggestion that the matter of the most suitable bargaining unit and sole bargaining agent for our Company should be submitted to the Industrial Court, for reference to the Commission on Industrial Relations. I shall now take the appropriate steps to that end.

Yours sincerely,

NOTE:
In the initial stages, I think it highly unlikely that any union will agree to the Court or the Commission having jurisdiction where this can be avoided. However, the situation may change.

135 Withdrawal of reference

Dear Mr Black,

I confirm that as agreement has now been reached concerning sole bargaining rights within our organisation, I have withdrawn the reference to the Industrial Court and hence to the Commission on Industrial Relations. I do hope that the new arrangements will work out to the mutual benefit of all.

Yours sincerely,

NOTE:
(1) *Like civil actions—but unlike criminal prosecutions—applications to the Court may be withdrawn. At any time before the Commission has actually reported to the Court, a reference may be withdrawn 'on the grounds that a satisfactory and lasting settlement of the questions in issue has already been reached'.*

(2) *It is the Government's earnest hope that, in practice, comparatively few applications or complaints will actually reach the Court or the Commission—or, for that matter, the Industrial Tribunal. They had better be right, or the entire system is, in my view, likely to collapse.*

(3) *Detailed provisions as to application and withdrawal of application are contained in Sections 45 to 53.*

136 Suggested withdrawal of recognition of sole bargaining agent

Dear Mr Brown,

I think you will agree that the arrangements whereby the Union of ______ and the Union of ______ formed a joint negotiating panel which was recognised as a sole bargaining agent for our factory has not worked out very well. In particular, we have had grave difficulties with the Union of ______ and the Union of ______, who have felt very much left out of things. In the circumstances, the management proposes that we reconsider this matter—and invites you to consider the setting up of a joint negotiating panel which would include the other Unions concerned. Please let me know your views.

Yours sincerely,

NOTE:

(1) *Here you tread on dangerous ground—but there are occasions when the management cannot avoid getting involved in inter-union rivalries.*

(2) *There are many reasons why recognition might be withdrawn—this letter can be adapted in numerous ways.*

(3) *If necessary, application may be made to the Court for withdrawal of a sole bargaining agency, on the ground that 'the organisation of workers or joint negotiating panel does not adequately represent the employees comprised in that bargaining unit, or does not adequately represent a particular section of it to which the applicant belongs' [Section 51 (1)].*

(4) *The Court will only entertain an application where at least one-fifth of the employees comprised in the bargaining unit 'has signified in writing their concurrence to the application'—and if there is a previously made Order of the Court setting up a sole bargaining agency, this can only be overruled after two years of operation.*

Chapter 16

Emergency Procedures—'Cooling-Off Periods' and Secret Strike Ballots

IT WAS THE (maximum 60 days) 'cooling-off period' and the compulsory strike ballot that caused many industrialists to welcome the Industrial Relations Act. They thought that these new procedures would place a considerable restraint on actual or potential strikers—and at least force them to consider their step and, where no majority was available, to call off the battle. What they did not realise is that the Act only allow these procedures to operate in case of real emergency.

Unions have always contended that these procedures would probably lead to the American situation—fewer strikes, but longer ones. And who wants to strike and to see his pay evaporating, when there is any reasonable hope of some sensible settlement?

Anyway, Part VIII of the Act is actually headed 'Emergency Procedures', so that no one may be in doubt. To prevent the power being used other than in emergencies, the Act provides for '*cooling-off periods*' as follows:

1 The procedure can only be initiated by the Secretary of State for Employment. So if you want to invoke the procedure, you must convince the Secretary of State that he should make application to the Court.

2 The Secretary of State may only apply to the Court for an Order if he is satisfied as to three circumstances:

'(a) That, in contemplation or furtherance of an industrial dispute, industrial action, consisting of a strike, any irregular industrial action short of a strike, or a lock out, has begun or is likely to begin.'

This is unlikely to be particularly difficult in practice.

(b) This condition is dealt with separately under Section 138 (2). The Secretary of State must be satisfied 'that the industrial action in question has caused or (as the case may be) would cause, an interruption in the supply of goods or in the provision of services of such a nature, or on such a scale, as to be likely—

(i) to be gravely injurious to the national economy, to imperil national security, or to create a serious risk of public disorder,

or (ii) to endanger the lives of a substantial number of persons, or expose a substantial number of persons to serious risk of disease or personal injury.'

The conditions in (b) will apply to disputes in the docks or post offices, to strikes by electricity workers or seamen—but hardly to the ordinary business.

If there has already been a long process of haggling; if negotiations fail; if conciliation or arbitration are not on the cards—well, the Secretary of State may refuse to act. Now for—

'(c) That, having regard to all the circumstances of the industrial dispute, it will be conducive to a settlement of it by negotiation, conciliation or arbitration if the industrial action were discontinued or deferred'.

To extend the possibility of a *secret strike ballot* beyond that of a 'cooling-off period' and to make such ballots rather more available, Section 141 adds another, alternative condition:

'That the effects of the industrial action in question of a particular industry are, or are likely to be, such as to be seriously injurious to the livelihood of a substantial number of workers employed in that industry'. Naturally, for a ballot, there must also be 'reasons for doubting whether the workers who are taking part or are expected to take part in the strike or other industrial action are or would be taking part in it in accordance with their wishes, and whether they have had an adequate opportunity of indicating their wishes in this respect'.

So the strike ballot may be available where (for example) a small number of drivers are holding up delivery of motor cars and are about to close down the works as a result—or, for that matter, where people producing windscreen wipers or other accessories strike, and are liable as a result to close down the entire industry and throw hundreds of thousands of fellow workers out of their jobs.

Now suppose that you have satisfied the Secretary of State that you are entitled to invoke the emergency procedures—and to do that, you will probably have adopted one of the precedents in this Chapter. He in his turn will apply to the Court—and if (but only if) the Court is 'satisfied on the evidence that there are sufficient grounds for believing' that the various conditions have been fulfilled, it will make the appropriate Order—and the emergency procedures will roll into operation.

138 To the Minister asking for a cooling-off period

Dear Sir,

I write to you on the instructions of the Board of the above company. Unfortunately, production is about to cease, as a result of a strike which has been called by the Union of ——. In our view, were the strike action to be postponed, the matters complained of by the men, could be dealt with, if not directly through negotiation, then by conciliation or arbitration.

If our works were to cease production, the entire —— industry would come to a halt within weeks, with dire effect to the national economy. In the circumstances, we would be pleased if you would make urgent arrangements for your representatives to visit this works, so that you may be advised as to the necessity for a cooling-off period of the full maximum 60 days. Your urgent attention to this letter would be much appreciated. It is being sent to you by hand.

Yours faithfully,

139 Lives in danger

Dear Sir,

If the strike which is, as you know, now imminent were to take place, there would be considerable danger to lives because of . . .

In the circumstances, it is earnestly hoped that you will make the appropriate application to the Industrial Court, without further delay.

Yours faithfully,

140 Reply to refusal by Secretary of State

Dear Sir,

We are deeply distressed and disappointed by your refusal to invoke the procedures open to you under Section 138 of the Industrial Relations Act, and to apply for a cooling-off period in connection with the threatened strike at our —— works. We presume that you realise that if this strike proceeds, there will be a severe risk of personal injury, for the following reasons:

(a) . . .
(b) . . .
(c) . . .

We would ask you to give urgent reconsideration to your decision.

Yours faithfully,

141 Thanks to Minister

Personal and Confidential

Dear Mr ——,

I am writing on behalf of our Board to thank you for the swift action which you have taken in connection with the dispute at our above works. I shall now use every endeavour to ensure that the cooling-off period which the Court has ordered will be put to good effect. We should also like to express our appreciation for the efforts of Mr —— and Mr ——, representatives of your Department, in this matter.

Yours sincerely,

142 To union—after order for 'cooling-off period'

Dear Mr Jones,

We fully appreciate that the present 'cooling-off period' was ordered contrary to the wishes of your Union—and we respect the reasons for your attitude. However, faced with the situation that now exists, we earnestly hope that advantage can be taken of the present breathing space, so that a settlement of the present dispute may be hammered out. It really would be a tragedy if (as is, we fully appreciate, a possibility) the effect of the cooling-off period were to harden attitudes on both sides and to extend the dispute even further, when the 60 days have expired.

In the circumstances, I am pleased to invite your colleagues and yourself for a further meeting at our Boardroom, tomorrow morning at 9.15. I do hope that this will be a convenient time for you. If not, do please suggest some alternative time, or if you cannot manage tomorrow some alternative date. I have certain suggestions to make which may resolve the present dispute.

Yours sincerely,

143 Response to union's rejection of 'cooling-off period'

Dear Mr Green,

While understanding the reasons why your Union has rejected the Court's Order for a cooling-off period—the Board regrets this attitude most deeply. It has no wish whatsoever for further ill-feeling, which would doubtless be aroused by any attempt to enforce the Order against the officers of the Union—an attempt which we feel is now inevitable.

In any event, we are still open to negotiations—and we understand from a press report of the statement of your Mr ______ that you would be prepared to negotiate further.

Obviously, this dispute must sooner or later come to an end—so we suggest that—whatever the situation regarding 'cooling-off', a further meeting would be worthwhile. And while the company adheres to its firm position in this matter, there are nevertheless some suggestions which we are prepared to make which might—given goodwill and flexibility on your side—resolve the matter at this stage.

I look forward to hearing from you.

Yours sincerely,

NOTE:

(1) *As in all other cases, employers must be prepared for a union's refusal to obey a Court's Order. In the case of strike ballots and cooling-off periods, the Secretary of State may have initiated the procedure—and this should, where necessary, be emphasised.*

(2) *Whether or not there is a cooling-off period, negotiations must continue. The hardening of attitudes only makes things worse.*

144 To union—have you considered a ballot?

Dear Mr Brown,

May we respectfully suggest that it would be better for a strike ballot to be held voluntarily, rather than on the initiative of the Minister?

You and I have co-operated happily for a very long time, and I am confident that you will not take this suggestion amiss. The present strike is jeopardising all our hopes for improved wages and conditions—which must, after all, be born out of productivity, which is at present in the process of being utterly ruined.

Or why do we not meet once again to see whether we can hammer out a reasonable settlement? I am available to you at any time.

With best wishes,

Yours sincerely,

145 To union leader—re wild-cat strike

Dear Mr Brown,

I know that you deplore the present situation as much as I do. Neither of us wishes the Court to get involved in it, either. Is there any way in which pressure can be brought upon Mr ——?

I appreciate that in general it is better for the management to keep in the background in these matters—but what about an informal chat between us two? Perhaps you would phone me.

Yours sincerely,

NOTE:

While union and management are often at loggerheads, there are many situations in which the leaders of both are on good terms—and where a settlement is desired by both. Meetings—informal or formal—are invariably preferable to court action.

Chapter 17

Registration

THE WHOLE of Part 4 of the Act is devoted to the registration of conduct of trade unions, employers' associations and other organisations. It starts with some controversial definitions:

'In this Act "trade union" means an organisation of workers which is for the time being registered as a trade union under this Act.' Hence no registration means no 'trade union'—and no agency shop agreement (see Chapter 14).

Still, an 'organisation of workers' exists—and that means 'an organisation (whether permanent or temporary) which either—

(a) consists wholly or mainly of workers of one or more descriptions and is an organisation whose principal objects include the regulation of relations between workers and that description or those descriptions and employers or organisations of workers, or
(b) a federation of workers' organisations.'

So you do not have to be a union to enter into a bargaining arrangement, nor, indeed, to be recognised as a 'sole bargaining agency' (Chapter 15).

Still, if a union wishes to retain rights equivalent to those previously possessed by registered unions under the (now repealed) Trade Disputes Acts, registration is essential. The question as to whether unions prefer their independence—and the possibility of destroying the total effect of this legislation—by deregistering or by not registering, is a matter of (to say the least) interest and concern.

Anyway, the Chief Registrar of Trade Unions has been appointed and the provisional register has been set up. And unions are bound to comply with the 'principles as to conduct' laid down by Section 65—such as the right of a member not to be excluded 'by way of any arbitrary or unreasonable discrimination' from taking part in the union's affairs.

Any organisation which is 'an independent organisation of workers, and has power, without the concurrence of any parent organisation, to alter its own rules and to control the application of its own property and funds' is eligible for registration as a trade union. This excludes tame, puppet, staff associations (and the like) financed by the company for its own purposes.

Similar principles apply to employers' organisations. These, too, may register.

Of course, it is the power of the Registrar to 'examine and approve' the rules, which causes much of the dismay in the union ranks. While every union which was previously registered under the Trade Union Acts or under the Friendly Society's Acts is automatically on the provincial register, and it may be transferred automatically by the Registrar to the permanent register, the Act provides that 'the Registrar *shall* cancel the entry of an organisation in the provisional register, or the registration of an organisation under this Act as a trade union or as an employers' association' in appropriate cases. These are:

'(a) if he was requested by the organisation to do so, or
(b) if the Registrar is satisfied that the organisation has ceased to exist.' (Section 92). Note the word '*shall*'. He is not given a discretion. Query: If the Union's own rules require it to be registered, is an application by that union for deregistration a valid 'request' within Section 22? I doubt it.

Anyway, here are the sort of draft letters which are likely to be needed, in connection with Part 4 of the Act.

146 Worker alleges 'unfair or unreasonable disciplinary action'

Dear Mr Brown,

I regard the fine imposed upon me by the Association as unfair and unreasonable—and hence in contravention of Section 65 (7) of the Industrial Relations Act. I must now ask the Committee to reconsider its decision, failing which I shall take such steps as I am advised in order to protect my position.

Yours sincerely,

147 Complaint of disciplinary action without 'full and fair hearing'

Dear Mr White,

I have been fined without being given the opportunity to defend myself. This is in direct contravention of Section 65 (8) of the

Industrial Relations Act. I shall not pay the fine until I have had the opportunity of stating my case.

Yours sincerely,

148 Application for cancellation

Dear Sir,

I am instructed by the executive of my union, the Union of ———, to request that you cancel the entry of my organisation in the provisional register/the registration of my union under the Industrial Relations Act as a trade union, in accordance with Section 92 of the Act.

Yours faithfully,

Chapter 18

The Code of Industrial Practice

SECTION 4 of the Act says that a failure 'on the part of any person to observe any provision of a Code of Practice . . . shall not in itself render him liable to any proceedings; but in any proceedings before the Industrial Court or an Industrial Tribunal under this Act—

(a) any such Code of Practice shall be admissible in evidence and
(b) any provision of such a Code of Practice which appears to the Court or Tribunal to be relevant to any question arising in the proceedings shall be taken into account by the Court or Tribunal in deciding that question.'

In other words, it is not a criminal offence or a civil offence or even an 'unfair industrial practice' to act in breach of the Code. But such a breach may be used in evidence against you.

Hence the following letters.

149 Allegation of breach of Code

Dear Mr White,

May I respectfully draw your attention to paragraph ——— of the Code of Industrial Practice. Your Union/Organisation/Company is clearly in breach of that provision, for the following reasons:

(a) . . .
(b) . . .
(c) . . .

I do hope that you will put matters right. If you would care to see me about this matter, then I shall be very glad to arrange a mutually convenient appointment.

Yours sincerely,

150 Denial of breach of Code

Dear Mr Pink,

I emphatically deny that we/the Company/the Union is in breach of the alleged or any provision of the Code of Industrial Practice, as alleged or at all.

The facts/the answers to the points you make are as follows:

(a) . . .
(b) . . .
(c) . . .

I hope that this makes the matter clear. If not, then I suggest that we should meet, as soon as possible. Would you please contact me?

Yours sincerely,

151 Please see the Code

Dear Mr White,

I enclose herewith a copy of the current Code of Industrial Practice—and would respectfully refer you to paragraph ______, at page ______. Does this not deal precisely with the situation which now faces us?

I fully appreciate that a breach of the Code does not of itself amount to 'an unfair industrial practice'—but it does, I suggest, indicate that the approach which your Union/Company/organisation of workers is at present taking is unhelpful/incorrect/improper. Naturally, we all hope that this is not a matter which will have to be sorted out by the Industrial Court/an Industrial Tribunal—but I am sure you appreciate that if matters do reach that unhappy pass, a breach of the Code will then be admissible in evidence.

With best wishes,

Yours sincerely,

152 To managing director—suggesting that he read the Code

Dear Bill,

I enclose herewith a copy of the Code of Industrial Practice. I note your criticisms of the manner in which I have handled the current situation—but if you would care to have a look at clause ——, you will find that I have done so in strict accordance with the provisions of the Code. I hope that this will set your mind at rest.

With best wishes,

Yours sincerely,

NOTE:

Many personnel managers and others directly concerned with control of staff consider that the Code is largely useless to them, because it contains so many elementary rules, which any self-respecting manager of men follows in any event. But it is sometimes suggested that if Members of the Board would read and digest the Code, they might learn a lot.

153 Invitation to chairman to read Code

Dear Sir Robert,

I have pleasure in enclosing herewith a copy of the Code of Industrial Practice. I doubt whether you will find this particularly stimulating reading—but on the other hand, if you would care to dip into it (with special reference to pages —— and ——), you may find that it throws a little light on the current unhappy situation/on the methods which we are using in connection with ——.

With my best wishes to you,

Yours sincerely,

154 Copy of Code sent to union leader/shop steward

Dear Mr Smith,

I have pleasure in enclosing herewith a copy of the current Code of Industrial Practice. If you would care to refer to clauses ——/pages —— and ——, I think you will find that we are in fact following the suggested system. However, I shall be only too pleased to discuss with you/your colleagues and yourself/your Union representatives the matters which are worrying you.

With best wishes,

Yours sincerely,

CLOSED SHOP

Part Four

Contracts of Employment, Conclusions and in Conclusion

Introduction

THERE ARE two sources of English law. First, there is Statute law—created by Parliament, in its contemporary wisdom (or lack thereof). Second, there is so-called 'Common Law'—that is, law created by judges. They are either interpreting statutes—and trying to throw light upon varying shades of Parliamentary darkness—or applying precedents, created by their predecessors in judgment.

The Industrial Relations Act, of course, is a massive statute—which will, after practically no gestation period whatsoever, give birth to a mass of Common Law interpretations. But it also has a vast effect on other, preceding statutes.

The whole of Trade Union law has been shaken until the Movement itself shouts with dismay. For instance, the various Trade Union Acts and Trade Disputes Acts are almost entirely repealed—and replaced with rules which often give equivalent protection to those Unions which see fit to register.

In this Part, though, we look at changes in the *Contracts of Employment Act, 1963*—a thoroughly useful statute, which not only laid down minimum periods of notice but also provided (in Section 4) that an employer must supply written particulars of the main terms of employment to every employee, within thirteen weeks of the commencement of that employment. Some of the minimum periods of notice have now been extended (page 39). And new written particulars must be given (Chapter 19).

I have included a number of letters of appointment—which, of course, can be adapted or used as written particulars under the Contracts of Employment Act, as now amended. These may, if desired, be supplemented by the letters in Chapter 1 of my *Letters of the Law*, which I have not repeated here.

NOTE:

Written particulars supplied before 28 February 1972 when this part of the Act came into effect, remain valid. But they must be supplemented by an additional note containing any of the new particulars not contained in the original document.

Chapter 19

Contracts of Employment

THE ONLY CONTRACTS which have to be made in or evidenced by writing if they are to be enforceable are those involving (in broad terms) the transfer of an interest in land, contracts of guarantee and some contracts of insurance. All others—including contracts of employment—are just as binding on the parties if made orally, as if every word were written down.

Still, it is wise to put any important contract into writing, so that the terms may if necessary be proved. In any event, by setting terms into clear writing, potential disputes are avoided. Naturally, if the writing is obscure, the danger of trouble may be increased. So lucidity is essential.

Among other objects, the *Contracts of Employment Act, 1963*, sought to ensure that employers supplied employees with all the major terms of their contracts. This rule has worked well in practice —but the new Act fills in four omissions. These deal with:

1 Holidays and holiday pay.
2 An employee's rights under Section 5 of the Industrial Relations Act—in general terms, to join or not to join a trade union of his choice.
3 Identifying the person who deals with grievances.
4 Grievance procedures.

These will now be dealt with in letters—or in notes. Remember that existing written particulars remain valid. If these already include all four of the new particulars, then you need serve no additional document on your employees. But if any of the four new items are not included in documents already served, you should let your employees have an additional note as soon as possible, setting out the missing items. You could, for instance, put a note with wages slips, reading:

In addition to the written particulars of your terms of employment, which you have already received, please note the following additional items, detailed for you as required by the Industrial Relations Act: . . .

155 Holidays and holiday pay—as amended

Dear Mr Brown,

To avoid misunderstanding, I am happy to confirm that employees such as yourself who have been with us for over ______ years are entitled to ______ weeks holiday in each calendar year—in addition, of course, to the usual public holidays. If your employment is terminated during the course of a year, then you will be entitled to accrued holiday pay on a pro rata basis—that is, the appropriate proportion having regard to the part of the year which you have actually been with us since the date of your last holiday.

With best wishes,

Yours sincerely,

NOTE:

(1) *Section 20 (1) of the Act provides that the following details must now be given concerning holiday entitlement:*

'Entitlement to holidays, including public holidays, and holiday pay (the particulars being sufficient to enable the employee's entitlement, including any entitlement to accrued holiday pay on the termination of employment, to be precisely calculated).'

(2) *The object of this study is mainly to avoid some of the arguments and disputes which have tended to arise in the past when employment has come to an end. The employee has maintained that he is entitled to a pro rata payment, in respect of that period of the year which he has actually worked; and the employer has sometimes maintained that accrued holiday entitlement only arose after a full year's service.*

(3) *The new rule does not make any change in the basic law—that an employee is only entitled to agreed holidays, plus public holidays—except for holidays required by Wages Council Orders, where applicable. So the following arrangement is still proper:*

156 No holidays until full year served

Dear Mr Roberts,

I am sorry, but as appears from the written particulars of your contract of employment which we supplied to you in accordance with Section 4 of the *Contracts of Employment Act, 1963*, as amended, you are only entitled to a holiday or to the equivalent accrued holiday pay, after the completion of a full year's service with the company. Equally, on the termination of your employment, there is no pro rata entitlement—only those who leave at the end of a full year's service are entitled to their holiday money.

I am sorry that I cannot be of help to you on this occasion.

Yours sincerely,

157 No accrued holiday pay where dismissal for misconduct*

Dear Mr Jones,

Thank you for your letter. You have in fact received everything to which you are entitled. I would refer you to the written particulars of your contract of employment, supplied to you in accordance with Section 4 of the *Contracts of Employment Act, 1963*, as amended. You will see therefrom that where the company dismisses an employee as a result of his misconduct, the employee forfeits any right which he would otherwise have to accrued holiday money. As you well know, you were dismissed for serious misconduct and we are not prepared to waive our normal rule on this occasion.

Yours sincerely,

158 Dismissal for misconduct—no accrued holiday pay—Wages Council order applies

Dear Mr Hawk,

Further to my letter of dismissal dated ——, I enclose herewith, as promised, your pay, earned as at the date when your employment terminated. Details of the manner in which that payment is arrived at are contained in the wages slip attached.

I note your request for accrued holiday pay. I would refer you to the —— Wages Council Order, which specifically provides that where an employee is dismissed for misconduct, he forfeits any right to accrued holiday pay. That, as you know, is a circumstance which unfortunately applies in your case.

Yours sincerely,

159 Right to join trade union—no agency shop†

Dear Mr Green,

I note your enquiry regarding membership of a trade union. Please note, first, that the *Industrial Relations Act, 1971*, specifically gives every employee the right to be a member of such registered trade union as he may choose. There is no equivalent right in respect of an unregistered union.

Equally, an employee has the right, if he so desires, to be a member of no trade union—registered or otherwise—or to refuse to

* See also Chapter 8.
† See also Chapter 13.

join any other 'organisation of workers'. This is subject to the existence of an agency shop agreement—there are none, at present, in this plant.

I do hope that this makes the situation clear. It may be helpful if I set out the new clause which it is intended to insert in the written particulars of each contract of employment, supplied to employees from now on in accordance with Section 4 of the *Contracts of Employment Act, 1963*, as amended by Section 20 (2) (a) of the *Industrial Relations Act, 1971*:

Under Section 5 of the *Industrial Relations Act, 1971*, you (together with all other employees) have the following rights:

(a) The right to be a member of such trade union as you may choose;

(b) The right, if you so desire, to be a member of no trade union or other organisation of workers or to refuse to be a member of any particular trade union or other organisation of workers;

(c) Where you are a member of a trade union, the right, at any appropriate time, to take part in the activities of the trade union (including any activities as, or with a view to becoming, an official of the trade union) and the right to seek or accept appointment or election, and (if appointed or elected) to hold office, as such an official.

No agency shop agreement or approved closed shop agreement applies in the case of your employment, so the above general principles affect your rights to trade union membership and activities.

With best wishes,

Yours sincerely,

NOTE:

(1) *Every statement given to an employee after the commencement of the Act must include a note: 'indicating the nature of the employee's rights under Section 5 of this Act, including, where an agency shop agreement or an approved closed shop agreement is in force which applies to him, the effect of that agreement on those rights'.*

(2) *I suggest that you might well include Section 5 in its entirety—perhaps adapted from the impersonal third person to the personal second person, i.e. addressed to the employee as 'you'.*

(3) *Where an agency shop agreement is in force, details must be given—as appears from the next precedent. However, I think it wise to indicate (as appropriate) that no such agreement is in force.*

(4) *Section 20 (2) (a) only states that you must 'indicate the nature' of the employee's rights under Section 5—not that the terms of Section*

5 must be set out. Nevertheless, if you do set them out, you are likely to avoid misunderstanding and criticism.

(5) *An 'approved closed shop agreement' is a permitted pre-entry closed shop agreement—likely to apply only in the case of seamen, musicians and actors. All other pre-entry closed shop agreements are void.*

160 New particulars where agency shop agreement in force*

Dear Mr Green,

I confirm that an agency shop agreement is in effect in respect of the plant/office/shop/factory/grade of employee where you will work/to which you will belong. The agreement concerned is made between the above company and the Union of ______ and the Union of ______. Under this agreement, the terms and conditions of employment of each employee must include a condition that every worker covered by the agreement (and this of course includes yourself) must either be or become a member of one of those Trade Unions or agree to pay appropriate contributions to one of those Trade Unions. In exceptional cases, where the worker objects on 'grounds of conscience'—such as on grounds of religious belief—both to being a member of a trade union and to paying contributions to a trade union in lieu of membership of it, he may pay equivalent contributions to a charity to be determined by agreement between him and the trade union.

I understand from our conversation that you are willing to join the Union of ______ and that you have applied for membership. Kindly inform me of the result of your application.

With best wishes,

Yours sincerely,

NOTE:

(1) *The above draft really indicates 'the nature of the employee's rights under Section 5'—and in particular the effect of the 'agency shop agreement' in question, on those rights. The employee is entitled to know precisely where he stands in these matters.*

(2) *For details of arrangements alternative to joining one of the unions concerned, i.e. paying appropriate contributions or contributing to a charity, see Chapter* 13.

* See also Chapter 14.

161 For redress of grievances, apply personnel manager

Dear Mr White,

Please would you see your supervisor, who will deal with your complaint—and, if necessary, refer it to ______.

Yours sincerely,

162 Personnel manager deals with grievances

Dear Miss White,

Kindly note that, in addition to the matters set out in the written particulars of your contract of employment, employees may now apply to our (newly appointed) personnel manager, for the purpose of seeking redress of any grievance relating to their employment. He is available in his room (No. ______) from ______ am to ______ am/pm each working day—or otherwise by appointment.

Yours sincerely,

163 Named person deals with grievances

Dear Mr White,

Mr James Brown is now the person to whom employees can apply for the purpose of seeking redress of any grievances relating to their employment. Please see him personally in room ______.

Yours sincerely,

164 Grievance procedure—reference to another document

Dear Mr White,

I was sorry to learn of your difficulties. I expect that you have discussed the matter with the Personnel Manager, who is dealing with it. The details of further steps in our grievance procedure are available from . . . / in . . .

Yours sincerely,

NOTE:

Section 20 (2) (c) requires the written particulars either to explain the steps consequent upon an application by an employee to a person for redress of a grievance relating to his employment, 'or referring to a document which is reasonably accessible to the employee and which explains those steps'. In my view, the contract itself—or the written particulars supplied thereunder—should set out the nature of the employee's rights under Section 5 and should identify them. Precisely because Section 20 (2) (c) says that the 'steps consequent upon such application' may be referred to in a reasonably accessible document, the implication is that the other particulars must be supplied directly to the individual employee.

165 Sample letter containing all written particulars now required

Dear Mr Wood,

I am happy to confirm your appointment, upon the following terms:

(a) Employment by: The ______ Company Limited.
(b) Employment to begin on the ______, 19__.
(c) Your scale or rate of remuneration and the method of calculating remuneration (including bonus and/or commission—if appropriate), to be as follows . . .
(d) Payment to be made every ______, i.e. weekly/monthly on the ______.
(e) Your normal working hours to be as follows . . .
(f) Overtime as follows . . .
(g) You will be entitled to usual public holidays. Your holidays and holiday pay to be calculated as follows . . .

Your entitlement to accrued holiday pay on the termination of your employment will be:

(h) In the event of your being absent from work due to sickness or injury, you will receive sick pay as follows . . .
(i) We operate the following pension scheme arrangements/there will be no pension arrangements made by the company and applicable to you . . .
(j) You will be entitled to receive the following periods of notice (assuming that you do not yourself repudiate your contract of service) . . .
(k) You will be obliged to give the following periods of notice, if you wish to leave the company's employment . . .
(l) By virtue of Section 5 of the *Industrial Relations Act, 1971*, you have the right to be a member of such trade union as you may choose; and as there is no agency shop agreement in force, you also have the right to be a member of no trade union or other organisation of workers or to

refuse to be a member of any particular trade union or other organisation of workers. If you are a member of a trade union, you also have the right, at any appropriate time, to take part in the activities of the trade union (including any activities as, or with the view to becoming, an official of the trade union) and the right to seek or accept appointment or election, and (if appointed or elected) to hold office as such an official. (If agency shop agreement or approved closed shop agreement in effect, then give particulars—see, for example, Letter 160, above.)

(m) In the event of your having any grievance relating to your employment, kindly see your supervisor/foreman/personnel manager/shop steward. Details of grievance procedures are available, if required, from . . ./are in the collective agreement which applies to you and which is available from . . .

If you have any questions concerning the above, please do not hesitate to contact me—or Mr ——, your ——, who will normally be found in ——, from —— am to —— pm.

Hoping that this will be the start of a long and happy association between the company and yourself and with my best wishes,

Yours sincerely,

NOTE:

The above is only the bare bones of a typical contract. The sort of additional terms which you may wish to include are set out in the following supplementary letters.

166 Right to search

Dear Mr Green,

Please note that, as I explained to you when we met, all employees are required to agree to submit to their person or property being searched, while on the company's premises, at any time at the request of ——. This is, of course, essential having regard to the nature of the company's business.

Yours sincerely,

NOTE:

To search an employee's person without his permission is an assault. To search his property without consent is a trespass. Permission may be obtained in advance—but should be confirmed at the time of the search. If you are satisfied that a theft has occurred and a suspect refuses to be searched, then the police should be called.

167 **Restraint clause**

Dear Mr Green,

I now confirm that the Board are prepared to employ you upon the terms set out in my letter of the ——, subject to your agreeing that you will not engage, directly or indirectly, in any branch of the —— trade/industry, within a radius of —— miles, for a period of —— months/years after leaving the company's service, and that you will not during that period solicit custom from or deal with or employ or be instrumental in the employing of persons who were customers or employees (as the case may be) of the company, during the period of your service with the company.

With best wishes,

Yours sincerely,

NOTE:

Restraint clauses should be drafted or at least approved by the company's solicitors. They are only enforceable if 'reasonable' from all viewpoints. In the absence of a valid restraint clause, an ex-employee may compete with his former company, as and where and when he sees fit—provided only that he does not divulge the company's confidential information—and to prove that he has done this is, in general, an impossibility.

168 **Obligation to move**

Dear Mr White,

I have discussed your place of employment with the Board. They are agreeable to your being stationed at —— for a minimum period of —— years. But bearing in mind the nature of the company's business, it must be understood that you will if necessary accept transfer to any of our factories/shops/branches/offices in the —— area, if given —— weeks/months notice of such transfer. The company will pay all reasonable moving expenses, including the cost of moving house.

I hope that the above suggestion will be acceptable to you. Please inform me at your earliest convenience.

Yours sincerely,

NOTE:

There is, of course, almost no end to the variations which may be played on the theme of a contract of employment. I strongly advise that all major terms be confirmed (if not made) in writing—clearly and lucidly—and discussed with the employee where necessary. Do not attempt to introduce new terms, though, under the guise of 'confirming' terms already made.

Chapter 20

Disclosure of Information*

AN EMPLOYER still need not tell all. But Sections 56 and 57 of the Act place an extremely important new duty of disclosure upon him—first, in the course of collective bargaining and in any event at least once a year.

Section 56 (1):

'For the purposes of all the stages of collective bargaining between an employer and trade union representatives, it shall (subject to Section 158 of this Act)'—which makes certain exceptions—'be the duty of the employer to disclose to those representatives all such information relating to his undertaking as is in the possession of the employer, or of any associated employer, and is both—

(a) Information without which the trade union representatives would be to a material extent impeded in carrying on collective bargaining with him, and
(b) Information which it would be in accordance with good industrial relations practice that the employer should disclose to them for the purposes of collective bargaining.'

To find out what 'would be in accordance with good industrial relations practice', the Section says that regard must be had to the principles relating to the disclosure of information by employers as set out in the Code of Practice.

Any disclosure of information required by trade union representatives must be confirmed in writing—see hereafter.

Section 57 only applies to 'undertakings' which (in general) employ more than 350 people—whether at the same or at different places. An 'undertaking' is defined (by Section 167) as including 'a business and, in relation to any body of persons (whether corporate or unincorporate) whose activities would not, apart from this provision, be regarded as constituting an undertaking, it includes the aggregate of those activities'. So if your business—or the aggregate of the

* As we go to press, the date when these rules will come into force has yet to be announced.

undertakings engaged in by your business—exceeds 350 people, Section 57 applies.

In that case, it will be your duty as owner of the undertaking 'to issue in respect of that financial year a statement . . . to persons employed in the undertaking. Every such statement shall be issued not later than six months after the end of the financial year to which it relates. Every such statement shall be in writing and' (subject again to Section 158 of the Act) 'shall contain all such information as may be required in accordance with regulations made by the Secretary of State . . . and shall be issued to every person who, on the date on which it is issued, is employed in the undertaking to which the statement relates, and who is not on that date an excepted person'. Regulations will also state who is to be excepted.

Now Section 158:

'No employer shall, by virtue of Section 56 or Section 57 of this Act, be required to disclose—

(a) Any information the disclosure of which would be against the interests of national security, or
(b) Any information which he could not disclose without contravening a prohibition imposed by or under an Enactment . . . or
(c) Any information which has been communicated to the employer in confidence, or which the employer has otherwise obtained in consequence of the confidence reposed in him by another person, or
(d) Any information relating specifically to an individual, unless he has consented to it being disclosed, or
(e) Any information the disclosure of which would be seriously prejudicial to the interests of the employer's undertaking for reasons other than its effect on collective bargaining, or
(f) Any information obtained by the employer for the purpose of bringing, prosecuting, or defending any legal proceedings.'

Sub-paragraph (c) may be useful. Sub-paragraph (d) would prevent the union leaders from knowing your salary. And sub-paragraph (e) would provide a happy hunting ground for the commercial or industrial barrack-room lawyer—after all, what confidential information would *not* be potentially 'seriously prejudicial' to the interests of your undertaking, if it were to be disclosed to the wrong people?

If there is a dispute as to whether or not employers have disclosed all proper information, the Industrial Court or Tribunal would rule, depending on the circumstances.

169 Written request by employees for disclosure of information during collective bargaining

Dear Mr White,

In accordance with Section 56 (1) of the Industrial Relations Act, I require you on behalf of the Union of ______ to disclose the following information concerning your plant, without which we are to a material extent impeded in carrying on collective bargaining with you:

(a) . . .
(b) . . .
(c) . . .

It is, of course, particularly important to us to have full details as to the productivity achieved in the ______ workshop. Without knowing how our efforts have contributed to the increase in profits arising from the production obtained in the shop concerned, we cannot possibly know whether you are correct in saying that no substantial wage increase can be afforded.

Yours sincerely,

170 Refusal to disclose—against interests of national security

Dear Mr Green,

I am in receipt of your request for information concerning ______. I regret that it would not be proper for me to disclose this, having regard to the top secret nature of the work in the department concerned. Such disclosure would be against the interests of national security. I am sure that on reconsideration you will agree with this.

Nevertheless, if you would care to meet me to discuss this matter, I think that I can provide you with sufficient information for your purposes, without going beyond the bounds of my proper authority—and I would be pleased to meet you at any mutually convenient time.

Yours sincerely,

171 Refusal—information supplied in confidence

Dear Mr Redd,

The information which you request was communicated to the management in confidence, and in the circumstances I regret that it cannot be revealed. I would refer you to Section 158 (1) (c) of the Act, which applies in the present circumstances.

We have already revealed to you a great deal of information—and it is hoped that you will now be able to proceed with the negotiations. If there are any further matters which can be disclosed to you without betrayal of a confidence and without contravening Section 158 of the Act, I shall of course be pleased to co-operate with you. We are only too anxious that our negotiations should be carried on in the most frank and friendly manner.

With best wishes,

Yours sincerely,

172 Refusal of information relating to an individual

Dear Mr Stone,

I am sorry. You ask for information relating to payments made to specific individuals. At your request, I consulted them to see whether they would be prepared to have their salaries or wages revealed—and they have declined. In the circumstances, Section 158 (1) (d) applies and I am not required to disclose this information to you.

In any event, the information which you have received should, I hope, be sufficient for your purposes—and the management is only too ready to co-operate with you in all respects, in the hope of achieving a mutually satisfactory agreement.

I look forward to seeing you, as arranged, at tomorrow's meeting.

Yours sincerely,

173 Refusal of information disclosure of which would be 'seriously prejudicial'

Dear Mr Jones,

To reveal to you the nature of the overdrafts granted to the Company would, I am informed, be highly prejudicial to the Company's interests, for reasons which have nothing whatsoever to do with their effect on collective bargaining. You will appreciate that this information is highly confidential and its revelation might lead to a leak—which could seriously affect the Company—and, of course, the jobs of the people whom we employ and whom you so ably represent.

I am sorry to have to convey this refusal to you, but I am

sure that you will understand the position. If there is any other information which you require for the purposes of the current negotiations, please do not hesitate to inform me.

Yours sincerely,

174 Refusal of information prepared for legal proceedings

Dear Mr Jones,

The information you require was prepared by our accountants specifically for the purpose of defending a legal action brought against the Company by ——. In the circumstances, Section 158 (1) (f) of the Industrial Relations Act applies so as to ensure that the Company is not required to disclose that information. You will appreciate, I am sure, that the legal proceedings concerned are of great importance to the Company and the material to which you refer is privileged in law.

Yours sincerely,

175 Union's rejection of 'excuse'

Dear Mr Peters,

Thank you for your letter. I regret that I cannot accept the excuse you give for non-disclosure of the information requested. I ask you to reconsider the matter, failing which I shall have no alternative other than to refer your refusal to the Court. I will be pleased to hear from you within the course of the next seven days.

Yours sincerely,

176 Letter enclosing annual statement to employees

Dear Mr Black,

I am happy to enclose herewith a statement concerning the Company's business during the financial year ending ——. We are always anxious that our employees should have as much information as possible concerning the business of which they form a vital part. I hope that you will find the report interesting.

Yours sincerely,

NOTE:

You might as well make a virtue out of a necessity. There is no need to say that you are only sending the report because Section 57 of the Act requires you to do so. You could, of course, send a more formal note. Thus:

177 Note enclosing statutory statement

Dear Mr Smith,

As required by Section 57 of the *Industrial Relations Act 1971*, I enclose herewith a statement concerning the affairs of the Company during the financial year ended ______.

Yours sincerely,

178 Refusal—information not necessary for carrying on collective bargaining

Dear Mr Jones,

The information you request is not necessary for the purposes of collective bargaining. It concerns matters outside the scope of the current negotiations. In the circumstances, I would not feel justified in revealing it to you.

However, I think that the ground which really would interest you would be . . . May I suggest that we discuss the question of . . .? I would be pleased to look into the question of . . . with you.

Yours sincerely,

NOTE:

It is always good tactics—in negotiating with employees, in the same way as in bargaining with potential suppliers or customers—not merely to say no. Use the positive approach, whenever you can. This is both helpful, fair and constructive. In other words, suggest an alternative.

179 Refusal—in reliance upon the code

Dear Mr Smith,

I really do not consider that the information you request comes within the scope of the Code. What you would like to know, I expect, is . . . And that I shall be pleased to tell you—and to explain it all in detail, if you will be kind enough to call on me.

With my best wishes to you,

Yours sincerely,

NOTE:
Section 56 (4) frees an employer from liability to produce or even allow the inspection of any document—other than one prepared for the purpose of conveying or confirming the information. The employee is not even entitled to make a copy of extracts from any document. Thus:

180 Refusal to allow documents to be produced or copied

Dear Mr Green,

I have given you all the information to which you are entitled —and I am sorry, but I cannot properly produce or allow inspection of the documents or accounts—still less is it possible for me to allow you to make a copy of them. I would refer you to Section 56 (4) of the Act.

On the other hand, I do feel that I can help you with certain further information of interest, so let us by all means meet again tomorrow morning, as arranged.

With kind regards,

Yours sincerely,

181 Reply to non-registered trade union

Dear Mr Brown,

I note your requirement that we disclose information to you for the purposes of collective bargaining. We shall be pleased to let you have as much information as we properly can—but I hope that you will bear in mind that the Sections to which you refer only enable a registered trade union to apply to the Court. Employers are not bound to disclose information to non-registered unions. However, this Company is only too pleased to co-operate with you, and, without prejudice to the foregoing, to provide you with a great deal of information.

With my kind regards,

Yours sincerely,

182 Union maintains that Section 57 statement insufficient

Dear Mr Brown,

Thank you for the statement supplied to me and to other members of my Union in purported compliance with Section 57 of the Industrial Relations Act. In my view, this statement does not comply with the Regulations, in the following respects:

(a) . . .
(b) . . .
(c) . . .

I shall be pleased to have your observations.

Yours sincerely,

NOTE:
Regulations will be published, specifying what must be included in a Section 57 statement.

183 Employer's reply to criticisms of Section 57 statement

Dear Mr Green,

Thank you for your letter. I have carefully considered the points you make, and would reply to them as follows:

(a) The information concerning ______ relates specifically to an individual who has not consented to its being disclosed.
(b) It would be seriously prejudicial to the Company's interests if the information concerning ______ were to be disclosed.
(c) The information requested concerning ______ is highly secret; its disclosure would be against the interests of national security.

Now that you know the reasons for the non-disclosure, I hope that you will appreciate our difficulties—and that you will accept that we have in fact set out in the statement as much as we properly can, in accordance with not only the Regulations (and Section 158 of the Act), but also in accordance with our firm wish that our employees—including, of course, members of your Union—should have the fullest possible information, consistent with good industrial relations practice.

Yours sincerely,

Chapter 21

An Executive's Letters

INEVITABLY, A BOOK of this sort is designed for executives in their business capacities. If, for instance, a man has to hire and fire, he must do his job as well and as fairly as he can—even if sometimes he finds it distasteful.

Similarly, the Industrial Relations Act is law—however distasteful that may be for many people. And the executive must cope with it not only from his viewpoint as an employer's representative, but also from his own.

Here, then, in this chapter and in the next—as an antidote to some of the miseries doled out to others—are some letters which the executive may like to use—and to adapt—for his own purposes, if he is dismissed. Naturally, the object of the exercise is to ensure that his dismissal is 'unfair'—and that he receives a handsome, tax-free sum if he cannot get other work. Remember you normally only have 4 weeks from the date when your employment terminates, within which to apply to the Tribunal. Delay too long and you will lose your rights.

184 Claim by dismissed employee for compensation

Dear Mr Brown,

I was shocked to be dismissed. The pay in lieu of notice which I received has in no way compensated me for the loss arising out of my dismissal. I have been unable to obtain other work at anything like the equivalent status or pay, and in the circumstances, I shall have to seek my remedy from the Industrial Tribunal.

I am advised that the burden of proving that the dismissal was 'fair' rests upon the company. I am also advised—and am confident—that this is a burden which the company will be unable to discharge.

I shall be pleased, in the circumstances, to receive an admission of liability from you. I shall then be prepared to discuss terms. And we can, if necessary, call in a conciliation officer to approve them.

If this matter is not dealt with swiftly and satisfactorily, then

I shall have no alternative other than to lay my complaint before a Tribunal.

This is indeed an unhappy ending to a long association.

Yours truly,

NOTE:

You may, of course, prefer to put the matter in the hands of your solicitors—and if there is much money involved, this may be wise. Thus:

185 Threat to instruct solicitors

Dear Mr Brown,

As you have not seen fit to make any substantial offer of compensation for my unfair dismissal, I have decided that I must put the matter in the hands of my solicitors. I have now been out of work for ______. Taking my pay at its previous level, I have therefore lost £______. I appreciate that this loss cannot be set off at a rate higher than £40 per week, but even that amounts to over ______. And as I have a wife and children to keep, I can delay my claim no longer.

I repeat: Unless I hear from you by return with a sensible and substantial offer, I shall pass the matter to my solicitors for their immediate attention.

Yours faithfully,

186 Denial of allegations made by employers

Dear Mr White,

I am in receipt of your letter in which you see fit to allege that I have been dismissed for misconduct/lack of qualification/lack of aptitude. This allegation I strenuously deny. By any standard, my dismissal was as unfair as it was unexpected. Unless I hear from you with an offer of a very substantial payment, I shall bring a claim for unfair dismissal before the Industrial Tribunal.

Yours faithfully,

NOTE:

Just as it is important for employers to put their case on to paper as soon as possible, so it is vital for the employee to do the same. If you are dismissed in writing, then answer the letter—and keep a copy of the answer. Deal with any allegations made, as briefly and lucidly as you can.

187 Executive unfairly dismissed

Dear Mr Green,

My dismissal has been unfair, in every sense of that word. I have been unable to find alternative employment—doubtless due to your failure to provide me with a satisfactory reference. In the circumstances, I shall apply to the Industrial Tribunal for compensation—which, I would remind you, may rise to £4,160.

It would, of course, enable me to mitigate my loss considerably if I were to obtain other work. Perhaps you would bear this in mind, when you are next asked for a reference for me. Meanwhile, I am informing prospective employers that my ——— years of service with the Company are likely to provide the best reference that I can get in the circumstances.

Yours sincerely,

188 Passing the buck

Dear Mr Director,

Before I dismissed James Brown, I discussed the matter with the Company solicitors/the Personnel Director/Mr White. We both appreciated that there were risks involved in taking this course, and that we might end up having to pay compensation for unfair dismissal. However, it was felt that this was a risk worth taking in the circumstances.

With best wishes,

Yours sincerely,

NOTE:

In all borderline cases involving 'unfair dismissal', management should confer—and, in general, advice should be taken either from a superior, or from the Company's solicitor—or both. This is, of course, a form of buck passing—but is entirely legitimate. When you deal with unfair dismissal, there is (potentially at least) over £4,000 at stake. And if you are trying to cope with an actual or potential industrial dispute, even an hour's break in production may cost the Company a small fortune.

Still, it is as well to do any buck passing with appropriate dignity—and to attempt, where possible, to be taking your fair share of responsibility. The above letter is intended to strike a sensible balance.

189 Refusal to resign

Dear Mr Green,

I know that I have been overruled. I appreciate that I am in a minority of one. And I adhere to my view that the step which it is proposed to take is not in the interests of the Company.

But I shall not resign.

Yours sincerely,

NOTE:

Never resign unless you have actually got a better job to go to. Only if you are **dismissed** *can you hope to get compensated for unfair dismissal—or redundancy pay, for that matter.*

190 Refusal to contract out of right to claim compensation for unfair dismissal on expiry of fixed term

Dear Mr Brown,

Thank you for your letter, suggesting that—in return for my long expected increase in salary—I should contract out of my possible right to claim compensation for unfair dismissal, if the company decides not to renew my employment when the present term comes to an end.

I am sure that if you look at this matter from my point of view, you will appreciate that this is not something that I could possibly do. I appreciate that the company is not bound to increase my salary, as I am on a fixed-term arrangement. However, the managing director has made it quite plain to me on numerous occasions that—having regard to the completely unexpected and enormous increase in the cost of living and the fall in the value of money—it is unreasonable to expect me to continue to work as I am, on the basis of the agreed salary. Equally, it is not reasonable to expect me to give up my potential statutory rights against the company.

In the circumstances, could you kindly arrange for me to see the Managing Director personally?

Meanwhile, you may be sure that I shall continue to use my best endeavours on the company's behalf.

Yours sincerely,

NOTE:

(1) *Meet the Managing Director face to face, and you will probably get better results than you could do through any correspondence.*

(2) *When you turn down a suggestion, it is important to do so in an amicable and dignified manner. After all, you will be continuing to work for the company, at least until your term does expire. And you do not want to give anyone any chance of showing that you have given grounds for 'fair dismissal'. Hence*

(3) *Always state that the company has the assurance of your loyalty, support, conscientious work, etc., etc.*

(4) *For details on fixed term contracts, please see Chapter 10.*

191 Denial that executive 'ordinarily works outside Great Britain'

Dear Mr Sparrow,

It is true that I have been employed by the company outside Great Britain for the past six months. It is not correct that I 'ordinarily work' outside the UK. In the circumstances, I am advised that I am entitled to rely upon those sections of the Industrial Relations Act which give a man in my position a right to compensation for 'unfair dismissal'. And, from my point of view, that is just as well—since you have seen fit to dismiss me, I have not been able to obtain alternative work. My loss is therefore enormous.

I hope that you will now deal with this matter speedily.

Yours sincerely,

NOTE:

(1) *Go on saying 'Yours sincerely'—you can be sincere, even if you do not like the man. 'Yours faithfully' is generally reserved for strangers (to whom the letter begins 'Dear Sir') or for a thoroughly brusque ending. (For details of this—and other essentials of letter writing techniques—you may like to see my:* Businessman's guide to letter-writing and to the law on letters, *Business Books, 1970.*)

(2) *Any facts which would tend to show that you 'ordinarily' work in Great Britain should be stated—assuming, that is, that they could be proved.*

192 Claim for compensation—not redundancy pay

Dear Mr Jones,

I note that you say that I am being 'made redundant'. This I do not accept. If I am dismissed, then such a dismissal is thoroughly unfair—and I shall take such steps as I may be advised in order to protect my position generally, and in particular in order to claim compensation for unfair dismissal, under the Industrial Relations Act.

Perhaps you will now reconsider the matter.

Yours sincerely,

193 Denial of misconduct

Dear Mr Brown,

I emphatically deny that I have been guilty of the alleged or any misconduct. I am putting this matter into the hands of my solicitors and, unless some satisfactory offer of settlement is made, I shall take such steps as they advise, in order to protect my position. In particular, I shall bring a claim for compensation for unfair dismissal.

Yours faithfully,

194 Denial that lack of qualification a 'reasonable' ground for dismissal

Dear Mr Williams,

I am astonished that you should have seen fit to dismiss me for lack of qualification, without giving me the opportunity to acquire such qualification. I appreciate that the new computer which you have introduced into the office has affected my work, but I was and remain fully prepared to take such courses as may be necessary in order to acquire the technical qualifications which I shall now need. You gave me no such opportunity, but instead have given me my notice.

In the circumstances, it is quite clear that I have been dismissed—and in my view, completely unfairly. I would ask you to be good enough to reconsider this matter—and in particular my wish to undergo training, in order to cope with the new machinery and methods.

I look forward to hearing from you at your early convenience.

Yours sincerely,

NOTE:
As we saw in Chapter 8, it is not enough to show a reason relating to 'capability' or 'qualifications' or 'conduct'—Section 24 (6) requires that the employer show that he acted 'reasonably'. When disputing 'fair' dismissal, you should always allege that the employer was 'unreasonable' in the action he took, If that denial is made from the start, it is more likely to be accepted at the end. And in any event, even if the claim will be settled in due course, it is important to put your case on record. As important, in fact, when you are acting for yourself as when you are doing your duty for your company.

Chapter 22

The Executive Complains

THE EXECUTIVE must communicate with the Company, on his own behalf, in the best possible manner. If he does so within the framework of the Act, then the same rules of good sense apply to him as when he is wearing his Company hat. There is one exception—if he has been shown to the door and wishes to obtain compensation for unfair dismissal, then he should note carefully the rules (and the precedents) in Part 2—and (standing them on their head, where necessary) employ them for his own purposes.

Here are some other cases in which individual letters may be of help, from the executive's own viewpoint.

195 Section 5—and a worker's rights

Dear Mr Director,

I fear that unless middle management gets organised, it is likely to be squeezed out of all negotiations, and to find itself in an impossible position. As you know, Mr ——, General Secretary of the Union of ——, came to see us recently. We were most impressed with both him and with the case he had presented. And I, along with a number of my colleagues, have definitely decided to join his Union and to exercise the right given to me by Section 5 of the Industrial Relations Act.

I hope that this step will be treated as a constructive one—it is certainly intended as such.

With best wishes,

Yours sincerely,

196 Refusal to superior to contravene Act

Dear Mr Jones,

I have given very careful consideration to your suggestion that we should . . .

May I respectfully refer you to Section . . . of the Industrial

Relations Act? I think that you will agree with me that if we were to take the step proposed by the Board, we would be flying in the teeth of the Act—and while the Union might not wish to invoke the procedures provided by this controversial legislation, I would not count on it.

In the circumstances, I would suggest that this matter deserves careful reconsideration, so as to avoid even worse dislocation in our production.

I will be pleased to call upon you to discuss this matter if you will be good enough to let me know what time would be convenient to you.

Meanwhile, I trust that you will appreciate the reason for my reluctance to carry out the procedure referred to in your letter.

With my best wishes,

Yours sincerely,

197 Refusal to dismiss unfairly

Dear Mr Jenkins,

I must ask you to reconsider your decision to dismiss Mr Green. I fully appreciate the grounds for that decision—but I fear that we may run into very serious difficulty under the provisions of the Industrial Relations Act which enable an employee, on occasion, to obtain as much as £4,160 as compensation for so-called 'unfair dismissal'.

Under the Act, a dismissal which we would regard as fair may nevertheless be 'unfair'. And once an employee has been dismissed, there is a presumption of unfairness—the burden of proving 'fair' dismissal rests upon the employers.

In the circumstances, I think that we would be well advised to exercise further patience with regard to Mr ——. However, if the Board decides despite my views to proceed with the dismissal, I know that it will take into account the potential financial risks—which I have felt it my duty to draw to your attention.

With best wishes,

Yours sincerely,

198 Executive warns Board—strike lawful

Dear Mr Green,

There seems to be some misunderstanding on the Board regarding the effect of the Industrial Relations Act. It does not make strikes unlawful, except in certain circumstances—none of which apply in the present case. Section 147 of the Act says that 'due notice given by or on behalf of an employee of his intention to take part in a strike shall not, unless it otherwise expressly provides, be construed as a notice to terminate his contract of employment, or as a repudiation of that contract'. And 'due notice' is defined as meaning 'notice of a duration not less than that which (whether by virtue of any enactment or otherwise) he would be required to give to terminate his contract of employment'.

So proper notice has been given—and we shall have to deal with the matter accordingly and as best we can. You may be sure that I am doing everything I possibly can to bring this dispute to an early end.

Thank you for taking the trouble to contact me.

Yours sincerely,

NOTE:

(1) *What this letter is really saying—very politely—is:*

(a) *You do not know what you are talking about;*

(b) *The Industrial Relations Act is highly complicated—and has made life pretty fair hell for executives in charge of personnel; so*

(c) *Please let me get on with it.*

(2) *Of course, to say those things directly would lead to potentially horrible consequences. The above draft is a tactful alternative.*

199 Explaining to chairman why collective bargain not 'legally enforceable'

Dear Mr Green,

You are, of course, quite right. The agreement with the Union of ______ is not legally enforceable, because of the inclusion of the clause to which you refer. And I am not at all surprised that you query this.

However, whether we would like the clause in or not, the Union is insisting—so we were really faced with the alternative: either we excluded the effect of Section 34 of the Industrial Relations Act by contracting out, or we would be left without an agreement. So there was really no alternative at all, as we saw it. I hope that you will agree.

With kind regards,

Yours sincerely,

200 Alternative explanation—contracting out in the company's interest

Dear Sir Robert,

Even had the Union of ——— not wanted to contract out of legal enforceability, I think we should still have done so. We have been advised that it is not wise for us to get embroiled in the toils of the law in connection with the enforcement of such agreements—the time element would be against us.

In addition, quite apart from any question of losing—and that is always a possibility, litigation being a somewhat doubtful business—we would run great risks, were we to win. If an order were made against the Union which the Union then saw fit to flout, we might personally rejoice to see one or two of its leaders incarcerated, but this would hardly be likely to keep the production lines flowing! And I am under the firm impression that the Unions would not take an adverse decision lying down.

I hope that you will understand the reasons, even if neither you nor I are very happy about them. Would you like me to call on you? If so, perhaps you would be good enough to get your secretary to let me know when you will next be at HQ and I shall be delighted to do so—alternatively, I would be pleased to come to you, at your convenience.

With kindest regards—and my warm thanks for your keen and continued interest in my work for the Company—which has not really been made any easier as a result of the new legislation.

Yours sincerely,

201 Why no secret ballot?

Dear Mr Brown,

You suggest that we ought to apply to the Court for a secret ballot. Unfortunately, this is not on the cards. I enclose herewith a copy of the relevant Sections* of the Industrial Relations Act, and you will see that however important our troubles may be to us, they do not come within the very specialised categories within which the law is prepared to force a ballot upon unwilling Unions. Alas!

Yours sincerely,

* Sections 141 and 142.

202 Thanks for the compliment

Dear Sir James,

I greatly appreciated your note. I am so pleased that we emerged from the recent troubles in good heart, and without loss of production—and I am glad that you feel that I was able to contribute to this happy result.

This was, as always, a team job—and I would like to pay special tribute to Mr ———, and to my assistant, Mr ———. I know that they—like the rest of us—are delighted to be working under your tactful leadership.

Yours sincerely,

203 Thanks to subordinate

Dear Mr Bright,

Your understanding of the Industrial Relations Act passeth all belief! I never thought that we would emerge intact—and without massive loss of production—from the recent dispute. I would like you to know how greatly I appreciated your constant assistance—and the tremendous number of hours which you put into your work, during the recent, very difficult weeks. I shall not forget it.

With best wishes to Mrs Bright,

Yours sincerely,

PS: I am sending a copy of this letter to the Chairman.

NOTE:

(1) *The words 'thank you' cost nothing but are worth a great deal—particularly when conveyed to those in real positions of power. They are all too often forgotten.*

(2) *There is a much shorter version of the above letter:*

204 Thanks

Dear Mr Green,

Thank you!

Yours sincerely,

205 Congratulations

Dear Mr Green,

Many congratulations on your success in handling the recent dispute. Had it reached me, I do not know how I would have coped. Your efforts are enormously appreciated.

Yours sincerely,

NOTE:
No one minds being congratulated. If you have no time to dictate a letter, then just write one, like this:

206 Again, congratulations

Dear Bob,

Well done!

Yours,

Bill

Chapter 23

Miscellaneous

IT HAS NOT been possible, of course, to follow the Act from Section to Section, page to page. The subjects leap around the Act, with gay abandon—and I have tried to bring some sort of order into the industrial letter-writer's world by concentrating on those areas which appear logically to come together—even if this has meant some repetition.

But there are some Sections which just fit in nowhere. And this is even recognised by the parliamentary draughtsmen, who have set aside Part 9 as 'Miscellaneous and Supplementary'. Here you find the rules as to conciliation officers (Section 146); the effects of a strike notice (Section 147); the *Race Relations Act, 1968*—as affected by the Act (Section 149—letter follows); and so on.

So here are a few supplementary and miscellaneous letters—starting with a glance back at 'peaceful picketing' (Section 134), which is now allowed outside business premises, but not outside a person's home.

207 **Picketing at home**

Dear Mr Brown,

You are fully entitled, of course, to keep your pickets outside our works. But I have received complaints that they have seen fit to picket homes of various employees. I do hope that you will ensure that this is stopped. You will recall that Section 134 (1) of the Industrial Relations Act does not permit picketing outside a place where an employee resides.

Yours sincerely,

NOTE:
Even picketing outside a place of work is only permitted 'for the purpose of peacefully obtaining information from' the person picketed 'or peacefully communicating information to him or peacefully persuading him to work or not to work'. Intimidation is unlawful.

208 Too short a strike notice

Dear Mr Brown,

I am in receipt of your strike notice, but would draw your attention to Section 147 of the Industrial Relations Act. Whereas 'due notice' given by or on behalf of an employee of his intention to take part in a strike shall not, unless it otherwise provides, be construed either as a notice to terminate his contract of employment, or as a repudiation of that contract, 'due notice' means 'notice of a duration not less than that which (whether by virtue of any enactment or otherwise) he would be required to give to terminate his contract of employment.

Seven days' notice may be enough for some of your members—but there are many whose employment is subject to up to a month's notice on their part. I trust that you have considered the serious effects which could result from your giving too short a notice—and that you will reconsider the entire matter.

We have no wish, of course, for anything other than a peaceful settlement to this dispute—and I shall be pleased to discuss the whole matter with you, if you wish.

Yours sincerely,

NOTE:

Even if the short strike notice does 'terminate the contract of employment', it is highly unlikely that the strike will come to an end without the promise of no victimisation—and reinstatement of each worker in his job. However, the above summarises Section 147. Strikes are both lawful and not in breach of contract, if the employees give the same notice of their proposal to strike as they should give in order to terminate their contracts of service.

209 Race Relations Act proceedings held over

Dear Mr Ahmed,

You are alleging (in our view without justification) that you have been unfairly dismissed because of your ethnic origin.

We understand that you have also made a complaint to the Race Relations Board with regard to the same matter. In the circumstances, we must refer you to Section 149 of the Industrial Relations Act, 1971, which, in effect, would postpone the Race Relations Board application until the unfair dismissal allegation has been dealt with.

In the circumstances, we would respectfully suggest that you might do well to consult your trade union/a solicitor. [You should be able to get his initial advice at a low fee under the Legal Aid and Advice Act or the Law Society's Scheme]. Alternatively, we suggest that you might go to a Citizens' Advice Bureau.

I would like to emphasise that I have caused full enquiries to be made into your case and I can find no evidence whatsoever of any discrimination against you, whether because of your ethnic origin or otherwise. We are proud in this company of the good relations which exist between our employees of various backgrounds. We are therefore very sorry that you should have seen fit to have raised the present allegations against us, either in the form of a complaint to the Race Relations Board or an allegation of unfair dismissal or at all.

Yours sincerely,

210 To Northern Ireland subsidiary

Dear Roger,

I confirm that the Industrial Relations Act does not apply to Northern Ireland. Apart from a few (and comparatively unimportant) Sections, the rules apply in England, Wales and Scotland only.

However, the Parliament of Northern Ireland is given (by Section 165) power to make laws for purposes similar to the purposes of the Industrial Relations Act.

Yours sincerely,

211 To subsidiary in Scotland

Dear Bill,

Yes, the Industrial Relations Act most emphatically does apply North of the border. You are thinking of Northern Ireland, where it will not apply unless the Stormont Parliament so decides.

Yours sincerely,

212 'No compulsion to work'

Dear Bill,

Unfortunately, we will not get an order for specific performance, requiring Roger Jones—or anyone else, for that matter—to carry out the terms of his contract of employment. Under the charming heading, 'No Compulsion to Work', Section 128 of the Industrial Relations Act makes it plain that no court may make an order for specific performance 'or specific implement of a contract of employment . . . or compel an employee to do any work or to attend any place for the purpose of doing any work'.

So there we are. An Industrial Tribunal may recommend that an employee who has been unfairly dismissed be re-engaged—but it cannot force him to come back, nor us to have him.

Yours sincerely,

213 Public servants—and employees of the Crown

Dear William,

You enquire whether the provisions of the Industrial Relations Act apply to public servants. In general, the answer is: Yes. Section 162 of the Act says so. But the armed forces are excluded.

Yours sincerely,

214 Wait for the regulations

Dear Roger,

Unfortunately, everything is not contained in the Industrial Relations Act—nor, still less, in the Code of Practice. Regulations are due to be made, in respect of many items—and we shall just have to keep our eyes open for them, as and when they arrive. There is no end to the new learning, thrust upon us by this incredible legislation.

Yours sincerely,

* * *

No end to learning? None. But at least if you know the rules explained and illustrated in this book, you will have made a very good beginning.

Chapter 24

Keeping the Peace—Letters of Explanation—Elucidation—and Apology

NO ONE KNOWS how long the Act as such will remain in force. Any Labour Government will have to consider repealing it in its entirety and replacing it with some other form of legislation. And as the pendulum swings—whether man so wisheth or no—the time will doubtless come when Labour will return to power, and the Act will come once again into the Parliamentary sphere.

At that stage, I think it highly probable that the following will happen:

1 The control of the Registrar over trade unions will be modified, if not removed altogether.
2 The pre-entry closed shop will cease to be illegal.
3 Other restrictions over the operations of unions—including restrictions on certain sympathy strikes will be removed—or at least adapted.

Conversely:

1 The right of an employee who is unfairly dismissed to obtain compensation will be retained.
2 The duties of employers to reveal information to employees will be extended.
3 Further changes will be made in the Contracts of Employment Act, to extend the effect of some made under the Industrial Relations Act.

All this may be achieved by repealing the main Statute and bringing in other legislation. Alternatively, the appropriate Sections of the Act may be amended or repealed. This is a matter of technical and political expediency. Certainly, in my view, no Labour Government—which, of course, depends for its moral and financial support upon trade union colleagues—can let the Act remain as it is.

So problems come in two stages, insofar as employers are concerned. First, they must cope with the Act, now and as it stands. Second, they must look ahead and plan for the future.

Like tax, the Act is with us—whether we like it or not. For reasons which will by now have become apparent to my readers, I think that it is likely to cause quite as much dismay and difficulty to employers as to employees. However, that is—for present purposes—irrelevant. It must be lived with, and letters in this book have been designed to show how—and to make such life bearable.

Equally, those of us who think that (for instance) the new bargaining arrangements—combined with the agency 'shop' provisions—are likely to lead to trouble in far too many cases—must nevertheless curb our desire for change and reform, and consider the law as it stands. Unions (registered) and 'organisations of workers' (unregistered) may register their protests and refuse their co-operation, even to the extent of declining to provide members for those Tribunals which may award compensation for unfair dismissal against unfair employers. That is entirely a matter for them. Equally, each union must decide whether it is prepared to go off or to stay off the Register (as the case may be)—and to put up with loss of protection (see Chapter 17) in return for the hope of killing the Act—or rendering it unworkable—or maintaining solidarity, keeping faith with its members—or however else it may put its case.

Employers, on the other hand, do have to keep their businesses going—and for that purpose they must get on with their workers—organised or unorganised, registered or unregistered. As Confucius is said to have remarked: 'If you are going to get raped, you might as well lie back and enjoy it. . . .' Well, that was dealing with an entirely different sort of relations—from the industrial viewpoint, the Act must be lived with until amendment or repeal do you part therefrom.

I hope, then, that the letters in this book will have proved helpful to you, in your quest for a way to live with the Act and with its rules. I have selected those parts of the Act which, I think, are most likely to lead to correspondence. And I would like to thank the many delegates to my BIS Public and In-Company Conferences on the Act who have (albeit unknowingly) contributed to this book by their observations, questions and suggestions.

It is also largely thanks to them that I have been able to reduce my explanations of the most vital Sections of the Act to a reasonably digestible minimum. If the meal has nevertheless proved too heavy, then I apologise. The pill must be swallowed, however thick the sugar coating. It is easy to quote from the Act—and often possible to indicate the legal meaning of otherwise obscure words. But equally, many words cannot properly be defined until seen in the context of their practical day-to-day application—and after they have been duly interpreted by the Courts.

Meanwhile, I repeat—you must live with the Act, and cope with the problems which it inevitably presents. The precedents in this book are designed to assist you in the proper pursuit of peace—if not on earth, then at least in the factory, office, plant, depot or whatever other 'shop' may dominate your working life.

I have also included a number of letters for employees. I hope that—in spite of the Act, or because of it, it matters not—you will be on good terms with those whom you employ and their representatives. You may wish, from time to time, to suggest precedents for their use.

Equally (and probably far more important), however mighty your own position, you are on someone's payroll. As an employed executive, there are parts of the Act which you must use to your own best advantage, as and when possible. Hence (for instance) many letters designed for your potential use, if you have the misfortune to be dismissed. Nowadays, if you want a financial fate worse than death, you do not have to resign—it is bad enough if you are dismissed 'fairly'.

Anyway, to round off the book I now offer three letters which may serve as useful drafts, as you seek to blame the Act for unpleasant tasks which you have to perform . . . to apologise for steps which (probably entirely genuinely) you would much prefer not to take, which the Act has thrust upon you . . . and which may help you to restore peace, if your plans for it are in pieces.

215 Blaming the Act

Dear Mr Jones,

I am sorry. You know my views on the Industrial Relations Act, and these to a considerable extent accord with your own. But we are both stuck with it, aren't we? And I fear that Section ______ makes the Company's position unavoidable. Meet me, though, and let's see whether we cannot sort out some legitimate and legal compromise.

With best wishes,

Yours sincerely,

216 Blaming the Act—simpliciter

Dear Mr Smith,

I know that you keep a copy of the Industrial Relations Act by your side, as I do. Have a look at Section ______ and you will see that I really have no alternative.

Yours sincerely,

217 **Can you suggest how to achieve results while keeping within the law?**

Dear Mr Brown,

I would willingly agree to a (for example, pre-entry closed shop) were an agreement to put one into effect not rendered void by the Industrial Relations Act. As it is, some sort of agency shop arrangement would appear to be the only lawful basis for an agreement between the Company and your Union/Unions. However, if you can suggest some lawful way in which we can get around this particular provision of the Act—which I know that neither of us cares for—then I shall be only too pleased to discuss this with you.

With best wishes,

Yours sincerely,

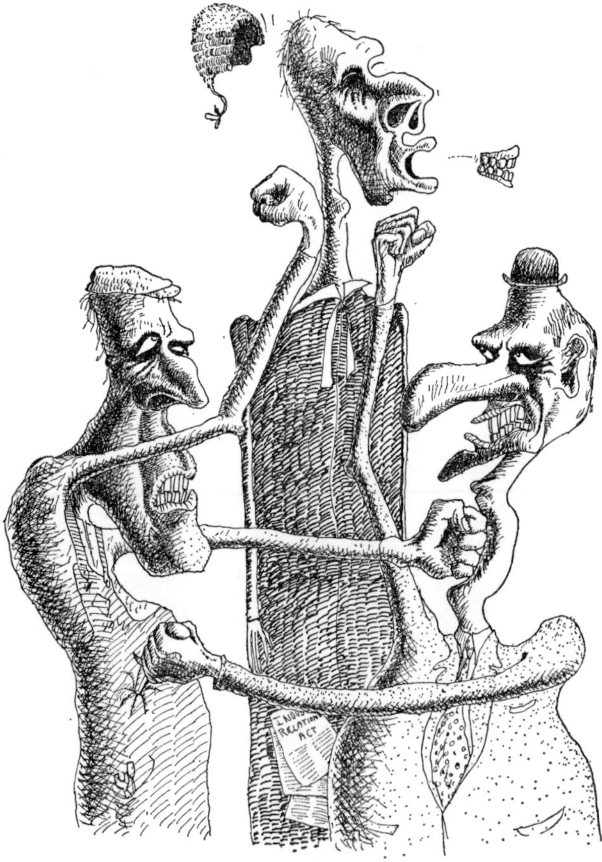
RELATION
ACT

Appendix 1

Vital Sections of the Industrial Relations Act, 1971

ARRANGEMENT OF SECTIONS

PART I

INTRODUCTORY

The Act

PART I

INTRODUCTORY

Use of code of practice in proceedings under this Act.

4. A failure on the part of any person to observe any provision of a code of practice which is for the time being in force under this Part of this Act shall not of itself render him liable to any proceedings ; but in any proceedings before the Industrial Court or an industrial tribunal under this Act—

(*a*) any such code of practice shall be admissible in evidence, and

(*b*) any provision of such a code of practice which appears to the Court or tribunal to be relevant to any question arising in the proceedings shall be taken into account by the Court or tribunal in determining that question.

PART II

RIGHTS OF WORKERS

Trade union membership and activities

Rights of workers in respect of trade union membership and activities.

5.—(1) Every worker shall, as between himself and his employer, have the following rights, that is to say,—

(*a*) the right to be a member of such trade union as he may choose ;

(*b*) subject to sections 6 and 17 of this Act, the right, if he so desires, to be a member of no trade union or other organisation of workers or to refuse to be a member of any particular trade union or other organisation of workers ;

(*c*) where he is a member of a trade union, the right, at any appropriate time, to take part in the activities of the trade union (including any activities as, or with a view to becoming, an official of the trade union) and the right to seek or accept appointment or election, and (if appointed or elected) to hold office, as such an official

(2) It shall accordingly be an unfair industrial practice for any employer, or for any person acting on behalf of an employer,—

(*a*) to prevent or deter a worker from exercising any of the rights conferred on him by subsection (1) of this section, or

(*b*) to dismiss, penalise or otherwise discriminate against a worker by reason of his exercising any such right, or

(*c*) except in accordance with the next following section,

to refuse to engage a worker on the grounds that, at the time when he applied for engagement, he was a member of a trade union or of a particular trade union, or that he was not then a member of a trade union or other organisation of workers or of a particular trade union or other organisation of workers or of any of two or more particular trade unions or other such organisations

(3) For the purposes of subsection (2)(*a*) of this section an employer, or a person acting on behalf of an employer, shall not be regarded as preventing or deterring a worker from exercising the rights conferred on the worker by subsection (1)(*b*) of this section by reason only that (without any suggestion of reward for compliance or penalty for non-compliance) he seeks to encourage the worker to join a trade union which the employer recognises as having negotiating rights in respect of him

(4) Where an employer offers a benefit of any kind to any workers as an inducement to refrain from exercising a right conferred on them by subsection (1) of this section, and the employer—

(*a*) confers that benefit on one or more of those workers who agree to refrain from exercising that right, and

(*b*) withholds it from one or more of them who do not agree to do so,

the employer shall for the purposes of this section be regarded, in relation to any such worker as is mentioned in paragraph (*b*) of this subsection, as having thereby discriminated against him by reason of his exercising that right.

(5) In this section " appropriate time ", in relation to a worker taking part in any activities of a trade union, means time which either—

(*a*) is outside his working hours, or

(*b*) is a time within his working hours at which, in accordance with arrangements agreed with, or consent given by or on behalf of, his employer, it is permissible for him to take part in those activities;

and in this subsection " working hours ", in relation to a worker, means any time when, in accordance with his contract with his employer, he is required to be at work.

(6) In this section any reference to a trade union shall be construed as including a reference to an organisation of workers which is for the time being entered in the provisional register.

Pre-entry closed shop agreements to be void.

7.—(1) In so far as any provision in any agreement purports—

(*a*) to preclude an employer, or employers of a description specified in the agreement, from engaging workers who are not members of a trade union or other organisation of workers, or from engaging workers who are not members of a particular trade union or other organisation of workers specified in the agreement, or are not members of any of two or more trade unions or other such organisations so specified, or

(*b*) to preclude an employer, or employers of a description specified in the agreement, from engaging workers who have not been recommended or approved for engagement by a trade union or other organisation of workers specified in the agreement, or by any of two or more trade unions or other such organisations so specified,

that provision shall be void.

(2) Any worker who, on application to an employer, has been refused engagement, and who claims that the refusal was attributable (wholly or in part) to a provision in an agreement which had the effect of precluding the employer as mentioned in paragraph (*a*) or paragraph (*b*) of subsection (1) of this section may apply to the Industrial Court for an order under the next following subsection.

(3) If on such an application the Industrial Court finds—

(*a*) that an agreement is in force consisting of or including a provision so formulated as to have the effect specified in subsection (2) of this section, however that provision is expressed and whether it purports to have that effect or not;

(*b*) that the refusal of the employer to engage the worker was wholly or partly attributable to that provision; and

(*c*) that the provision in question constitutes a substantial derogation from the rights conferred on workers by section 5 of this Act,

the Industrial Court shall make an order declaring that provision to be void.

8.—(1) Any reference in this Act to appropriate contributions to a trade union in lieu of membership of the trade union shall be construed in accordance with the following provisions of this section.

Appropriate contributions to trade union in lieu of membership.

(2) Appropriate contributions to a trade union in lieu of membership may be either—

(*a*) periodical payments only, or

(*b*) periodical payments and an initial payment,

as any particular agency shop agreement may provide; and, subject to the following provisions of this section and to section 10 of this Act, the amount of any such contribution payable by any person under an agency shop agreement shall be such amount as may be determined in accordance with the agreement.

(3) In so far as they consist of periodical payments, appropriate contributions payable by a person to a trade union for any year in pursuance of an agency shop agreement shall not in the aggregate exceed the aggregate amount which he would be required to pay for that year by way of periodical contributions in respect of membership if he were a member of the trade union, excluding any such contribution which (subject to his giving any requisite notice) he would not be obliged to pay.

(4) An agency shop agreement may provide for appropriate contributions to include an initial payment to a trade union where, under the rules of the trade union, a new member of the trade union would be required, on joining the union, to pay an initial contribution in addition to any periodical contributions; but, where the rules of the trade union do require such an initial contribution, any initial payment for which the agreement provides shall not exceed the initial contribution so required by the rules of the trade union.

(5) In the case of a person who, on the date on which an agency shop agreement takes effect, is a worker to whom the agreement applies, the agreement shall not require him to pay any such contribution as is mentioned in this section in respect of any period beginning earlier than three months from that date; and, in the case of a person who on that date is not a worker to whom the agreement applies, but subsequently becomes such a worker, the agreement shall not require him to pay any such contribution in respect of any period beginning earlier than one month from the date on which his employment as such a worker begins.

(6) The Secretary of State may by order made by statutory

instrument provide that, in so far as any agency shop agreement relates to workers engaged, or seeking to be engaged, in work of a description specified in the order, subsection (5) of this section shall have effect as if, for the references to three months and one month, there were substituted references to such shorter periods as are specified in the order.

Contributions to charity instead of contributions to trade union

9.—(1) Any worker who—

(*a*) in accordance with an agency shop agreement would, unless otherwise permitted under this or the next following section, be required to agree to pay appropriate contributions to a trade union, but

(*b*) objects on grounds of conscience both to being a member of a trade union and to paying contributions to a trade union in lieu of membership of it,

may propose to the trade union that, instead of paying such contributions, he should agree to pay equivalent contributions to a charity to be determined by agreement between him and the trade union.

(2) If the trade union agrees to the proposal, and the amount of the contributions, and the charity to which they are to be paid, are agreed between the worker and the trade union, the contributions so agreed shall be taken to be the equivalent contributions for the purposes of this Act.

(3) In this Part of this Act " charity " means any institution or other organisation established for charitable purposes only; and in relation to Scotland " charitable " shall be construed in the same way as if it were contained in the Income Tax Acts.

Reference to industrial tribunal of dispute relating to contribution.

10.—(1) Where any worker claims that a contribution which a trade union requires him to pay, as being an appropriate contribution payable in accordance with an agency shop agreement,—

(*a*) is not payable in accordance with the agreement, or

(*b*) exceeds the limit permitted by section 8 of this Act,

he may, in accordance with industrial tribunal regulations, require that claim to be referred to and determined by an industrial tribunal.

(2) If, in consequence of a proposal made by a worker under section 9 of this Act, a dispute arises between him and the trade union to which the proposal is made on any question—

(*a*) whether his objections to paying contributions to the

trade union are genuinely objections on grounds of conscience, or

(*b*) to which charity the contributions should be payable, or

(*c*) what contributions to a charity would be equivalent to appropriate contributions to the trade union,

the question in dispute may, in accordance with industrial tribunal regulations, be referred to and determined by an industrial tribunal.

(3) Any matter determined by the decision of an industrial tribunal on a reference under this section shall have the like effect for the purposes of this Act as if it had been agreed between the worker and the trade union.

Agency shop agreements

11.—(1) In this Act " agency shop agreement " means an agreement made between one or more employers and one or more trade unions or between an employers' association and one or more trade unions, whereby it is agreed, in respect of workers of one or more descriptions specified in the agreement, that their terms and conditions of employment shall include a condition that every such worker must either— **Agency shop agreement.**

(*a*) be or become a member of that trade union or of one of those trade unions, as the case may be, or

(*b*) agree to pay appropriate contributions to that trade union, or (as the case may be) to one of those trade unions, in lieu of membership or (where permitted to do so in accordance with section 9 or section 10 of this Act) agree to pay equivalent contributions to a charity.

(2) Where one or more trade unions desire to enter into an agency shop agreement with an employer in respect of workers of one or more descriptions, or a joint negotiating panel desires an employer to enter into such an agreement with one or more trade unions represented on the panel, and (in either case) the employer is unwilling to do so, either the trade union or trade unions or the joint negotiating panel or the employer may make an application to the Industrial Court, specifying—

(*a*) the description or descriptions of workers in question, and

(*b*) the employer and the trade union or trade unions who (if the agreement were made as desired) would be the parties to the agreement.

(3) If, on any such application, the Industrial Court is satisfied—

(*a*) that it is not precluded by section 13(4) or section 15(3) of this Act from entertaining the application, and

(*b*) that the trade union (or, as the case may be, each of the trade unions) or the joint negotiating panel specified in the application is recognised by the employer as having negotiating rights, or rights corresponding to negotiating rights, in respect of workers of the description or descriptions so specified,

the Court shall request the Commission to proceed in accordance with the next following section with a view to the taking of a ballot on the question whether an agency shop agreement should be made between the employer and the trade union or trade unions specified in the application.

(4) In this Part of this Act " rights corresponding to negotiating rights " means rights to participate, on behalf of one or more descriptions of workers who are not employees, in negotiations relating to those workers, with a view to the conclusion or modification of one or more collective agreements.

Ballot as to agency shop agreement.

12.—(1) If, on a request made by the Industrial Court under section 11(3) of this Act, it appears to the Commission that, in relation to workers of one or more descriptions specified in the application,—

(*a*) there is a question in dispute in respect of which an application has been or could be made to the Industrial Court under section 45 of this Act, and that, until that question has been settled, an agency shop agreement is likely to be ineffective, or

(*b*) such a question, although not yet in dispute, is likely to become the subject of a dispute if an agency shop agreement is made in pursuance of the application, and would in that event be likely, until settled, to make that agreement ineffective,

the Commission shall make a report to that effect to the Industrial Court, and to the trade union, trade unions, joint negotiating panel or employer who made the application, and shall not proceed further in relation to that request.

(2) Subject to the preceding subsection, the Commission shall determine—

(*a*) whether the ballot should extend to all workers falling within the range specified in the application (whether that range consists of one description or two or more descriptions of workers) or should be limited to part of that range, and (*b*) whether (in addition to workers falling within that range or part of it, as the case may be) the ballot should extend to workers of one or more descriptions not specified in the application, in respect of whom the trade union (or, as the case may be, each of the trade unions) or the joint negotiating panel is recognised by the employer as having negotiating rights or rights corresponding to negotiating rights,

and shall make a report to the Industrial Court specifying the description or descriptions of workers who, in accordance with the conclusions of the Commission under this subsection, are to take part in the ballot.

(3) The Commission shall also determine whether the ballot is to be taken by the Commission or is to be taken under the supervision of the Commission by some other body, and in either case what arrangements would best secure that the ballot will be properly conducted, and that the voting in the ballot will be kept secret.

(4) The Commission shall thereupon arrange for the ballot to be taken in accordance with their conclusions under subsections (2) and (3) of this section, and shall report the result of the ballot to the Industrial Court and to the employer and the trade union or trade unions specified in the application under section 11 of this Act and, where the applicant was a joint negotiating panel, to that panel.

Effect of ballot. under s. 12.

13.—(1) If the result of a ballot as reported to the Industrial Court under section 12 of this Act is that either a majority of the workers eligible to vote in the ballot or not less than two-thirds of those who voted in it have voted in favour of an agency shop agreement, then it shall be the duty of the employer to take all such action as is requisite on his part for the purposes—

(*a*) of entering into an agency shop agreement in respect of the description or descriptions of workers comprised in the ballot, and

(*b*) after such an agreement has been made, of carrying out the agreement so long as it remains in force.

(2) It shall be an unfair industrial practice for any person (including any trade union or other organisation of workers or any official of a trade union or of such an organisation)—

(*a*) by calling, organising, procuring or financing a strike, or threatening to do so, or

(*b*) by organising, procuring or financing any irregular

industrial action short of a strike, or threatening to do so,

knowingly to induce or attempt to induce an employer not to perform a duty imposed on the employer by the preceding subsection.

(3) If the result of a ballot as reported by the Commission to the Industrial Court is that neither a majority of the workers eligible to vote in the ballot nor two-thirds of those who voted in it have voted in favour of an agency shop agreement, the Industrial Court shall make an order directing—

(*a*) that no agency shop agreement in respect of workers of any description comprised in the ballot shall, during the period of two years beginning with the date on which that result was reported by the Commission to the Court, be made between the employer and the trade union (or, as the case may be, any of the trade unions) specified in the application in pursuance of which the ballot was taken, and

(*b*) that any such agency shop agreement purporting to be made between those parties during that period shall be void.

(4) Where the Industrial Court has made an order under subsection (3) of this section, the Court shall not entertain any application under section 11 of this Act if—

(*a*) it is made before the end of the period specified in that subsection, and

(*b*) it relates (wholly or in part) to workers of any descriptions comprised in the ballot.

Application for ballot on continuance of agency shop agreement.

14.—(1) Subject to the following provisions of this section, at any time when an agency shop agreement is in force any worker to whom the agreement applies may make an application to the Industrial Court under this section.

(2) The Industrial Court shall not entertain such an application unless the Court is satisfied that not less than one-fifth of the workers to whom the agreement for the time being applies have signified in writing their concurrence in the application.

(3) In the case of an agency shop agreement made in pursuance of a ballot taken under section 12 of this Act, the Industrial Court shall not entertain an application under this section if the application is made before the end of the period of two years beginning with the date on which the result of that ballot was reported by the Commission to the Court.

(4) Where the Industrial Court entertains an application under this section, the Court shall request the Commission to arrange for a ballot to be taken on the question whether the agency shop agreement to which the application relates should continue in force.

(5) The persons eligible to vote in the ballot shall be the workers to whom the agency shop agreement for the time being applies.

15.—(1) For the purpose of complying with a request made by the Industrial Court under section 14 of this Act with respect to an agency shop agreement, the Commission shall determine whether the ballot is to be taken by the Commission or is to be taken under the supervision of the Commission by some other body, and in either case what arrangements would best secure— **Ballot on application under s. 14.**

(*a*) that the ballot will be properly conducted, and

(*b*) that the voting in the ballot will be kept secret,

and shall arrange for the ballot to be taken accordingly.

(2) After a ballot has been taken under this section, the Commission shall report the result of the ballot to the Industrial Court and to each of the parties to the agency shop agreement.

(3) If the result of the ballot, as so reported, is that neither a majority of the workers eligible to vote in the ballot nor two-thirds of those who voted in it have voted in favour of continuance of the agency shop agreement, the Industrial Court shall make an order rescinding the agreement, and directing—

(*a*) that no agency shop agreement in respect of workers of any description comprised in the ballot shall, during the period of two years beginning with the date on which the result of the ballot was so reported, be made between the employer and the trade union (or, as the case may be, any of the trade unions) who were parties to the agency shop agreement to which the ballot related, and

(*b*) that any such agency shop agreement purporting to be made between those parties during that period shall be void ;

and during that period the Industrial Court shall not entertain any application under section 11 of this Act if it appears to the Court to relate (wholly or in part) to a description of workers which is substantially the same as the description, or one of the descriptions, of workers comprised in the ballot.

(4) If the result of the ballot, as so reported, is that either a majority of the workers eligible to vote in the ballot or not less than two-thirds of those who voted in it have voted in favour of continuance of the agency shop agreement, the Industrial Court shall not entertain any application under section 14 of this Act if—

(*a*) it relates to the same agency shop agreement, and

(*b*) it is made before the end of the period of two years beginning with the date on which the result of the ballot was so reported.

Pressure to anticipate result of ballot.

16.—(1) It shall be an unfair industrial practice for an employer, by instituting, carrying on, organising, procuring or financing a lock-out, or threatening to do so, knowingly to induce or attempt to induce a trade union or joint negotiating panel, or any other person, to refrain from making an application under section 11 or section 14 of this Act.

(2) It shall be an unfair industrial practice for any person (including any trade union or any official of a trade union) by calling, organising, procuring or financing a strike or threatening to do so, or by organising, procuring or financing any irregular industrial action short of a strike, or threatening to do so,—

(*a*) except in the circumstances specified in section 13(1) of this Act, knowingly to induce or attempt to induce an employer to enter into an agency shop agreement in respect of workers of any description after an application relating (wholly or in part) to workers of that description has been made under section 11 of this Act, or

(*b*) knowingly to induce or attempt to induce an employer to refrain from making an application under section 11 of this Act.

Contracts of Employment Act 1963

Minimum periods of notice to terminate contracts of employment. 1963 c. 49.

19.—(1) In subsections (1) and (2) of section 1 of the Contracts of Employment Act 1963 (which specify the minimum periods of notice required to terminate the contracts of employment of employees who have been continuously employed for twenty-six weeks or more), for the words " twenty-six ", in each place where they occur, there shall be substituted the word " thirteen "

(2) In paragraph (*c*) of subsection (1) of that section (which specifies the minimum period of notice where an employee's

period of continuous employment is five years or more), after the words "five years or more" there shall be inserted the words "but less than ten years, and", and after that paragraph there shall be inserted the following paragraphs:—

"(*d*) shall be not less than six weeks' notice if his period of continuous employment is ten years or more but less than fifteen years, and

(*e*) shall be not less than eight weeks' notice if his period of continuous employment is fifteen years or more".

Written particulars of terms of employment.

20.—(1) In section 4 of the Contracts of Employment Act 1963 (which requires employers to give to their employees a written statement containing particulars of their terms of employment), for sub-paragraph (i) of subsection (1)(*d*) there shall be substituted the following sub-paragraph:—

"(i) entitlement to holidays, including public holidays, and holiday pay (the particulars given being sufficient to enable the employee's entitlement, including any entitlement to accrued holiday pay on the termination of employment, to be precisely calculated)".

(2) Every statement given to an employee under subsection (1) of that section after the commencement of this Act shall include a note—

(*a*) indicating the nature of the employee's rights under section 5 of this Act, including, where an agency shop agreement or an approved closed shop agreement is in force which applies to him, the effect of that agreement on those rights, and

(*b*) specifying by description or otherwise a person to whom the employee can apply for the purpose of seeking redress of any grievance relating to his employment, and the manner in which any such application should be made, and

(*c*) either explaining the steps consequent upon any such application or referring to a document which is reasonably accessible to the employee and which explains those steps.

Unfair dismissal

Right of employee not to be unfairly dismissed.

22.—(1) In every employment to which this section applies every employee shall have the right not to be unfairly dismissed by his employer; and accordingly, in any such employment, it shall be an unfair industrial practice for an employer to dismiss an employee unfairly.

(2) This section applies to every employment except in so far as its application is excluded by or under any of sections 27 to 31 of this Act.

(3) In the following provisions of this Part of this Act "the claimant" means the employee who claims that he has been unfairly dismissed by his employer.

Meaning of "dismissal". **23.**—(1) In this Act "dismissal" and "dismiss" shall be construed in accordance with the following provisions of this section.

(2) Subject to the next following subsection, for the purposes of this Act an employee shall be taken to be dismissed by his employer if, but only if,—

(*a*) the contract under which he is employed by the employer is terminated by the employer, whether it is so terminated by notice or without notice, or

(*b*) where under that contract he is employed for a fixed term, that term expires without being renewed under the same contract.

(3) Where an employer gives notice to an employee to terminate his contract of employment and, at a time within the obligatory period of that notice, the employee gives notice in writing to the employer to terminate the contract of employment on a date earlier than the date on which the employer's notice is due to expire, the employee shall for the purposes of this Act be taken to be dismissed by his employer, and the reasons for the dismissal shall be taken to be the reasons for which the employer's notice is given.

(4) For the purposes of subsection (3) of this section—

(*a*) if the actual period of the employer's notice (that is to say, the period beginning at the time when the notice is given and ending with the time when it expires) is equal to the minimum period which (whether by virtue of any enactment or otherwise) is required to be given by the employer to terminate the contract of employment, "the obligatory period", in relation to that notice, means the actual period of the notice;

(*b*) in any other case, "the obligatory period", in relation to an employer's notice, means that period which, being equal to the minimum period referred to in the preceding paragraph, expires at the time when the employer's notice expires.

(5) In this Act " the effective date of termination "—

(*a*) in relation to an employee whose contract of employment is terminated by notice, whether given by his employer or by the employee, means the date on which that notice expires;

(*b*) in relation to an employee whose contract of employment is terminated without notice, means the date on which the termination takes effect; and

(*c*) in relation to an employee who is employed under a contract for a fixed term, where that term expires without being renewed under the same contract, means the date on which that term expires.

24.—(1) In determining for the purposes of this Act whether the dismissal of an employee was fair or unfair, it shall be for the employer to show— Fair and unfair dismissal

(*a*) what was the reason (or, if there was more than one, the principal reason) for the dismissal, and

(*b*) that it was a reason falling within the next following subsection, or some other substantial reason of a kind such as to justify the dismissal of an employee holding the position which that employee held.

(2) In subsection (1)(*b*) of this section the reference to a reason falling within this subsection is a reference to a reason which—

(*a*) related to the capability or qualifications of the employee for performing work of the kind which he was employed by the employer to do, or

(*b*) related to the conduct of the employee, or

(*c*) was that the employee was redundant, or

(*d*) was that the employee could not continue to work in the position which he held without contravention (either on his part or on that of his employer) of a duty or restriction imposed by or under an enactment.

(3) Where the employer has fulfilled the requirements of subsection (1) of this section, then, subject to sections 25 and 26 of this Act, the question whether the dismissal was fair or unfair shall be determined in accordance with the following provisions of this section.

(4) For the purposes of this Act the dismissal of an employee by an employer shall be regarded as having been unfair if the

reason for it (or, if more than one, the principal reason) was that the employee had exercised, or had indicated his intention to exercise, any of the rights conferred on the employee by section 5(1) of this Act.

(5) Where the reason or principal reason for the dismissal of an employee was that he was redundant, but it is shown that the circumstances constituting the redundancy applied equally to one or more other employees in the same undertaking who held positions similar to that held by him and who have not been dismissed by the employer, and either—

(*a*) that the reason (or, if more than one, the principal reason) for which he was selected for dismissal was that he had exercised, or had indicated his intention to exercise, any of the rights conferred on him by section 5(1) of this Act, or

(*b*) that he was selected for dismissal in contravention of a customary arrangement or agreed procedure relating to redundancy and there were no special reasons justifying a departure from that arrangement or procedure in his case,

then for the purposes of this Act the dismissal shall be regarded as unfair.

(6) Subject to subsections (4) and (5) of this section, the determination of the question whether the dismissal was fair or unfair, having regard to the reason shown by the employer, shall depend on whether in the circumstances he acted reasonably or unreasonably in treating it as a sufficient reason for dismissing the employee; and that question shall be determined in accordance with equity and the substantial merits of the case.

(7) In this section, in relation to an employee,—

(*a*) " capability " means capability assessed by reference to skill, aptitude, health or any other physical or mental quality;

(*b*) " qualifications " means any degree, diploma or other academic, technical or professional qualification relevant to the position which the employee held; and

(*c*) any reference to redundancy or to being redundant shall be construed as a reference to the existence of one or other of the facts specified in paragraphs (*a*) and (*b*) of section 1(2) of the Redundancy Payments Act 1965.

1965 c. 62.

Dismissal in connection with a lock-out.

25.—(1) The dismissal of an employee by way of a lock-out (whether the lock-out extends to all the employees of the employer or only to some of them, and whether the dismissal occurs at the beginning of the lock-out or during the course of it) shall not be regarded as unfair if the employee is offered re-engagement as from the date of resumption of work.

(2) Where an employee who has been so dismissed, and has not been offered re-engagement as from the date of resumption of work, claims that he was unfairly dismissed by his employer, the provisions of section 24 of this Act shall apply as if in that section, for any reference to the reason or principal reason for which the employee was dismissed by his employer, there were substituted a reference to the reason or principal reason for which he was not offered re-engagement as from that date.

(3) In this section any reference to an offer of re-engagement, in relation to an employee, is a reference to an offer (made either by the original employer or by a successor of that employer or by an associated employer) to re-engage that employee, either in the position which he held immediately before the effective date of termination or in a different position which would be reasonably suitable to him.

(4) In this section—

(*a*) "the date of resumption of work" means the date as from which, at or after the termination of the lock-out, the other comparable employees of the original employer, or a majority of those employees, were offered re-engagement, and

(*b*) "the original employer" means the employer who dismissed the claimant;

and in this subsection "comparable employees", in relation to the claimant, means such of the employees of the original employer to whom the lock-out extended as, immediately before the effective date of termination, held positions similar to that held by the claimant.

26.—(1) The provisions of this section shall have effect in relation to an employee who claims that he has been unfairly dismissed by his employer, where on the date of dismissal he was taking part in a strike or in any irregular industrial action short of a strike. Dismissal in connection with a strike or other industrial action.

(2) If the reason or principal reason for the dismissal was that the claimant took part in the strike or other industrial action, the dismissal shall not be regarded as unfair unless it is shown—

(*a*) that one or more employees of the same employer (in this section referred to as "the original employer"), who also took part in that action, were not dismissed for taking part in it, or (*b*) that one or more such employees, who were dismissed for taking part in it, were offered re-engagement on the termination of the industrial action and that the claimant was not offered such re-engagement,

and that the reason (or, if more than one, the principal reason) for which the claimant was selected for dismissal, or not offered re-engagement, was his having taken action to which the next following subsection applies.

(3) This subsection applies to any action on the part of the claimant which consisted of exercising, or indicating his intention to exercise, any of the rights conferred on him by section 5(1) of this Act.

(4) In this section any reference to the date of dismissal—

(*a*) where the claimant's contract of employment was terminated by notice, whether given by his employer or by him, is a reference to the date on which that notice was given, and

(*b*) in any other case, is a reference to the effective date of termination;

and any reference to an offer of re-engagement, in relation to an employee, is a reference to an offer (made either by the original employer or by a successor of that employer or by an associated employer) to re-engage that employee, either in the position which he held immediately before the date of dismissal or in a different position which would be reasonably suitable to him.

Excluded cases

Excluded classes of employment.

27.—(1) Section 22 of this Act does not apply to any of the following, that is to say,—

(*a*) any employment in an undertaking in which immediately before the effective date of termination there were in the aggregate (including the claimant) less than four employees who had been continuously employed for a period of not less than thirteen weeks, whether they are, or had been, all employed at the same place or are, or had been, employed at different places;

(*b*) any employment where the employer is the husband or wife or a close relative of the employee;

(*c*) any employment as a registered dock worker, as defined by any scheme for the time being in force under the

1946 c. 22.

Dock Workers (Regulation of Employment) Act 1946,

not being employment by virtue of which the employee is wholly or mainly engaged in work which is not dock work as defined by the scheme;

(*d*) any employment as master or as a member of the crew of a fishing vessel, where the employee is not remunerated otherwise than by a share in the profits or gross earnings of the vessel;

(*e*) any employment as a teacher to whom section 85 of the Education (Scotland) Act 1962 (dismissal of teachers) applies; 1962 c. 47.

(*f*) any employment under a contract which normally involves employment for less than twenty-one hours weekly.

(2) Section 22 of this Act does not apply to any employment where under his contract of employment the employee ordinarily works outside Great Britain.

(3) For the purposes of subsection (2) of this section a person employed to work on board a ship registered in the United Kingdom (not being a ship registered at a port outside Great Britain) shall, unless—

(*a*) the employment is wholly outside Great Britain, or

(*b*) he is not ordinarily resident in Great Britain,

be regarded as a person who under his contract ordinarily works in Great Britain.

(4) In this section " close relative ", in relation to a person, means that person's father, mother, grandfather, grandmother, stepfather, stepmother, son, daughter, grandson, granddaughter, stepson, stepdaughter, brother, sister, half-brother or half-sister.

(5) The preceding provisions of this section shall have effect subject to any order made under section 29 of this Act.

Qualifying period and upper age limit.

28. Subject to the next following section, section 22 of this Act does not apply to the dismissal of an employee from any employment if the employee—

(*a*) was not continuously employed for a period of not less than 104 weeks ending with the effective date of termination, or

(*b*) on or before the effective date of termination attained the age which, in the undertaking in which he was employed, was the normal retiring age for an employee holding the position which he held, or, if a man, attained the age of sixty-five, or, if a woman, attained the age of sixty.

Supplementary provisions relating to ss. 27 and 28.

29.—(1) Paragraph (*a*) of section 27(1) and section 28 of this Act shall not apply to the dismissal of an employee if it is shown that the reason (or, if more than one, the principal reason) for the dismissal was that the employee had exercised, or had indicated his intention to exercise, any of the rights conferred on him by section 5(1) of this Act.

(2) The Secretary of State may by order made by statutory instrument add to or vary any of the provisions of sections 27 and 28 of this Act or exclude the operation of any of those provisions.

(3) No order shall be made under this section unless a draft of the order has been laid before Parliament and approved by a resolution of each House of Parliament.

Exclusion of certain contracts for a fixed term.

30. Section 22 of this Act does not apply—

(*a*) to dismissal from employment under a contract for a fixed term of two years or more, where the contract was made before the commencement of this Act and is not a contract of apprenticeship, and the dismissal consists only of the expiry of that term without its being renewed, or

(*b*) to dismissal from employment under a contract for a fixed term of two years or more, where the dismissal consists only of the expiry of that term without its being renewed, if before the term so expires the employee has agreed in writing to exclude any claim in respect of rights under that section in relation to that contract.

Supplementary

Pressure on employer to infringe rights of workers.

33.—(1) In determining, for the purposes of this Part of this Act, any question as to the reason, or principal reason, for which a worker was dismissed, penalised, or otherwise discriminated against, or any question whether the reason or principal reason for which a worker was dismissed was a reason fulfilling the requirements of section 24(1)(*b*) of this Act or whether the employer acted reasonably in treating it as a sufficient reason for dismissing him,—

(*a*) no account shall be taken of any pressure which, by means of any action to which this section applies, was exercised on the employer to dismiss, penalise or otherwise discriminate against the worker, and

(*b*) any such question shall be determined as if no such pressure had been exercised.

(2) This section applies to action of any of the following descriptions, that is to say—

(*a*) calling, organising, procuring or financing a strike, or threatening to do so;

(*b*) organising, procuring or financing any irregular industrial action short of a strike, or threatening to do so.

(3) It shall be an unfair industrial practice for any person (including any trade union or other organisation of workers or any official of a trade union or of such an organisation) to take any action to which this section applies, if the purpose or principal purpose for which that action is taken is—

(*a*) knowingly to induce an employer, or a person acting on behalf of an employer, to take any action which (whether by virtue of subsection (1) of this section or otherwise) is or would be an unfair industrial practice, in accordance with section 5(2) or section 22(1) of this Act, on the part of the employer or of the person acting on the employer's behalf, or

(*b*) knowingly to induce an employer to comply with any provision in an agreement in so far as that provision is void by virtue of subsection (1) of section 7 of this Act, or knowingly to induce an employer to enter into an agreement consisting of or including a provision which would be void by virtue of that subsection, or

(*c*) knowingly to induce an employer to comply with a provision declared to be void by an order of the Industrial Court under section 7(3) of this Act, or

(*d*) knowingly to induce an employer or an employers' association to join in making an application under Part I of Schedule 1 to this Act.

(4) In this Act "irregular industrial action short of a strike" means any concerted course of conduct (other than a strike) which, in contemplation or furtherance of an industrial dispute,—

(*a*) is carried on by a group of workers with the intention of preventing, reducing or otherwise interfering with the production of goods or the provision of services, and

(*b*) in the case of some or all of them, is carried on in breach of their contracts of employment or (where they are not employees) in breach of their terms and conditions of service.

PART III

COLLECTIVE BARGAINING

Effect of collective agreements

Presumptions relating to collective agreements.

34.—(1) Every collective agreement which—

(*a*) is made in writing after the commencement of this Act, and

(*b*) does not contain a provision which (however expressed) states that the agreement or part of it is intended not to be legally enforceable,

shall be conclusively presumed to be intended by the parties to it to be a legally enforceable contract.

(2) Where a collective agreement made in writing after the commencement of this Act contains a provision which (however expressed) states that a part of the agreement specified in that provision is intended not to be legally enforceable, the agreement, with the exception of that part, shall be conclusively presumed to have been intended by the parties to it to be a legally enforceable contract.

Breach of collective agreement.

36.—(1) It shall be an unfair industrial practice for any party to a collective agreement—

(*a*) where the agreement is a legally enforceable contract, to break the agreement, or

(*b*) where part (but not the whole) of the agreement is a legally enforceable contract, to break that part of the agreement.

(2) Where a collective agreement made after the commencement of this Act, or part of such a collective agreement, is a legally enforceable contract, it shall be an unfair industrial practice for any party to the agreement not to take all such steps as are reasonably practicable for the purposes—

(*a*) of preventing persons acting or purporting to act on behalf of that party from taking any action contrary to an undertaking given by that party and contained in the collective agreement or in that part of the agreement, as the case may be;

(*b*) where the party in question is an organisation, of preventing members of the organisation from taking any such action; and

(*c*) where any action has been taken as mentioned in paragraph (*a*) or paragraph (*b*) of this subsection, of securing that the action is not continued and that further action as mentioned in those paragraphs does not occur.

(3) For the purposes of subsection (2) of this section action taken by a person other than the party who gave the undertaking in question (in this subsection referred to as " the contracting party ") shall be regarded as action taken contrary to the undertaking if either—

(*a*) it is action which, if taken by the contracting party, would have been a breach of the undertaking by the contracting party, or

(*b*) it consists in doing that which, in accordance with the undertaking, was not to be done, or in not doing that which, in accordance with the undertaking, was to be done.

Remedial action where procedure agreement non-existent or defective

37.—(1) The Secretary of State, or any other party to whom this section applies, may make an application to the Industrial Court with respect to any particular unit of employment on the grounds that the unit suffers from one or both of the following defects, that is to say—

Application to Industrial Court relating to procedural provisions.

(*a*) the absence of a procedure agreement, or the unsuitability of such procedure agreement as may exist for the purpose of settling disputes or grievances promptly and fairly;

(*b*) where a procedure agreement is in existence, recourse to industrial action (whether consisting of lock-outs, strikes or irregular industrial action short of a strike) contrary to the terms or intentions of that agreement.

(2) The parties to whom this section applies in relation to a unit of employment, other than the Secretary of State, are the employer and—

(*a*) any trade union which the employer recognises as having negotiating rights in relation to that unit, and

(*b*) where a procedure agreement is in existence which applies to that unit, any trade union (not falling within the preceding paragraph) which is a party to that agreement.

(3) Before the Secretary of State makes an application under this section with respect to a unit of employment, he shall

consult the parties appearing to him, in relation to that unit, to be the parties to whom this section applies.

(4) The Industrial Court shall not entertain an application made under this section by a party other than the Secretary of State unless that party, before making the application, has given notice to the Secretary of State of the proposal to make it; and, where such a notice has been given,—

(*a*) the Secretary of State shall offer such advice and assistance to the party giving the notice, and to such other parties as appear to him to be directly concerned, as he may consider appropriate with a view to promoting agreement between them with respect to the matters to which the application would relate, and for that purpose may refer any question relating to those matters to the Commission for examination by them, but

(*b*) nothing in the preceding paragraph shall prevent the party giving the notice from making an application under this section at any time after the notice has been given.

(5) Subject to the last preceding subsection, if on an application under this section it appears to the Industrial Court that there are reasonable grounds for believing that the unit of employment to which the application relates suffers from one or both of the defects specified in subsection (1) of this section and that, by reason of its doing so,—

(*a*) the development or maintenance of orderly industrial relations in that unit has been seriously impeded, or

(*b*) there have been substantial and repeated losses of working time in that unit,

the Court shall refer to the Commission the question whether the unit does suffer from one or both of those defects and, if so, what remedy (if any) in accordance with the provisions of section 40 of this Act is to be recommended

(6) In this section and in sections 38 to 42 of this Act " unit of employment " means an undertaking or part of an undertaking.

Recognition of sole bargaining agent

Definitions relating to bargaining structure.

44. In this Act—

(*a*) " bargaining unit " means those employees or descriptions of employees of an employer, or of two or more associated employers, in relation to whom collective bargaining, in respect of such matters as are not dealt with under more extensive bargaining arrangements, is, or could appropriately be, carried on by an organisation of workers or a joint negotiating panel, or partly by an organisation of workers and partly by a joint negotiating panel;

(*b*) " negotiating rights " means rights, recognised by an employer or by two or more associated employers, to participate, on behalf of all or some of the employees comprised in a bargaining unit, in negotiations relating to that unit, with a view to the conclusion or modification of one or more collective agreements;

(*c*) " sole bargaining agent ", in relation to a bargaining unit, means the organisation of workers or joint negotiating panel having negotiating rights in relation to that unit to the exclusion of all other organisations of workers and joint negotiating panels, except in respect of matters which are dealt with under more extensive bargaining arrangements;

(*d*) " joint negotiating panel " means a body consisting of representatives of two or more organisations of workers which is established for purposes of collective bargaining and is authorised by or on behalf of those organisations to enter into collective agreements on their behalf;

(*e*) " joint negotiating panel of trade unions " means a joint negotiating panel where all the organisations of workers represented on it are trade unions; and

(*f*) " more extensive bargaining arrangements ", in relation to any particular employees or descriptions of employees of an employer, or of two or more associated employers, means arrangements for collective bargaining in respect of matters common to those employees or descriptions of employees and to other employees or descriptions of employees, whether of the same employer or employers or of one or more different employers.

45.—(1) An application may be made to the Industrial Court for the reference to the Commission, for examination by them, of the following two questions relating to the employees of an

Application to Industrial Court for reference as to

recognition of sole bargaining agent

employer, or to the employees of two or more associated employers, that is to say—

(*a*) whether a specified group of those employees should, as a whole, be recognised (or, if already recognised, should continue to be recognised) by the employer or employers as a bargaining unit, or a part or parts of such a specified group should be so recognised (or should continue to be so recognised) as a separate bargaining unit or separate bargaining units; and

(*b*) whether, for any bargaining unit which is or should be so recognised, a sole bargaining agent should be recognised by the employer or employers and, if so, what organisation of workers or what joint negotiating panel (whether already in existence or to be formed for the purpose) should be the sole bargaining agent for that bargaining unit.

(2) Subject to the next following subsection, an application under this section relating to the employees of one or more employers may be made—

(*a*) by one or more trade unions, or

(*b*) by the employer or (as the case may be) by any of the employers, or

(*c*) by the employer, or (as the case may be) any of the employers, jointly with one or more trade unions, or

(*d*) by the Secretary of State.

(3) Before making an application under this section with respect to a group of employees, the Secretary of State shall consult—

(*a*) their employer or employers, and

(*b*) any organisation of workers or joint negotiating panel appearing to him to be directly concerned in the matters to which the proposed application would relate.

(4) The Industrial Court shall not entertain an application made under this section otherwise than by the Secretary of State unless, before the application was made, notice of the proposal to make it had been given to the Secretary of State; and where such a notice has been given—

(*a*) the Secretary of State shall offer such advice and assistance to the party or parties giving the notice, and to such other parties as appear to him to be directly concerned, as he may consider appropriate with a view to promoting agreement between them with respect to the matters to which the application would relate, and for that purpose may refer any question relating to those matters to the Commission for examination by them, but

(*b*) nothing in the preceding paragraph shall prevent the party or parties giving the notice from making an application under this section at any time after the notice has been given.

(5) In this section and in section 46 of this Act " group ", in relation to an application relating to the employees of an employer or of two or more associated employers, means a group consisting either of all those employees or of such of them as fall within one or more descriptions specified in the application.

47.—(1) At any time after a reference has been made to the Commission under section 46 of this Act, and before the Commission have reported on it, the Commission may apply to the Industrial Court to withdraw the reference on the grounds that a satisfactory and lasting settlement of the questions in issue has already been reached; and, if the Industrial Court is satisfied that such a settlement has been reached, the Court shall withdraw the reference.

Withdrawal or extension of reference under s. 46.

(2) If, at any time after such a reference has been made and before the Commission have reported on it, it appears to the Commission that, with a view to promoting a satisfactory and lasting settlement of the questions in issue, it is necessary or expedient to extend the scope of the reference, the Commission, subject to the next following subsection, may formulate proposals for extending it; and, where the Commission have formulated any such proposals, they shall—

(*a*) transmit the proposals to the Industrial Court, and

(*b*) cause notice of the proposals to be given or published as may appear to the Commission to be appropriate for bringing them to the attention of persons who in the opinion of the Commission would be affected by them.

(3) No such proposals shall provide for extending the scope of a reference to any employer unless he is an associated employer in relation to the employer or employers to whom the reference originally related.

(4) At any time within the period of two weeks from the

date (or, if more than one, the latest date) on which notice of any such proposals is given or published under subsection (2)(*b*) of this section, any person claiming to be affected by the proposals may apply to the Industrial Court to consider whether the proposals are necessary or expedient; and on any such application the Industrial Court may—

(*a*) extend the scope of the reference in accordance with the proposals, or

(*b*) extend its scope to a lesser extent than that proposed, or

(*c*) direct that its scope shall remain unchanged,

as the Court may consider appropriate.

(5) If no such application as is mentioned in subsection (4) of this section is made within the period specified in that subsection, the Industrial Court shall confirm the proposals and extend the scope of the reference in accordance with them.

48.—

(6) Where it appears to the Commission that a joint negotiating panel ought to be formed in relation to a bargaining unit, the Commission, before recommending any organisation of workers for inclusion among those to be represented on the panel, shall in particular consider whether—

(*a*) it has or would have the support of a substantial proportion of the employees comprised in that bargaining unit, or of a substantial proportion of the employees of one or more descriptions comprised in that unit, and

(*b*) it has or would have such resources, and is or would be so organised, as to enable it to participate effectively in the work of the panel.

(7) Any recommendation contained in such a report may be made subject to such conditions as the Commission think fit; and in particular (but without prejudice to the generality of this subsection) any such condition—

(*a*) may require an organisation of workers recommended for recognition as sole bargaining agent for a bargaining unit, or for inclusion in a joint negotiating panel so recommended, to make sufficient trained officials available for purposes of collective bargaining, or

(*b*) may require any organisation of workers so recommended to undertake not to make or pursue any claim to be recognised as sole bargaining agent for any other bargaining unit consisting (wholly or in part) of employees of any employer to whom the recommendation relates.

(8) Where the Commission determine, in making a report under this section, to recommend the recognition of an organisation of workers or joint negotiation panel as sole bargaining agent for a bargaining unit, and it appears to the Commission that there are in existence more extensive bargaining arrangements which will be applicable to the employees comprised or to be comprised in that bargaining unit, the recommendation—

(*a*) may specify the more extensive bargaining arrangements in question, and

(*b*) may be made subject to the reservation that the organisation or panel, at any time when it is recognised as sole bargaining agent in pursuance of the recommendation, shall not have exclusive negotiating rights in respect of matters which are at that time being dealt with under the specified arrangements or which are then the subject of a collective agreement negotiated under those arrangements.

Application to Industrial Court for ballot as to recognition of sole bargaining agent.

49.—(1) Where in a report under section 48 of this Act the Commission have recommended (with or without a reservation under subsection (8) of that section) that a particular organisation of workers or joint negotiating panel should be recognised by one or more employers as sole bargaining agent for a bargaining unit, then at any time before the end of the period of six months beginning with the date on which that report is transmitted by the Commission to the Industrial Court, either—

(*a*) the employer (or, if more than one, any of the employers), or

(*b*) subject to the next following subsection, the organisation of workers or joint negotiating panel, as the case may be,

may make an application to the Industrial Court under this section.

(2) No application under this section shall be made—

(*a*) in respect of a recommendation relating to an organisation of workers, unless at the time of the application it is a trade union, or (*b*) in respect of a recommendation relating to a joint negotiating panel, unless at that time it is a joint negotiating panel of trade unions.

(3) If, on any such application, the Industrial Court is satisfied that the recommendation of the Commission was unconditional, or that any conditions subject to which it was made have been sufficiently complied with, the Court shall request the Commission to make arrangements for a ballot of employees comprised in the bargaining unit to be taken on the question whether the recommendation should be made binding.

(4) For the purpose of complying with any such request of the Industrial Court, the Commission shall determine whether the ballot is to be taken by the Commission or is to be taken under the supervision of the Commission by some other body, and in either case what arrangements would best secure that the ballot is properly conducted and that the voting in the ballot will be kept secret, and shall arrange for the ballot to be taken accordingly.

(5) The Commission shall secure that the ballot is not taken until such period as in their opinion is adequate has elapsed since the publication of the report under section 48 of this Act.

(6) After a ballot has been taken under this section, the Commission shall report the result of the ballot to the Industrial Court, to the employer or employers and to the trade union or joint negotiating panel, as the case may be.

Withdrawal of recognition of sole bargaining agent

Application to Industrial Court with a view to withdrawal of recognition.

51.—(1) Any person claiming to be an employee for the time being comprised in a bargaining unit may make an application to the Industrial Court on the grounds that an organisation of workers or joint negotiating panel specified in the application—

(*a*) is for the time being recognised by one or more employers so specified as sole bargaining agent for that bargaining unit, or

(*b*) is required, by an order under section 50 of this Act which is for the time being in force, to be so recognised,

and that (in either case) the organisation of workers or joint negotiating panel does not adequately represent the employees comprised in that bargaining unit, or does not adequately represent a particular section of it to which the applicant belongs.

(2) The Industrial Court shall not entertain an application under this section, in a case where there is no order for the time being in force under section 50 of this Act requiring the organisation of workers or joint negotiating panel in question to be recognised as mentioned in the preceding subsection, unless the Court is satisfied that not less than one-fifth of the employees for the time being comprised in the bargaining unit have signified in writing their concurrence in the application.

(3) The Industrial Court shall not entertain an application under this section, in a case where such an order as is mentioned in subsection (2) of this section is for the time being in force, unless—

(*a*) the application is made after the end of the period of two years beginning with the date on which the order was made, and

(*b*) the Court is satisfied that not less than two-fifths of the employees for the time being comprised in the bargaining unit have signified in writing their concurrence in the application.

Supplementary

Unfair industrial practices relating to pending questions as to recognition of sole bargaining agent.

54.—(1) Where notice of a proposal to make an application to the Industrial Court under section 45 of this Act has been given in pursuance of subsection (4) of that section, any question which—

(*a*) in accordance with that notice would be one of the questions proposed to be referred to the Commission, or

(*b*) on an application made in pursuance of that notice is one of the questions proposed to be so referred, or

(*c*) is referred to the Commission on such an application, or by virtue of section 47 of this Act is included in a reference made to the Commission on such an application,

shall be a question to which this section applies.

(2) Any question to which this section applies and which falls within paragraph (*b*) or paragraph (*c*) of the preceding subsection shall for the purposes of this section be taken to be pending at any time before whichever of the following events first occurs, that is to say—

(*a*) the Industrial Court determines not to refer any question to the Commission on the application mentioned in those paragraphs;

(*b*) a reference made to the Commission on that application is withdrawn;

(*c*) the period of six months, beginning with the date on which the report of the Commission on such a reference is transmitted to the Industrial Court, expires.

(3) A question to which this section applies, and which falls within paragraph (*a*), but neither within paragraph (*b*) nor within paragraph (*c*), of subsection (1) of this section, shall for the purposes of this section be taken to be pending at any time before such date as may be certified by the Secretary of State to be either—

(*a*) the date on which agreement was reached as to the matters to which the proposed application would have related, or

(*b*) the date on which, whether in consequence of a refusal of his offer of advice and assistance or otherwise, it became apparent that no such agreement was likely to be reached without an application to the Industrial Court.

(4) At any time when a question to which this section applies is pending in accordance with subsection (2) or subsection (3) of this section it shall be an unfair industrial practice—

(*a*) for any employer directly concerned in a dispute relating to that question to institute, carry on, organise, procure or finance a lock-out in furtherance of that dispute, or to threaten to do so, or

(*b*) for any person (including any trade union or other organisation of workers or any official of a trade union or of such an organisation) to call, organise, procure or finance a strike, or organise, procure or finance any irregular industrial action short of a strike, in furtherance of such a dispute, or to threaten to do so.

Unfair industrial practices in connection with collective bargaining procedures.

55.—(1) Where an order of the Industrial Court under section 50 of this Act is for the time being in force requiring an employer to recognise a trade union or joint negotiating panel as sole bargaining agent for a bargaining unit, it shall (subject to the following provisions of this section) be an unfair industrial practice for the employer—

(*a*) to carry on any collective bargaining in relation to that bargaining unit with any other organisation of workers, or

(*b*) not to take all such action, by way of or with a view to carrying on collective bargaining with that trade union or joint negotiating panel, as might reasonably be expected to be taken by an employer ready and willing to carry on such collective bargaining.

(2) Where such an order as is mentioned in subsection (1) of this section relates to a joint negotiating panel, it shall not by virtue of that subsection be an unfair industrial practice for the employer specified in the order to carry on collective bargaining with one or more of the trade unions represented on the panel, if he does so in pursuance of an agreement whereby the panel has consented to his carrying on such collective bargaining.

(3) Where such an order as is mentioned in subsection (1) of this section is for the time being in force, it shall be an unfair industrial practice for any person (including any trade union or other organisation of workers or any official of a trade union or of such an organisation)—

(*a*) by calling, organising, procuring or financing a strike, or threatening to do so, or

(*b*) by organising, procuring or financing any irregular industrial action short of a strike, or threatening to do so,

knowingly to induce or attempt to induce the employer specified in the order to do anything which, by virtue of subsection (1) of this section, is or would be an unfair industrial practice on the part of that employer.

(4) Subsections (1) to (3) of this section shall have effect in relation to an order made under section 50 of this Act in respect of two or more associated employers, but for that purpose shall have effect as if—

(*a*) any reference in those subsections to the employer were a reference to any of those employers;

(*b*) in subsections (1)(*a*) and (2) references to carrying on collective bargaining were references to carrying on such bargaining either alone or jointly with any other employer or employers comprised in the order;

(*c*) in subsection (1)(*b*) references to carrying on collective bargaining were references to carrying on such bargaining jointly with the other employer or employers comprised in the order.

(5) In relation to an order which is made subject to a reservation under section 50(2) of this Act, nothing in paragraph (*a*) or paragraph (*b*) of subsection (1) of this section shall be construed as applying to collective bargaining in respect of matters which, by virtue of that reservation, are excepted from the exclusive negotiating rights of the sole bargaining agent.

(6) At any time before the end of the period of two years beginning with the date on which the Commission transmit a report to the Industrial Court under section 48 of this Act, it shall be an unfair industrial practice for any person (including any trade union or other organisation of workers or any official of a trade union or of such an organisation), by any such means as are mentioned in paragraphs (*a*) and (*b*) of subsection (3) of this section, knowingly to induce or attempt to induce an employer—

(*a*) to recognise, as sole bargaining agent for the bargaining unit to which the report related, an organisation of workers or joint negotiating panel which was not recommended for such recognition in that report, whether the report recommended some other organisation or panel as sole bargaining agent for that bargaining unit or not, or

(*b*) to carry on, with any organisation of workers or joint negotiating panel which was not recommended as mentioned in the preceding paragraph, any collective bargaining in relation to employees of any description comprised in the bargaining unit to which that report related.

(7) Where the Industrial Court has made an order under section 53 of this Act, it shall be an unfair industrial practice for any person (including any trade union or other organisation of workers or any official of the trade union or of such an organisation), by any such means as are mentioned in paragraphs (*a*) and (*b*) of subsection (3) of this section, knowingly to induce or attempt to induce the employer to whom the order relates not to comply with the order.

(8) It shall be an unfair industrial practice for an employer, by instituting, carrying on, organising, procuring or financing a lock-out, or threatening to do so, knowingly to induce or attempt to induce any person to refrain from making an application under section 45 or section 51 of this Act.

56.—(1) For the purposes of all the stages of collective bargaining between an employer and trade union representatives, it shall (subject to section 158 of this Act) be the duty of the employer to disclose to those representatives all such information relating to his undertaking as is in the possession of the employer, or of any associated employer, and is both— General duty of employers to disclose information.

(*a*) information without which the trade union representatives would be to a material extent impeded in carrying on collective bargaining with him, and

(*b*) information which it would be in accordance with good industrial relations practice that the employer should disclose to them for purposes of collective bargaining.

(2) In determining, for the purposes of subsection (1)(*b*) of this section, what would be in accordance with good industrial relations practice, regard shall be had to the principles relating to disclosure of information by employers set out in the code of practice for the time being in force under Part I of this Act, so far as those principles are applicable to the circumstances of the collective bargaining in question, but not so as to exclude any other evidence of what that practice is.

(3) Where an employer is required by virtue of this section to disclose any information to trade union representatives, the disclosure of it shall be, or be confirmed, in writing if they so request.

(4) In the performance of his duty under subsection (1) of this section an employer shall not be required—

(*a*) to produce, or allow inspection of, any document (other than a document prepared for the purpose of conveying or confirming the information) or to make a copy of or extracts from any document, or

(*b*) to compile or assemble any information where the compilation or assembly of it would involve an amount of work or expenditure out of reasonable proportion to the value of the information in the conduct of the collective bargaining.

(5) In this section "trade union representative" means any person who, being either—

(*a*) an official of a trade union, or

(*b*) any other person authorised by or on behalf of a trade union to carry on the collective bargaining in question,

is a person or one of the persons with whom, as representing the workers or some of the workers to whom it relates, the collective bargaining is carried on.

Disclosure of information to employees by major employers.

57.—(1) In the case of any undertaking in which, on any date within a financial year of the undertaking, more than 350 persons, other than excepted persons, are employed (whether they are employed at the same place or at different places) it shall, subject to the following provisions of this section, be the duty of the employer who is the owner of the undertaking to issue in respect of that financial year a statement under this section to persons employed in the undertaking.

(2) Every such statement shall be issued not later than six months after the end of the financial year to which it relates.

(3) Every such statement shall be in writing and (subject to section 158 of this Act) shall contain all such information as may be required in accordance with regulations made by the Secretary of State under this section, and shall be issued to every person who, on the date on which it is issued, is employed in the undertaking to which the statement relates, and who is not on that date an excepted person.

(4) Regulations under this section may provide that, in such cases and to such extent as may be prescribed, the information to be contained in a statement issued under this section by a company—

(*a*) where the company owns other undertakings, shall extend to those other undertakings, and

(*b*) where there are other companies which are associated employers in relation to the company, shall extend to the undertakings of those other companies.

(5) Subject to the next following subsection, regulations under this section may confer such exemptions from the duty imposed by subsection (1) of this section as the Secretary of State may consider necessary or expedient.

(6) Any such exemptions shall be so conferred either—

(*a*) on employers of a prescribed description, or

(*b*) in respect of matters of a prescribed description, or

(*c*) on employers of a prescribed description in respect only of matters of a prescribed description, or

(*d*) on one or more particular employers specified in the regulations, but only in respect of matters of a description prescribed in relation to them.

(7) The Secretary of State may by order made by statutory instrument provide that, in subsection (1) of this section, for the words " 350 " (or such other number as may have been

substituted for those words by virtue of this subsection) there shall be substituted such other number (whether larger or smaller) as may be specified in the order.

(8) No regulations or order shall be made under this section unless a draft of the regulations or order has been laid before Parliament and approved by a resolution of each House of Parliament.

(9) In this section "financial year", in relation to an undertaking, means a period for which the accounts of the undertaking are made up (including any such period part of which is before and part after the commencement of this Act); and for the purposes of this section a person is an excepted person on any date if on that date—

(*a*) he is employed under a contract which normally involves employment for less than twenty-one hours weekly, or

(*b*) he has been employed in the undertaking in question for less than thirteen weeks, or

(*c*) he is outside Great Britain and is a person who under his contract of employment ordinarily works outside Great Britain.

PART IV

REGISTRATION AND CONDUCT OF TRADE UNIONS, EMPLOYERS' ASSOCIATIONS AND CERTAIN OTHER ORGANISATIONS

Introductory

61.—(1) In this Act (subject to section 86) "organisation of workers" means an organisation (whether permanent or temporary) which either— Trade unions and other organisations of workers.

(*a*) consists wholly or mainly of workers of one or more descriptions and is an organisation whose principal objects include the regulation of relations between workers of that description or those descriptions and employers or organisations of employers, or

(*b*) is a federation of workers' organisations.

(3) In this Act "trade union" means an organisation of workers which is for the time being registered as a trade union under this Act.

Principles as to conduct of organisations of workers, other than federations of workers' organisations

Guiding principles for organisations of workers.

65.—(1) The principles set out in the following provisions of this section shall be guiding principles in the conduct of every organisation of workers, other than federations of workers' organisations.

(2) Any person who applies for membership of the organisation, or of a branch or section of the organisation, and who—

(*a*) is a worker of the description, or (as the case may be) of one of the descriptions, of which, in accordance with the rules of the organisation, the organisation or that branch or section, as the case may be, is intended wholly or mainly to consist, or of which it wholly or mainly consists, and

(*b*) is appropriately qualified for employment as a worker of that description,

shall not, by way of any arbitrary or unreasonable discrimination, be excluded from membership of the organisation or of that branch or section of it.

(3) Every member of the organisation shall have the right, on giving reasonable notice and complying with any reasonable conditions, to terminate his membership of the organisation at any time.

(4) No member of the organisation, or of any branch or section of the organisation, shall, by way of any arbitrary or unreasonable discrimination, be excluded from—

(*a*) being a candidate for or holding any office in the organisation or in a branch or section of it;

(*b*) nominating candidates for any such office;

(*c*) voting in any election for any such office or in any ballot of members of the organisation or of a branch or section of it; or

(*d*) attending and taking part in meetings of the organisation or of any branch or section of the organisation.

(5) The voting in any ballot of members of the organisation, or of a branch or section of the organisation, shall be kept secret.

(6) In any ballot, and on any motion, in respect of which he is entitled to vote, every member of the organisation shall have a fair and reasonable opportunity of voting without interference or constraint.

(7) No member of the organisation shall be subjected by or on behalf of the organisation to any unfair or unreasonable disciplinary action; and in particular (but without prejudice to the generality of this subsection) no disciplinary action shall be taken against any member of the organisation by reason of his refusing or failing—

(*a*) to take any action which, in accordance with any provision of this Act, would constitute an unfair industrial practice on his part, or

(b) to take part in a strike which the organisation, or any other person, has called, organised, procured or financed otherwise than in contemplation or furtherance of an industrial dispute, or in such circumstances as, in accordance with any provision of this Act, to constitute an unfair industrial practice on the part of the organisation or of that person, or

(*c*) to take part in any irregular industrial action short of a strike which the organisation, or any other person, has organised, procured or financed as mentioned in paragraph (*b*) of this subsection.

(8) Except in respect of non-payment of any contribution which under the rules of the organisation he is required to pay, no member of the organisation shall be subjected to any disciplinary action by or on behalf of the organisation unless—

(*a*) he has had written notice of the charges brought against him and has been given a reasonable time to prepare his defence;

(*b*) he is afforded a full and fair hearing;

(*c*) a written statement of the findings resulting from the hearing is given to him; and

(*d*) where under the rules of the organisation he has a right of appeal, his appeal has been heard or the time for appealing has expired without his having exercised that right.

(9) A person's membership of the organisation shall not be terminated unless reasonable notice of the proposal to terminate his membership, and of the reason for it, has been given to him.

(10) No restriction shall, whether by the rules of the organisation or otherwise, be placed on any member of the organisation in respect of his instituting, prosecuting or defending

proceedings before any court or tribunal or giving evidence in any such proceedings.

(11) For the purposes of subsection (7) of this section, section 33(4) of this Act, and the definition of " strike " in section 167(1) of this Act, shall apply as if—

(*a*) in section 33(4) the words " in contemplation or furtherance of an industrial dispute ", and

(*b*) in the definition of " strike " the words " in contemplation or furtherance of an industrial dispute, whether they are parties to the dispute or not ",

were omitted.

Unfair industrial practices in connection with principles stated in s. 65.

66. It shall be an unfair industrial practice for any organisation of workers, or any official of or person acting on behalf of such an organisation, to take or threaten to take any action against any member of the organisation or other person in contravention of the principles set out in section 65 of this Act.

Registration of organisations of workers as trade unions

Organisations eligible for registration as trade unions.

67.—(1) Subject to the next following subsection, any organisation which—

(*a*) is an independent organisation of workers, and

(*b*) has power, without the concurrence of any parent organisation, to alter its own rules and to control the application of its own property and funds,

shall be eligible for registration as a trade union under this Act.

(2) A federation of workers' organisations shall not be eligible for such registration (notwithstanding that it fulfils the conditions specified in the preceding subsection) unless all the constituent or affiliated organisations of which it consists, or which are represented on it, are either trade unions or organisations for the time being entered in the special register.

(3) In this section " parent organisation ", in relation to an organisation of workers, means an organisation of which it is a branch or section.

Application for registration as trade union.

68.—(1) Any organisation of workers, whether formed before or after the passing of this Act, may apply to the registrar for registration as a trade union under this Act.

(2) Any such application shall be made in such form and manner as the registrar may require.

(3) Together with any such application there shall be sent to the registrar—

(*a*) a copy of the rules of the organisation and a list of its officers;

(*b*) the names and addresses of the branches (if any) of the organisation; and

(*c*) if the organisation has been in operation for more than a year before the date of the application, a statement setting out the like information as would be required to be contained in an annual return of the organisation under section 88 of this Act, if such a return were made on the date of the application.

(4) If on any such application the registrar is satisfied—

(*a*) that the body making the application is an organisation of workers and that it is eligible for registration as a trade union, and

(*b*) that the requirements of subsection (3) of this section have been complied with,

the registrar, subject to the next following subsection, shall register the organisation as a trade union under this Act and shall issue to it a certificate of such registration.

(5) Except as provided by section 79(5) of this Act, the registrar shall not register an organisation under this section except on payment of a fee of £25 or such other sum as may be prescribed.

Examination and approval of rules by registrar.

75.—(1) As soon as practicable after issuing to an organisation a certificate of registration under this Act, the registrar shall examine the rules of the organisation; and if on such examination it appears to him that the rules are defective in that—

(*a*) in the case of a trade union, they are in any way inconsistent with the principles set out in section 65 of this Act, or

(*b*) in the case of an employers' association, they are in any way inconsistent with the principles referred to in section 69 of this Act, or

(*c*) in either case, they do not comply with the requirements set out in Schedule 4 to this Act,

the registrar shall serve notice on the organisation, indicating what alterations in the rules are needed for the purpose of remedying the defect.

(2) Where the registrar serves a notice under the preceding subsection, he shall fix a reasonable period for the organisation to alter its rules in accordance with the notice and to submit them as altered to him for his approval, and the notice shall specify the period fixed by him under this subsection.

(3) If an organisation submits its rules to the registrar before the end of the period specified in a notice served under subsection (1) of this section, but it appears to the registrar that the rules have not been altered so as to comply with the requirements of the notice, the registrar may, if he thinks fit, allow to the organisation a further reasonable period for it to make the required alterations and to submit the rules to him as further altered.

(4) Except as provided by the next following section, the registrar shall not approve the rules of an organisation under this Act unless—

(*a*) he is satisfied that they are not defective as mentioned in subsection (1) of this section, and

(*b*) where he has served a notice under that subsection, they have been submitted to him, altered as required by that notice, before the end of the period specified in the notice or any further period allowed under subsection (3) of this section.

Application to Industrial Court as to approval of rules.

76.—(1) The registrar may apply to the Industrial Court for an order directing the registration of an organisation as a trade union or an employers' association under this Act to be cancelled on the grounds—

(*a*) that the organisation has not submitted its rules to him within the period specified in a notice served under subsection (1) of section 75 of this Act, or within a further period allowed under subsection (3) of that section or under this section, or

(*b*) that the rules submitted to him by the organisation were defective as mentioned in subsection (1) of that section and that the defect was not remedied within the period so specified or within any further period so allowed.

(2) If, on any such application, the Industrial Court finds that the grounds of the application are well-founded, the Court shall either—

(*a*) make an order allowing to the organisation a further period for altering its rules and submitting them as altered to the registrar, or

(*b*) make an order directing the registrar to cancel the registration of the organisation as a trade union or an employers' association under this Act,

as the Court considers appropriate in the circumstances.

(3) Where a trade union or employers' association has submitted its rules to the registrar within the period specified in a notice served under subsection (1) of section 75 of this Act, or within a further period allowed under subsection (3) of that section or under this section, but the registrar has not approved the rules, the trade union or employers' association may apply to the Industrial Court for an order—

(*a*) allowing it a further period for altering its rules and submitting them as altered to the registrar, or

(*b*) directing the registrar to approve the rules as already submitted to him;

and if, on any such application, the Industrial Court considers that it would be appropriate to do so, the Court may make an order in accordance with paragraph (*a*) or paragraph (*b*) of this subsection.

Application to Industrial Court for cancellation of registration on other grounds.

77.—(1) The registrar may apply to the Industrial Court for an order directing the registration of an organisation as a trade union or an employers' association under this Act to be cancelled on any of the following grounds, that is to say,—

(*a*) that the registration was obtained by fraud or mistake;

(*b*) that, by reason of a change in its rules or other change of circumstances, the organisation has ceased to be eligible for registration under this Act;

(*c*) that the organisation has refused or failed to comply with any requirement (other than a requirement relating to its rules) imposed on it by or under this Part of this Act, and has persisted in its default after the registrar has given it notice specifying the default and fixing a time (not being less than two months) for remedying the fault, and that time has expired.

(2) If, on an application made on the grounds specified in paragraph (*a*) or paragraph (*b*) of the preceding subsection, the Industrial Court finds that the grounds of the application are well-founded, the Court shall make an order in accordance with the application.

(3) If, on an application made on the grounds specified in subsection (1)(*c*) of this section, the Industrial Court finds that the grounds of the application are well-founded, the Court shall either—

(*a*) make an order extending the time for remedying the default, or

(*b*) make an order directing the registrar to cancel the registration of the organisation under this Act,

as the Court considers appropriate in the circumstances.

Provisional register

Entry of organisations in provisional register.

78.—(1) As soon as practicable after the passing of this Act, the registrar shall institute a register under this section (in this Act referred to as "the provisional register") and shall maintain that register until all entries in it have been cancelled.

(2) The registrar shall forthwith enter in the provisional register every organisation which, immediately before the passing of this Act, is for the time being registered as a trade union under the Trade Union Acts 1871 to 1964.

(3) The registrar shall also enter in the provisional register any organisation which—

(*a*) is not registered as mentioned in subsection (2) of this section, but

(*b*) before the end of the period of six months beginning with the passing of this Act makes an application to the registrar to enter it in the provisional register, on the grounds that it is a trade union within the meaning of those Acts.

Transfer from provisional register and cancellation of entries.

79.—(1) In the case of each organisation which is entered in the provisional register, the registrar shall consider whether it appears to him to be eligible for registration as a trade union or as an employers' association in accordance with section 67 or section 71 of this Act; and if, before the end of the period of six months beginning with the date of its entry in the provisional register, the registrar is satisfied that it is so eligible, he shall cancel that entry and register the organisation under this Act as a trade union or as an employers' association, as the case may be, and shall issue to it a certificate of such registration.

(2) If, in the case of any organisation which is entered in the provisional register, the registrar is not satisfied as mentioned in the preceding subsection before the end of the period specified

in that subsection, he shall serve on the organisation a notice stating that fact; and, where the registrar has served such a notice, he shall cancel the entry of the organisation in the provisional register unless, before the end of the period of six months beginning with the date of service of that notice, he is satisfied—

(*a*) that the organisation would have to alter its rules in order to be eligible for registration under this Act as a trade union or as an employers' association, and

(*b*) that the organisation is taking all necessary steps for the purpose of so altering its rules.

(3) Where the registrar refrains from cancelling the entry of an organisation in the provisional register by reason that he is satisfied as mentioned in paragraphs (*a*) and (*b*) of subsection (2) of this section, he shall serve on the organisation a notice allowing it such further period as he may consider appropriate for enabling it to make the requisite alterations in its rules.

(4) If, before the end of a further period allowed to an organisation under subsection (3) of this section, the organisation does not make an application for registration under section 68 or section 72 of this Act, the registrar shall cancel its entry in the provisional register at the end of that period; but, where the organisation does make such an application before the end of that period, then—

(*a*) if in consequence of that application the organisation is registered under this Act as a trade union or as an employers' association, the registrar shall cancel its entry in the provisional register as soon as the organisation is so registered, or

(*b*) in any other case, the registrar shall cancel that entry as soon as he has given his decision on the application and the time for appealing to the Industrial Court against that decision has expired without any such appeal having been brought or, on any such appeal, his decision has been upheld by the Court.

(5) No fee shall be payable for the registration of an organisation in pursuance of an application made in accordance with subsection (4) of this section.

Effect of entry in provisional register.

80. The entry of an organisation in the provisional register shall not constitute registration of the organisation under this Act as a trade union or as an employers' association; but, in relation to any organisation for the time being entered in the provisional register, the provisions of section 5, of Parts V to VII and of section 153 of this Act shall have effect to the extent specified in those provisions.

Power of registrar to investigate

Application to registrar to investigate.

81.—(1) Any person who—

(*a*) is a member of an organisation to which this section applies, or

(*b*) was a member of such an organisation and has ceased to be a member of it otherwise than by voluntary resignation, or

(*c*) has sought to become a member of it and has been refused admission to it or has, by any other action taken by or on behalf of the organisation, been prevented from obtaining admission to it,

shall be eligible to make an application under this section in relation to the organisation.

(2) This section applies to any organisation which is either—

(*a*) a trade union registered under this Act as being an organisation of workers other than a federation of workers' organisations, or

(*b*) an employers' association registered under this Act as being an organisation of employers other than a federation of employers' organisations.

(3) Any person who, in relation to an organisation to which this section applies, is eligible to do so may make an application to the registrar on the grounds that action specified in the application has been taken against him by or on behalf of the organisation and either—

(*a*) in accordance with section 66 or section 70 of this Act constituted an unfair industrial practice on the part of the organisation, or on the part of a person acting on its behalf, or

(*b*) constituted a breach of the rules of the organisation, other than a breach to which the next following subsection applies.

(4) This subsection applies—

(*a*) to any breach of any rules made in pursuance of section 3, section 4(1) or section 5(1) of the Trade Union Act 1913 (which relate to political funds), and 1913 c. 30 (2 & 3 Geo. 5).

(*b*) to any breach of rules in taking a vote on a resolution to approve an instrument of amalgamation or transfer within the meaning of the Trade Union (Amalgamations, etc.) Act 1964). 1964 c. 24

(5) In this section " person " does not include a body of persons, whether corporate or unincorporate.

82.—(1) The registrar shall not proceed with an application made to him under section 81 of this Act unless he is satisfied that it was made by a person who is eligible to make it and that the application is made on grounds falling within subsection (3) of that section. Action by registrar on application under s. 81.

(2) The registrar shall not proceed with such an application unless either he is satisfied that it was made before the end of the period of four weeks beginning with whichever is the latest of the following dates, that is to say—

(*a*) the date of the action to which the application relates (or, if that action occurred on two or more dates, the latest of those dates);

(*b*) the earliest date on which that action came to the knowledge of the applicant;

(*c*) the date on which a complaint made by the applicant to the organisation to which the application relates, having been referred for determination in accordance with a procedure established for that purpose under the rules of the organisation, was finally determined (whether by being rejected or otherwise),

or he is satisfied that in the circumstances it was not practicable for the application to be made before the end of that period.

(3) Where on any such application it appears to the registrar that in accordance with the rules of the organisation an adequate procedure has been established for determining complaints, and that a complaint with respect to the action to which the application relates could be, but has not been, referred for determination in accordance with that procedure, the registrar shall defer consideration of the application, but shall resume consideration of it if it is re-submitted—

(*a*) after such a complaint has been referred for determination in accordance with that procedure, and a reasonable time has been allowed for it to be so determined, but

(*b*) not later than the end of the period of four weeks beginning with the date on which such a complaint is finally determined in accordance with that procedure.

(4) The registrar shall not be required to proceed with any such application if in his opinion it is frivolous or vexatious.

(5) Where the registrar proceeds with an application under section 81 of this Act, he shall investigate the matter to which the application relates and shall give notice of his conclusions to the applicant and to the organisation.

(6) If on carrying out that investigation it appears to him that the grounds of the application are well-founded, he shall endeavour to promote a settlement of the matter to which the application relates without its becoming the subject of a complaint to an industrial tribunal.

(7) Anything communicated to the registrar, or to a person acting on behalf of the registrar, in connection with the performance of his functions under subsection (6) of this section shall not be admissible in evidence in any proceedings before the Industrial Court or an industrial tribunal, except with the consent of the person who communicated it to the registrar or to that person.

Investigation initiated by registrar.

83.—(1) Where, otherwise than in consequence of an application under section 81 of this Act, the registrar, in the case of a trade union or an employers' association, has reason to suspect—

(*a*) that there has been a serious breach, or have been persistent breaches, of its rules, other than such rules as are mentioned in subsection (2) of this section, or

(*b*) that action has been taken by it or on its behalf which is in serious contravention of the principles set out in section 65 or (as the case may be) the principles referred to in section 69 of this Act, or that action in contravention of those principles has been persistently taken by it or on its behalf,

the registrar shall investigate the matter.

(2) For the purposes of paragraph (*a*) of the preceding subsection the registrar shall disregard any breach of rules to which section 81(4) of this Act applies.

(3) If, on carrying out an investigation under subsection (1) of this section, it appears to the registrar that one or more breaches have occurred as mentioned in paragraph (*a*) of that subsection, or that action has been taken as mentioned in paragraph (*b*) of that subsection, he shall give notice of his conclusions to the trade union or employers' association and endeavour to secure such action or such an undertaking on its part as, in his opinion, would be appropriate for either or both of the following purposes, that is to say, to remedy or mitigate the consequences, and to prevent a continuance or repetition, of the breaches of rules or of the action in question.

(4) Where the registrar gives notice in accordance with subsection (3) of this section, but is unable to secure such action or such an undertaking as is mentioned in that subsection and is satisfied that, in default of such action or such an undertaking, it would be an appropriate case for him to present a complaint to the Industrial Court under Part VI of this Act, the registrar shall give notice to the trade union or employers' association stating that, unless such action or such an undertaking as is specified in that notice is taken or given within a period so specified, it is his intention to present such a complaint.

Supplementary

Cancellation by registrar on request or where organisation ceases to exist.

92.—(1) The registrar shall cancel the entry of an organisation in the provisional register, or the registration of an organisation under this Act as a trade union or as an employers' association,—

(*a*) if he is requested by the organisation to do so, or

(*b*) if the registrar is satisfied that the organisation has ceased to exist.

(2) Where under this section the registrar cancels the registration of an organisation, he shall cause notice of the cancellation to be published in the London and Edinburgh Gazettes.

Examination and approval of changes in rules.

93.—(1) As soon as practicable after the registrar has, in pursuance of section 89(3) of this Act, registered a change in the rules of an organisation, he shall examine the rules as they have effect in consequence of that change (in this section referred to as " the amended rules ") ; and, if on such examination it appears to him that the amended rules are defective in any of the ways specified in paragraphs (*a*), (*b*) and (*c*) of section 75(1) of this Act, he shall serve on the organisation a notice indicating what alterations in the amended rules are needed for the purpose of remedying the defect.

(2) The provisions of subsections (2) to (4) of section 75 and the provisions of section 76 of this Act shall have effect in relation to a notice served under subsection (1) of this section as they have effect in relation to a notice served under section 75(1) of this Act, as if in those provisions—

(*a*) any reference to a notice served under section 75(1) were a reference to a notice served under subsection (1) of this section, and

(*b*) any reference to the rules were a reference to the amended rules.

Relaxation of restrictions on changes in rules.

94.—(1) The provisions of this section shall have effect for enabling any organisation to which this section applies to make a change in its rules, whether by altering or revoking existing rules or adding new rules,—

(*a*) for the purpose of becoming eligible for registration as a trade union or as an employers' association, or

(*b*) for the purpose of complying with the requirements of a notice served under section 75(1) or section 93(1) of this Act, or otherwise for the purpose of securing that its rules will be consistent with the principles set out in section 65 of this Act, or with the principles referred to in section 69 of this Act, as the case may be, or that they will comply with the requirements set out in Schedule 4 to this Act.

(2) This section applies to any organisation which is for the time being entered in the provisional register or which is a trade union or an employers' association.

(3) Where at any time after the commencement of this Act the steps which, by the rules of an organisation to which this section applies, are required for making a change in the rules for any of the purposes specified in subsection (1) of this section could not, apart from this section, be initiated, by reason of a restriction imposed by the rules as to the interval which must elapse between successive changes, or successive proposals for changes, in the rules, the steps so required may be initiated, and any procedures consequential upon those steps may be entered upon and completed, notwithstanding that restriction.

PART V

OTHER UNFAIR INDUSTRIAL PRACTICES

96.—(1) It shall be an unfair industrial practice for any person, in contemplation or furtherance of an industrial dispute, knowingly to induce or threaten to induce another person to break a contract to which that other person is a party, unless the person so inducing or threatening to induce the breach of contract— Inducement of, or threat to induce, breach of contract.

(*a*) is a trade union or an employers' association, or

(*b*) does so within the scope of his authority on behalf of a trade union or an employers' association.

(2) In this Part of this Act any reference to a trade union or an employers' association shall be construed as including a reference to an organisation which is for the time being entered in the provisional register.

(3) In this section " contract "—

(*a*) does not include a collective agreement or any part of a collective agreement, but

(*b*) notwithstanding anything in the preceding paragraph, includes so much of any contract of employment as is implied or incorporated in that contract by reference to a collective agreement.

97.—(1) Subject to subsection (3) of this section, it shall be an unfair industrial practice for any person, in contemplation or furtherance of an industrial dispute, to take or threaten to take any of the steps specified in the next following subsection, if his purpose or principal purpose in doing so is to further any action which has been taken, whether by him or by any other person, and which, in accordance with any provision of this Act, constituted an unfair industrial practice. Industrial action in support of unfair industrial practice.

(2) The steps referred to in the preceding subsection are—

(*a*) calling, organising, procuring or financing a strike;

(*b*) organising, procuring or financing any irregular industrial action short of a strike;

(*c*) instituting, carrying on, organising, procuring or financing a lock-out.

(3) Any steps taken or threatened to be taken by a trade union or an employers' association for the purpose of furthering any action which—

(*a*) has been taken by one or more officials or members of the trade union or employers' association, and

(*b*) constituted an unfair industrial practice by virtue only of section 96 of this Act,

shall not be an unfair industrial practice by virtue of this section.

Industrial action against extraneous parties.

98.—(1) It shall be an unfair industrial practice for any person, in contemplation or furtherance of an industrial dispute, to take or threaten to take any of the steps specified in section 97(2) of this Act if—

(*a*) he knows or has reasonable grounds for believing that another person has entered into a contract (not being a contract of employment) with a party to that industrial dispute;

(*b*) his purpose or principal purpose in taking or threatening to take those steps is knowingly to induce that other person to break that contract or to prevent him from performing it; and

(*c*) that other person is an extraneous party in relation to that industrial dispute.

(2) For the purposes of this section a person shall be regarded as an extraneous party in relation to an industrial dispute if—

(*a*) he is not a party to that dispute, and

(*b*) he has not, in contemplation or furtherance of that dispute, taken any action in material support of a party to it.

(3) A person shall not be regarded for the purposes of this section as a party to an industrial dispute or as having taken action as mentioned in subsection (2)(*b*) of this section by reason only that he—

(*a*) is an associated employer in relation to an employer who is a party to the industrial dispute, or

(*b*) is a member of an organisation of employers of which a party to the industrial dispute is also a member, or

(*c*) has contributed to a fund which may be available to such a party by way of relief in respect of losses incurred or to be incurred in consequence of the dispute, where the fund was established, and his contribution to it was paid, without specific reference to that industrial dispute, or (*d*) supplies goods to, or provides services for, a party to the industrial dispute in pursuance of a contract entered into before the industrial dispute began, or is a party to such a contract under which he is or may be required to supply goods to, or provide services for, a party to the industrial dispute.

PART VI

NATIONAL INDUSTRIAL RELATIONS COURT, INDUSTRIAL TRIBUNALS, COMMISSION ON INDUSTRIAL RELATIONS AND INDUSTRIAL ARBITRATION BOARD

Complaint to Industrial Court of unfair industrial practice.

101.—(1) A complaint may be presented to the Industrial Court by any person (in this section referred to as "the complainant") that—

(*a*) action specified in the complaint has been taken by a person so specified (in this section referred to as "the respondent");

(*b*) in accordance with any provision of this Act, other than sections 5 and 22, that action constituted an unfair industrial practice on the part of the respondent; and

(*c*) the complainant is the person against whom the action was taken.

(2) If, on such a complaint, the Industrial Court finds that the grounds of the complaint (as specified in paragraphs (*a*) to (*c*) of the preceding subsection) are well-founded, the Court may, if it considers that it would be just and equitable to do so, grant to the complainant such one or more of the remedies specified in the following provisions of this section as the Court considers appropriate.

(3) Subject to the next following subsection, the remedies which may be so granted are—

(*a*) an order determining the rights of the complainant and of the respondent in relation to the action specified in the complaint;

(*b*) an award of compensation, to be paid by the respondent to the complainant, in respect of that action;

(*c*) an order directing the respondent to refrain from continuing to take that action, and to refrain from taking any other action of a like nature in relation to the complainant.

(4) Where, in any proceedings on a complaint under this section against an official of a trade union or an employers' association in respect of action taken by him in his capacity as such an official, it is shown that he took that action within the scope of his authority on behalf of the trade union or employers' association,—

(*a*) the Industrial Court shall not make an award or order against him in pursuance of paragraph (*b*) or paragraph (*c*) of subsection (3) of this section, but

(*b*) nothing in this subsection shall affect the granting of any remedy against the trade union or employers' association, whether in the same proceedings or in any other proceedings.

Complaint of breach of duty under s. 13(1) or s. 56.

102.—(1) A complaint may be presented to the Industrial Court by a trade union that an employer—

(*a*) in contravention of his duty under section 13(1) of this Act, has not taken all such action as was requisite on his part for the purpose of entering into an agency shop agreement with the trade union, or for the purpose of carrying out an agency shop agreement to which he and the trade union are parties, or

(*b*) in contravention of his duty under section 56 of this Act, has refused or failed to disclose to officials or other representatives of the trade union information which he was required by that section to disclose to them, or to confirm any such information in writing when requested by them to do so.

(2) If, on such a complaint, the Industrial Court finds that the grounds of the complaint are well-founded, the Court may, if it considers that it would be just and equitable to do so, make any one or more of the following orders, that is to say—

(*a*) an order determining the rights of the trade union and of the employer in relation to the matters to which the complaint relates ;

(*b*) an order directing the employer to take such action in fulfilment of the duty in question as, in the opinion of the Court, it would be within the power of the employer to take and is action which in the circumstances he ought to be required to take ;

(*c*) where the complaint relates to section 56 of this Act, an order authorising the presentation of a claim to the Industrial Arbitration Board under section 126 of this Act.

106.—(1) A complaint may be presented to an industrial tribunal against an employer by any person (in this section referred to as "the complainant") that—

Complaint to industrial tribunal of unfair industrial practice under s. 5 or s. 22.

(*a*) action specified in the complaint has been taken by the employer or by a person acting on the employer's behalf;

(*b*) in accordance with section 5 or section 22 of this Act, that action constituted an unfair industrial practice on the part of the employer or of the person acting on the employer's behalf; and

(*c*) where the complaint relates to dismissal, the complainant is the person who was dismissed, or, in any other case, the complainant is the person who was prevented or deterred from exercising his rights, or was penalised or otherwise discriminated against, or was refused engagement, as the case may be.

(2) If on a complaint under this section, other than a complaint relating to dismissal, the industrial tribunal finds that the grounds of the complaint (as specified in paragraphs (*a*) to (*c*) of the preceding subsection) are well-founded, the tribunal may, if it considers that it would be just and equitable to do so, grant to the complainant either or both of the remedies specified in the next following subsection, as the tribunal considers appropriate.

(3) The remedies which may be so granted are—

(*a*) an order determining the rights of the complainant and of the employer in relation to the action specified in the complaint;

(*b*) an award of compensation, to be paid by the employer to the complainant, in respect of that action.

(4) Where on a complaint under this section relating to dismissal the industrial tribunal—

(*a*) finds that the grounds of the complaint (as specified in paragraphs (*a*) to (*c*) of subsection (1) of this section) are well-founded, and

(*b*) considers that it would be practicable, and in accordance with equity, for the complainant to be re-engaged by the employer, or to be engaged by a successor of the employer or by an associated employer,

the tribunal shall make a recommendation to that effect, stating the terms on which it considers that it would be reasonable for the complainant to be so re-engaged or engaged.

(5) Where on such a complaint the industrial tribunal finds that the grounds of the complaint are well-founded, but—

(*a*) the tribunal does not make such a recommendation as is mentioned in subsection (4) of this section, or

(*b*) the tribunal makes such a recommendation, and (for whatever reason) the recommendation is not complied with,

the tribunal shall make an award of compensation, to be paid by the employer to the complainant, in respect of the dismissal.

Complaint by individual of unfair industrial practice under s. 66 or s. 70, or of breach of rules.

107.—(1) Any person who—

(*a*) is a member of an organisation to which this section applies, or

(*b*) was a member of such an organisation and has ceased to be a member of it otherwise than by voluntary resignation, or

(*c*) has sought to become a member of it and has been refused admission to it or has, by any other action taken by or on behalf of the organisation, been prevented from obtaining admission to it,

shall be eligible to present a complaint under this section to an industrial tribunal against the organisation.

(2) This section applies to any organisation which is either—

(*a*) an organisation of workers, other than a federation of workers' organisations, or

(*b*) an organisation of employers, other than a federation of employers' organisations.

(3) Any complaint presented to an industrial tribunal under this section shall be a complaint that action specified in the complaint has been taken by or on behalf of the organisation and, where the organisation is a trade union or an employers' association, that it was taken against the person who presents the complaint, and (whether the organisation is a trade union or an employers' association or not) that the action specified in the complaint either—

(*a*) in accordance with section 66 or section 70 of this Act constituted an unfair industrial practice on the part of the organisation, or on the part of a person acting on the organisation's behalf, or

(*b*) constituted a breach of the rules of the organisation.

(4) An industrial tribunal to which a complaint is presented under this section shall not entertain the complaint if it appears to the tribunal that—

(*a*) it relates to a matter in respect of which an application has been made under section 81 of this Act, and

(*b*) the registrar has proceeded or is proceeding with that application and has not yet given notice of his conclusions on investigating the matter to which it related.

(5) In this section "person" does not include a body of persons, whether corporate or unincorporate.

108.—(1) The provisions of this section shall have effect where— Complaint by registrar to industrial tribunal in consequence of application under s. 81.

(*a*) a person (in this section referred to as "the original applicant") has made an application to the registrar under section 81 of this Act, and, on proceeding with that application and carrying out an investigation under section 82 of this Act, the registrar finds that the grounds of the application appear to him to be well-founded;

(*b*) a settlement with respect to the action to which the application related is not reached within such period as the registrar considers reasonable in the circumstances;

(*c*) the registrar does not propose to present a complaint to the Industrial Court under section 103 of this Act with respect to that action; but

(*d*) it appears to the registrar that it is a matter in respect of which a complaint ought to be presented to an industrial tribunal and that the original applicant has not presented and does not intend to present such a complaint.

(2) In the circumstances specified in the preceding subsection, a complaint in respect of the action to which the application related may be presented to an industrial tribunal by the registrar against the trade union or employers' association in relation to which the application was made.

109.—(1) Where on a complaint presented under section 107 or section 108 of this Act the industrial tribunal, on determining the complaint, finds that the action specified in the complaint was taken by or on behalf of the organisation against which the complaint was presented and— Determination of complaint under s. 107 or s. 108.

(*a*) in accordance with section 66 or section 70 of this Act constituted an unfair industrial practice on the part of the organisation, or on the part of a person acting on the organisation's behalf, or

(*b*) constituted a breach of the rules of the organisation,

the tribunal may, if it considers that it would be just and equitable to do so, grant to the relevant person either or both of the remedies specified in the next following subsection, as the tribunal considers appropriate.

(2) The remedies which may be so granted are—

(*a*) an order determining the rights of the relevant person and of the organisation in relation to the action specified in the complaint;

(*b*) an award of compensation, to be paid by the organisation to the relevant person, in respect of that action.

(3) In this section " the relevant person "—

(*a*) in relation to a complaint presented under section 107 of this Act, means the person who presented the complaint, and

(*b*) in relation to a complaint presented by the registrar under section 108 of this Act, means the original applicant within the meaning of that section.

Complaint of breach of duty under s. 57.

110.—(1) Any person employed in an undertaking may present to an industrial tribunal a complaint against the employer who is the owner of the undertaking that—

(*a*) under section 57 of this Act it was the duty of the employer to issue to him a statement relating to a period specified in the complaint and containing the information required in accordance with regulations made under that section, and

(*b*) the employer has not fulfilled that duty as required by that section.

(2) If, on such a complaint, the industrial tribunal finds that the grounds of the complaint are well-founded, the tribunal may, if it considers that it would be just and equitable to do so, make an order determining the rights of the person who presented the complaint and of the employer in relation to the matters to which the complaint relates.

(3) Where an industrial tribunal makes an order under this section, the tribunal may direct that, in relation to the period specified in the complaint, the time limited by section 57(2) of

this Act shall be extended for such further period as may be specified in the order; and in the next following subsection " the time allowed by the tribunal " means the time so limited together with any further period specified in the order.

(4) If a person whose rights have been determined by an order made by an industrial tribunal under this section claims that, notwithstanding the order, the employer has not, within the time allowed by the tribunal, issued to him a statement in accordance with his rights as so determined he may present a complaint to that effect to the Industrial Court.

(5) On a complaint presented under subsection (4) of this section the Industrial Court may, if it finds that the grounds of the complaint are well-founded and considers that it would be just and equitable to do so, make an order directing the employer, before the end of such period as may be specified in the order of the Court, to issue to the complainant a statement containing such information as the Court considers appropriate, having regard to the rights determined by the order of the industrial tribunal.

Transfer of cases between industrial tribunals and Industrial Court

111.—(1) An industrial tribunal to which a complaint is presented under this Act shall not determine the complaint if—

(*a*) in accordance with Industrial Court rules the Industrial Court has directed the tribunal to transfer the complaint to that Court, or

(*b*) in accordance with industrial tribunal regulations the tribunal itself transfers the complaint to the Industrial Court, and the Industrial Court does not transfer the complaint back to the industrial tribunal, as being more appropriate for determination by the tribunal.

(2) For the purpose of dealing with any complaint which an industrial tribunal is precluded from determining by virtue of subsection (1) of this section, the Industrial Court shall have the like jurisdiction as the industrial tribunal would have had, and shall be subject to the like provisions of this Act as to the remedies which are to be or may be granted in respect of it.

Application to Industrial Court for declaration

112.—(1) Any party to a collective agreement in writing may make an application to the Industrial Court for a declaration with respect to any question relating to any provisions of the agreement.

with respect to collective agreement.

(2) Any such application shall specify the question or questions on which a decision of the Industrial Court is sought and, with respect to each such question,—

(*a*) shall indicate the provisions of the collective agreement to which it relates, and

(*b*) shall contain, or be accompanied by, a statement of the facts in consequence of which it is claimed that the question arises.

(3) An application under this section—

(*a*) shall not be entertained by the Industrial Court if it relates to a collective agreement which contains a provision (however expressed) stating that the agreement is intended not to be legally enforceable, or

(*b*) if it relates to a collective agreement which contains a provision (however expressed) stating that part of the agreement is intended not to be legally enforceable, shall not be entertained by the Industrial Court in so far as it relates to that part of the collective agreement.

(4) On an application under this section the Industrial Court, having regard to its findings in respect of the facts stated by the applicant and in respect of the construction and effect of the provisions of the collective agreement to which the application relates, may, if the Court considers that it would be just and equitable to do so, make such declaration with respect to any question specified in the application as the Court considers appropriate.

Power to confer jurisdiction on industrial tribunals in respect of damages for breach of contract of employment.

113.—(1) This section applies to damages for breach, by any party to it, of any contract of employment or of any term of such a contract (whether it is a term expressly included in the contract or implied in it by virtue of any enactment or otherwise, or is a term of the contract as modified by virtue of any enactment), other than damages in respect of personal injuries to any person or in respect of a person's death.

(2) The Lord Chancellor may by order made by statutory instrument provide, either—

(*a*) generally in relation to claims for damages to which this section applies, or

(*b*) in relation to claims for such damages of any such description as may be specified in the order,

that, subject to such exceptions (if any) as may be so specified, proceedings for the recovery of damages to which this section applies, or for the recovery of such damages on claims of a description specified in the order, as the case may be, may in accordance with industrial tribunal regulations be brought before an industrial tribunal if, in accordance with the law for the time being in force, a court in England or Wales would have jurisdiction to hear and determine an action for the recovery of those damages.

(3) The Secretary of State may by order made by statutory instrument provide, either—

(*a*) generally in relation to claims for damages to which this section applies, or

(*b*) in relation to claims for such damages of any such description as may be specified in the order,

that, subject to such exceptions (if any) as may be so specified, proceedings for the recovery of damages to which this section applies, or for the recovery of such damages on claims of a description specified in the order, as the case may be, may in accordance with industrial tribunal regulations be brought before an industrial tribunal if, in accordance with the law for the time being in force, a court in Scotland would have jurisdiction to hear and determine an action for the recovery of those damages.

(4) Any jurisdiction conferred on industrial tribunals by virtue of this section shall not include power to award any relief other than damages and (in England and Wales) costs or (in Scotland) expenses.

(5) Any order made under this section may contain such incidental, supplementary or transitional provisions (including provisions modifying any other enactment) as the Minister making the order considers necessary or expedient.

(6) Provision may be made by industrial tribunal regulations for enabling an industrial tribunal to take proceedings brought by virtue of this section concurrently with any proceedings brought before the tribunal by virtue of any other enactment (including any enactment contained in this Act).

(7) Subject to section 130 of this Act, any jurisdiction conferred on an industrial tribunal by virtue of this section shall be exercisable concurrently with any court in England or Wales, or in Scotland, as the case may be, which has jurisdiction to hear and determine an action for the damages in question.

(8) In this section "personal injuries" includes any disease and any impairment of a person's physical or mental condition; and for the purposes of this section a claim for payment of any sum payable under a contract of employment shall be regarded as a claim for damages for breach of the contract, and any

reference in this section to damages shall be construed accordingly.

(9) No regulations or order shall be made under this section unless a draft of the regulations or order has been laid before Parliament and approved by resolution of each House of Parliament.

Compensation

General principles as to assessment of compensation.

116.—(1) Where in any proceedings on a complaint under this Act the Industrial Court or an industrial tribunal makes an award of compensation to be paid by a party to the proceedings (in this section referred to as " the party in default ") to another party (in this section referred to as " the aggrieved party "), the amount of the compensation shall, subject to the following provisions of this Part of this Act, be such amount as the Court or tribunal considers just and equitable in all the circumstances, having regard to the loss sustained by the aggrieved party in consequence of the matters to which the complaint relates, in so far as that loss was attributable to action taken by or on behalf of the party in default.

(2) The loss sustained by the aggrieved party, as mentioned in the preceding subsection, shall be taken to include—

(*a*) any expenses reasonably incurred by him in consequence of the matters to which the complaint relates, and

(*b*) loss of any benefit which he might reasonably be expected to have had but for those matters,

subject, however, to the application of the same rule concerning the duty of a person to mitigate his loss as applies in relation to damages recoverable under the common law of England and Wales or of Scotland, as the case may be.

(3) Where the Industrial Court or industrial tribunal finds that the matters to which the complaint relates were to any extent caused or contributed to by any action of the aggrieved party in connection with those matters (whether that action constituted an unfair industrial practice on his part or not), the Court or tribunal shall reduce its assessment of his loss to such extent as, having regard to that finding, the Court or tribunal considers just and equitable.

(4) Where, on a complaint under section 106 of this Act relating to dismissal, the industrial tribunal or (as the case may be) the Industrial Court has made a recommendation

in accordance with subsection (4) of that section, and that recommendation is not complied with, then—

(*a*) if the tribunal or Court finds that the reason for which it was not complied with was that the complainant refused an offer of re-engagement or engagement on the terms stated in the recommendation, and the tribunal or Court considers that he acted unreasonably in doing so, the tribunal or Court (without prejudice to the generality of the rule mentioned in subsection (2) of this section) shall reduce the assessment of his loss, or

(*b*) if the tribunal or Court finds that the reason for which the recommendation was not complied with was that the employer in question refused or failed to make such an offer, and the tribunal or Court considers that he acted unreasonably in doing so, the tribunal or Court shall increase that assessment,

to such extent (in either case) as in the circumstances the tribunal or Court considers just and equitable.

(5) In determining, on a complaint under section 106 of this Act, how far any loss sustained by the complainant was attributable to action taken by or on behalf of the employer, no account shall be taken of any pressure which was exercised on the employer as mentioned in section 33(1)(*a*) of this Act, and that question shall be determined as if no such pressure had been exercised.

Limit on compensation awarded against trade union.

117.—(1) In any proceedings before the Industrial Court on a complaint under this Act where an award of compensation is made by the Court against a trade union (whether such an award is also made against any other party to the proceedings or not) the compensation awarded against the trade union in those proceedings shall not exceed the appropriate limit.

(2) For the purposes of this section the appropriate limit—

(*a*) in the case of a trade union having a membership of less than 5,000, is £5,000;

(*b*) in a case of a trade union having a membership of 5,000 or more but less than 25,000, is £25,000;

(*c*) in the case of a trade union having a membership of 25,000 or more but less than 100,000, is £50,000; and

(*d*) in the case of a trade union having a membership of 100,000 or more, is £100,000.

(3) In this section any reference to a trade union shall be construed as including a reference to an organisation of workers which is for the time being entered in the provisional register.

Limit on compensation awarded under s. 103, s. 106 or s. 109.

118.—(1) Without prejudice to section 117 of this Act, the amount of the compensation which, on the determination of a complaint by the Industrial Court or an industrial tribunal, is awarded to a person under section 103, section 106 or section 109 of this Act shall not exceed—

(*a*) the amount which, in his case, represents 104 weeks' pay, or

(*b*) £4,160 (that is to say, 104 × £40),

whichever is the less.

(2) The Secretary of State shall make provision by regulations for calculating the amount of a week's pay for the purposes of the preceding subsection.

(3) The Secretary of State may by order made by statutory instrument provide that, subject to such transitional provisions (if any) as may be contained in the order, subsection (1) of this section shall have effect as if, for the references to £4,160 and £40, there were substituted references to such larger sums as may be specified in the order.

(4) No order shall be made under subsection (3) of this section unless a draft of the order has been laid before Parliament and approved by a resolution of each House of Parliament.

Contribution to compensation on complaint under s. 106.

119.—(1) The provisions of this section shall have effect where, in any proceedings on a complaint under section 106 of this Act, an industrial tribunal or the Industrial Court makes an award of compensation to be paid by an employer in consequence of action taken by the employer or by a person acting on his behalf, and the employer claims—

(*a*) that the action so taken by him or on his behalf was induced by pressure exercised on him by another person (in this section referred to as " the third party ") by means of action to which section 33 of this Act applies, and

(*b*) that by virtue of subsection (3) of that section the action taken by the third party, whereby pressure was so exercised on the employer, constituted an unfair industrial practice.

(2) In the circumstances specified in the preceding subsection the employer may, in accordance with industrial tribunal regulations or Industrial Court rules, as the case may be, require the third party to be joined as a party to the proceedings; and if in the proceedings the industrial tribunal or the Industrial Court finds that the claim of the employer (as specified in paragraphs (*a*) and (*b*) of the preceding subsection) is well-founded, then, subject to subsection (4) of this section, the tribunal or Court may, if it considers that it would be just and equitable to do so, make an order requiring the third party to pay to the employer a contribution in respect of the compensation awarded against him.

(3) The amount of any contribution ordered to be paid under this section in respect of any compensation—

(*a*) shall be such amount as the industrial tribunal or the Industrial Court, as the case may be, considers to be just and equitable in the circumstances, and

(*b*) may, if the tribunal or Court so determines, be such as to constitute a complete indemnity.

(4) Where the third party is an official of a trade union, and it is shown that, in taking the action in question, he was acting in his capacity as such an official and within the scope of his authority on behalf of the trade union—

(*a*) the industrial tribunal or the Industrial Court, as the case may be, shall not order him to pay any contribution to the employer under this section, but

(*b*) nothing in the preceding paragraph shall affect the power of the tribunal or Court to order a contribution to be paid by the trade union.

PART VII

RESTRICTIONS ON LEGAL PROCEEDINGS

Proceedings in contract

No compulsion to work or to take part in industrial action

128.—(1) No court shall, whether by way of—

(*a*) an order for specific performance or specific implement of a contract of employment, or

(*b*) an injunction or interdict restraining a breach or threatened breach of such a contract, compel an employee to do any work or to attend at any place for the purpose of doing any work.

1875 c. 90. (2) Any power conferred on a court by the Employers and Workmen Act 1875—

(*a*) to accept security for the performance of a person's contract, or

(*b*) having accepted such security, to order performance of the contract accordingly,

shall cease to be exercisable.

(3) No court shall, by granting an injunction or interdict restraining an employee from working in accordance with a lawful contract of employment, compel him to take part in a strike or in any irregular industrial action short of a strike.

Collective agreements.

129.—(1) Subject to the next following subsection, no court other than the Industrial Court shall entertain any proceedings brought by a party to a collective agreement against another party to it, if the purpose or principal purpose of the proceedings is—

(*a*) to obtain a decision of the court on the construction or effect of the collective agreement, or

(*b*) to enforce the collective agreement or claim damages for a breach of it.

(2) The preceding subsection does not apply to any proceedings on, or in consequence of, an appeal from a decision or order of the Industrial Court.

Unfair industrial practice in breach of contract of employment.
1925 c. 49.
1959 c. 22.

130.—(1) The power to make rules of court under section 99 of the Supreme Court of Judicature (Consolidation) Act 1925, and the power to make county court rules under section 102 of the County Courts Act 1959, shall each include power by any such rules to make provision for enabling the court in which any action for damages is pending, on the application of any party to the action, to stay the action if the court is satisfied—

(*a*) that the action relates to an employee's contract of employment;

(*b*) that proceedings on a complaint presented under Part VI of this Act by the employee against the same employer are pending before an industrial tribunal or the Industrial Court; and

(*c*) that by virtue of an order made under section 113 of this Act an industrial tribunal would have jurisdiction to hear and determine a claim for the damages claimed in the action.

(2) The Court of Session shall have power by Act of Sederunt to make provision enabling a court to sist an action in the circumstances described in the preceding subsection.

(3) Except as provided by rules or Act of Sederunt in accordance with the preceding provisions of this section, nothing in this Act shall prevent an employee from—

(*a*) presenting and prosecuting a complaint under Part VI of this Act, and

(*b*) bringing an action in respect of any breach of his contract of employment,

notwithstanding that the matters to which the complaint relates are the same as those alleged to constitute the breach of contract.

Proceedings in tort

Acts in contemplation or furtherance of industrial dispute.

132.—(1) An act done by a person in contemplation or furtherance of an industrial dispute shall not be actionable in tort on the ground only—

(*a*) that it induces another person to break a contract to which that other person is a party or prevents another person from performing such a contract, or

(*b*) that it consists in his threatening that a contract (whether one to which he is a party or not) will be broken or will be prevented from being performed, or that he will induce another person to break a contract to which that other person is a party or will prevent another person from performing such a contract.

(2) For the avoidance of doubt it is hereby declared than an act done by a person in contemplation or furtherance of an industrial dispute is not actionable in tort on the ground only that it is an interference with the trade, business or employment of another person, or with the right of another person to dispose of his capital or his labour as he wills.

(3) An agreement or combination by two or more persons to do or procure to be done any act in contemplation or furtherance of an industrial dispute shall not be actionable in tort, if the act in question is one which, if done without any such agreement or combination, would not be actionable in tort.

(4) Where in any court proceedings in tort are brought in respect of an agreement or combination by two or more persons

to do or procure to be done an act in contemplation or furtherance of an industrial dispute, and subsection (3) of this section does not afford a defence to the proceedings, the court shall nevertheless stay the proceedings if it is satisfied that either of the conditions specified in section 131(2) of this Act is fulfilled in relation to the act in question.

Criminal (or criminal and civil) proceedings

Peaceful picketing.

134.—(1) The provisions of this section shall have effect where one or more persons (in this section referred to as " pickets "), in contemplation or furtherance of an industrial dispute, attend at or near—

(*a*) a place where a person works or carries on business, or

(*b*) any other place where a person happens to be, not being a place where he resides,

and do so only for the purpose of peacefully obtaining information from him or peacefully communicating information to him or peacefully persuading him to work or not to work.

(2) In the circumstances specified in the preceding subsection, the attendance of the pickets at that place for that purpose—

(*a*) shall not of itself constitute an offence under section 7 of the Conspiracy, and Protection of Property Act 1875 (penalty for intimidation or annoyance by violence or otherwise) or under any other enactment or rule of law, and

(*b*) shall not of itself constitute a tort.

Illegality on grounds of restraint of trade excluded.

135. The purposes of any trade union or other organisation of workers, of any employers' association or other organisation of employers or of any body to which section 35 of this Act applies shall not, by reason only that they are in restraint of trade, be unlawful, so as—

(*a*) to make any member of the organisation or body liable to criminal proceedings for conspiracy or otherwise, or

(*b*) to make any agreement or trust void or voidable.

PART VIII

EMERGENCY PROCEDURES

Application to Industrial Court with a view to discontinuing or deferring industrial action.

138.—(1) Where it appears to the Secretary of State—

(*a*) that, in contemplation or furtherance of an industrial dispute, industrial action, consisting of a strike, any irregular industrial action short of a strike, or a lock-out, has begun or is likely to begin ;

(*b*) that the condition specified in the next following subsection is fulfilled ; and

(*c*) that, having regard to all the circumstances of the industrial dispute, it would be conducive to a settlement of it by negotiation, conciliation or arbitration if the industrial action were discontinued or deferred,

the Secretary of State may apply to the Industrial Court for an order under the next following section.

(2) The condition referred to in paragraph (*b*) of the preceding subsection is that the industrial action in question has caused, or (as the case may be) would cause, an interruption in the supply of goods or in the provision of services of such a nature, or on such a scale, as to be likely—

(*a*) to be gravely injurious to the national economy, to imperil national security or to create a serious risk of public disorder, or

(*b*) to endanger the lives of a substantial number of persons, or expose a substantial number of persons to serious risk of disease or personal injury.

(3) Any application made by the Secretary of State under this section—

(*a*) where it relates to a strike, or to irregular industrial action short of a strike, shall specify the persons (whether they are organisations of workers, officials of such organisations or other persons) appearing to the Secretary of State to be responsible for calling, organising, procuring or financing the strike or other action in question, or for a threat to do so, and

(*b*) where it relates to a lock-out, shall specify the persons (whether they are employers, organisations of employers or other persons) appearing to the Secretary of State to be responsible for instituting, carrying on, organising, procuring or financing the lock-out, or for a threat to do so ;

and the persons so specified shall, together with the Secretary of State, be the parties to any proceedings on that application.

Order of Industrial Court on application under s. 138.

139.—(1) Where an application is made to the Industrial Court under section 138 of this Act, the Court, subject to its being satisfied on the evidence that there are sufficient grounds for believing that the condition specified in subsection (2) of that section is fulfilled, shall make an order under this section.

(2) Any such order shall specify—

(*a*) the area of employment in respect of which the order is to have effect, that area being defined in the order by reference to (or to any combination of) any of the following, that is to say, one or more industries specified in the order, one or more undertakings or parts of undertakings so specified, and one or more descriptions of workers so specified;

(*b*) the persons who are to be bound by the order, who (subject to the next following subsection) shall be the persons specified in the application in accordance with section 138(3) of this Act; and

(*c*) the date on which the order is to take effect and the period, not exceeding sixty days, for which the order is to remain in force.

(3) The persons specified in pursuance of subsection (2)(*b*) of this section in an order relating to a strike, or to any irregular industrial action short of a strike, shall not include any person who in the opinion of the Industrial Court (notwithstanding that he is specified in the application for the order)—

(*a*) has, or (as the case may be) would have, no responsibility for the strike or other action in question beyond that of being included among the persons taking part in it, or

(*b*) has no responsibility for calling, organising, procuring or financing the strike or other action in question, or for threatening to do so, except in his capacity as an official of a trade union acting within the scope of his authority on behalf of the trade union.

(4) An order under this section made on an application relating to a strike, or to irregular industrial action short of a strike, shall be an order directing that, during the period for which the order remains in force, no person specified in the order in accordance with paragraph (*b*) of subsection (2) of this section shall—

(*a*) call, organise, procure or finance a strike, or threaten to do so, or (*b*) organise, procure or finance any irregular industrial action short of a strike, or threaten to do so,

within the area of employment specified in the order in accordance with paragraph (*a*) of that subsection or any part of that area.

(5) An order under this section made on an application relating to a lock-out shall be an order directing that, during the period for which the order remains in force, no person specified in the order in accordance with paragraph (*b*) of subsection (2) of this section shall institute, carry on, authorise, organise or finance a lock-out, or threaten to do so, within the area of employment specified in the order in accordance with paragraph (*a*) of that subsection or any part of that area.

(6) An order under this section may also require any one or more of the persons specified in the order, before the end of such period as may be specified in the order for the purposes of this subsection, to take such steps (whether by way of withdrawing or securing the withdrawal of any instructions issued by or on behalf of that person or those persons or otherwise) as may be so specified for the purpose of securing that the industrial action to which the application for the order related is discontinued or (as the case may be) deferred during the period for which the order remains in force.

(7) Any order under this section shall indicate the scope of the industrial dispute in consequence of which the order is made, in such manner as may appear to the Industrial Court to be sufficient to indicate the area of employment affected by the dispute and the extent of the matters to which the dispute relates.

Supplementary provisions where order made under s. 139.

140.—(1) The provisions of this section shall have effect where an order (in this section referred to as " the principal order ") has been made under section 139 of this Act.

(2) If the period specified in the principal order in accordance with section 139(2)(*c*) of this Act (or that period as previously extended under this subsection) is less than sixty days, then at any time before the end of that period the Industrial Court, on the application of the Secretary of State, may by order extend that period, but not so as to exceed sixty days in all.

(3) Where at a time within the period for which the principal order is in force it appears to the Secretary of State, that persons

other than those specified in the principal order in accordance with subsection (2)(*b*) of section 139 of this Act—

(*a*) are at that time responsible as mentioned in paragraph (*a*) or paragraph (*b*) of section 138(3) of this Act, but

(*b*) are not then persons required to be excluded from the order in accordance with section 139(3) of this Act,

the Secretary of State may make an application to the Industrial Court, specifying those persons and applying for the principal order to be extended to them; and the persons so specified shall, together with the Secretary of State, be the parties to any proceedings on that application.

(4) Subject to the next following subsection, on any application made by the Secretary of State under subsection (3) of this section the Industrial Court shall make an order specifying the persons who were specified in the application and directing that, in relation to any time after the order under this subsection takes effect, the principal order, while it remains in force, shall have effect as if those persons had been included among the persons specified in the principal order in accordance with section 139(2)(*b*) of this Act.

(5) The Industrial Court shall not make an order under subsection (4) of this section after the end of the period specified in the principal order, and, where it makes an order under that subsection, shall not include in it any person required to be excluded in accordance with section 139(3) of this Act.

(6) In relation to any person to whom the principal order applies by virtue of an order made under subsection (4) of this section (in this subsection referred to as "the supplementary order") the supplementary order may impose any requirement which, in pursuance of section 139(6) of this Act, could have been imposed on him by the principal order if—

(*a*) the principal order had been made at the time when, and in the circumstances in which, the supplementary order is made, and

(*b*) he were one of the persons specified in the principal order.

(7) After the period specified in the principal order has begun, the Industrial Court shall not, either during that period or at any time thereafter, entertain any application under section 138 of this Act in respect of the same industrial dispute, or in respect of any other industrial dispute in so far as it appears to the Court

that its scope falls within the scope (as indicated in the principal order in accordance with section 139(7) of this Act) of the industrial dispute in consequence of which the principal order was made.

Application to Industrial Court for order for ballot relating to industrial action

141.—(1) Where it appears to the Secretary of State—

(*a*) that in contemplation or furtherance of an industrial dispute a strike or any irregular industrial action short of a strike has begun or is likely to begin;

(*b*) that either or both of the conditions specified in the next following subsection are fulfilled; and

(*c*) that there are reasons for doubting whether the workers who are taking part or are expected to take part in the strike or other industrial action are or would be taking part in it in accordance with their wishes, and whether they have had an adequate opportunity of indicating their wishes in this respect,

the Secretary of State may apply to the Industrial Court for an order requiring a ballot to be taken.

(2) The conditions referred to in paragraph (*b*) of the preceding subsection are—

(*a*) the condition specified in section 138(2) of this Act; and

(*b*) the condition that the effects of the industrial action in question on a particular industry are, or are likely to be, such as to be seriously injurious to the livelihood of a substantial number of workers employed in that industry.

(3) Any application under this section shall specify the persons (whether they are organisations of workers, officials of such organisations or other persons) appearing to the Secretary of State to be responsible for calling, organising, procuring or financing the strike or other action in question, or for a threat to do so; and the persons specified in the application in accordance with this subsection shall, together with the Secretary of State, be the parties to any proceedings on that application.

(4) Before making any application under this section, the Secretary of State shall, so far as appears to him to be practicable in the circumstances, consult every employer, trade union or employers' association appearing to him to be a party to the industrial dispute in question.

Order of Industrial Court on application under s. 141.

142.—(1) Where an application is made to the Industrial Court under section 141 of this Act, the Court, subject to its being satisfied on the evidence that there are sufficient grounds for believing that either or both of the conditions mentioned in subsection (2) of that section are fulfilled, shall order a ballot to be taken.

(2) Any such order shall specify—

(*a*) the area of employment in relation to which the ballot is to be taken, that area being defined in the order by reference to (or to any combination of) any of the following, that is to say, one or more industries specified in the order, one or more undertakings or parts of undertakings so specified, and one or more descriptions of workers so specified;

(*b*) the question on which the ballot is to be taken; and

(*c*) the period within which the result of the ballot is to be reported to the Industrial Court.

(3) The order shall include provisions for enabling the workers eligible to vote in the ballot to be determined; and those provisions shall be formulated in such manner as in the opinion of the Industrial Court will secure that all workers falling within the area of employment specified in the order in accordance with subsection (2)(*a*) of this section will be eligible to vote.

(4) Any order under this section shall indicate the scope of the industrial dispute in consequence of which the order is made, in such manner as may appear to the Industrial Court to be sufficient to indicate the area of employment affected by the dispute and the extent of the matters to which the dispute relates.

(5) The Industrial Court may, if it thinks fit, invite the assistance of the Commission in formulating any order under this section.

PART IX

MISCELLANEOUS AND SUPPLEMENTARY

Conciliation officers.

146.—(1) The Secretary of State shall appoint officers to perform on his behalf the functions specified in the following provisions of this section, subject to the approval of the Minister for the Civil Service as to their numbers and as to their terms and conditions of service; and in this Act "conciliation officer" means an officer so appointed.

(2) Where a complaint has been presented to an industrial tribunal under section 106 of this Act, and a copy of it has been sent to a conciliation officer, it shall be the duty of the conciliation officer—

(*a*) if he is requested to do so by the employee who presented the complaint, and by the employer against whom it was presented, or

(*b*) if, in the absence of any such request, the conciliation officer considers that he could act under this subsection with a reasonable prospect of success,

to endeavour to promote a settlement of the complaint without its being determined by an industrial tribunal.

(3) For the purpose of promoting such a settlement, in a case where the employee has ceased to be employed by the employer against whom the complaint was made,—

(*a*) the conciliation officer shall in particular seek to promote re-engagement of the employee by the employer, or his engagement by a successor of the employer or by an associated employer, on terms appearing to the conciliation officer to be equitable ; but

(*b*) where such re-engagement or engagement is not practicable or cannot be agreed between the parties to the complaint, and they desire the conciliation officer to act under this paragraph, he shall seek to promote agreement between them as to a sum by way of compensation to be paid by the employer to the employee.

(4) Where at any time—

(*a*) after an employee has ceased to be employed by an employer, in circumstances where the employee claims that he was unfairly dismissed, or that other action on the part of the employer, or of a person acting on behalf of the employer, constituted an unfair industrial practice in accordance with section 5 of this Act, but

(*b*) before any complaint relating to that claim has been presented by the employee under section 106 of this Act,

a request is made to a conciliation officer (whether by the employer or by the employee) to make his services available to them, the conciliation officer shall act in accordance with subsections (2) and (3) of this section as if a complaint had been presented in pursuance of that claim.

(5) At any time when an order under section 113 of this Act is in force, the Secretary of State may direct conciliation officers to perform such services, in relation to claims for damages in respect of which jurisdiction is conferred on industrial tribunals by the order, as may be specified in the directions.

(6) Anything communicated to a conciliation officer in connection with the performance of his functions under this section shall not be admissible in evidence in any proceedings before the Industrial Court or an industrial tribunal, except with the consent of the person who communicated it to that officer.

(7) Nothing in this section shall be construed as derogating from any powers or duties of the Secretary of State under any other enactment.

Effect of strike notice.

147.—(1) Due notice given by or on behalf of an employee of his intention to take part in a strike shall not, unless it otherwise expressly provides, be construed—

(*a*) as a notice to terminate his contract of employment, or

(*b*) as a repudiation of that contract.

(2) Subject to the next following subsection, where an employee takes part in a strike after due notice of his intention to do so has been given by him or on his behalf, his action in taking part in the strike shall not be regarded as a breach of his contract of employment for the purposes of—

(*a*) any proceedings in contract brought against the employee in respect of breach of that contract, or

(*b*) any proceedings in tort, whether brought against the employee or brought against any other person, or

1875 c. 86.

(*c*) section 5 of the Conspiracy, and Protection of Property Act 1875 (breach of contract involving injury to persons or property), or

(*d*) section 96 of this Act.

(3) Subsection (2) of this section shall not apply to any action by an employee which is contrary to a term of his contract of employment (including any term implied or incorporated in that contract by reference to a collective agreement) excluding or restricting his right to take part in a strike.

(4) Nothing in subsection (2) of this section shall be taken to exclude or restrict any right which an employer would have apart from that subsection to dismiss (with or without notice) an employee who takes part in a strike.

(5) In this section "due notice", in relation to an employee, means notice of a duration not less than that which (whether by virtue of any enactment or otherwise) he would be required to give to terminate his contract of employment.

(6) In the application of this section to Scotland, "proceedings in tort" shall be construed in accordance with section 137(*a*) of this Act.

149.—(1) Where under the Race Relations Act 1968 a complaint is made to the Secretary of State or the Race Relations Board that action has been taken which is unlawful by virtue of section 3(1) of that Act, or a matter falling to be investigated by that Board raises the question whether any such action has been taken, then, if it appears to the Secretary of State or the Board— Race Relations Act 1968. 1968 c. 71.

(*a*) that the action in question is action in respect of which a complaint has been presented to an industrial tribunal under section 106 of this Act, or in respect of which a complaint could be so presented (or could have been so presented if the requirements of industrial tribunal regulations relating to it had been complied with), and

(*b*) that a complaint so presented to an industrial tribunal has not been dismissed by virtue of any provision contained in or made under sections 27 to 31 of this Act, or (as the case may be) would not fall or have fallen to be so dismissed,

the Secretary of State or the Board shall not proceed any further under that Act in relation to that action, except to the extent provided by the following provisions of this section.

(2) If, on determining a complaint presented under section 106 of this Act in respect of the action in question, an industrial tribunal or the Industrial Court has recorded a finding that the action was taken against the complainant and constituted an unfair industrial practice (whether by way of unfair dismissal or otherwise) and also that the reason, or one of the reasons, for which it was taken was the complainant's colour, race or ethnic or national origins, then the preceding subsection shall not preclude the Secretary of State or the Race Relations Board—

(*a*) from proceeding under that Act for the purpose of securing a written assurance against a repetition of that action, in accordance with section 15(3)(*b*) of that

Act or in accordance with paragraph 3 of Schedule 2 or paragraph 2 or paragraph 8 of Schedule 3 to that Act, or

(*b*) from proceeding under that Act (whether by way of bringing proceedings or otherwise) in consequence of forming an opinion or receiving a report that a written assurance so secured has been broken.

(3) The Secretary of State or the Race Relations Board may proceed in accordance with paragraph (*a*) or paragraph (*b*) of subsection (2) of this section notwithstanding any limitation
1968 c. 71. imposed by the Race Relations Act 1968 as to the time within which anything may be done under that Act.

(4) In this section any reference to the Race Relations Board shall be construed as including references—

(*a*) to any conciliation committee constituted under the Race Relations Act 1968, and

(*b*) to any other body of persons to whom a matter could be referred for investigation under Schedule 2 or Schedule 3 to that Act.

Redundancy payments.

150.—(1) Regulations made by the Secretary of State may make provision with respect to cases where a complaint relating to dismissal is presented to an industrial tribunal under section 106 of this Act, and a redundancy payment or an equivalent payment has been paid, or has been or is claimed, in respect of the same dismissal.

1965 c. 62. (2) Any such regulations may make such modifications of the provisions of Part VI of this Act, or of the Redundancy Payments Act 1965, as the Secretary of State may consider appropriate, including—

(*a*) provisions excluding the right to a redundancy payment or equivalent payment, or requiring any such payment to be repaid, or

(*b*) provisions requiring a rebate under section 30 of that Act or a sum payable under section 41(2) of that Act to be withheld or reduced, or (where already paid) to be recoverable in whole or in part, and on being so recovered to be paid into the Redundancy Fund,

in such circumstances as may be prescribed.

(3) In section 21 of the Redundancy Payments Act 1965

(claims for redundancy payments), at the end of paragraph (*c*) there shall be added the words " or

(*d*) a complaint relating to his dismissal has been presented by the employee under section 106 of the Industrial Relations Act 1971 ".

(4) In this section " redundancy payment " has the same meaning as in the Redundancy Payments Act 1965, and " equivalent payment " means any payment which is either—

(*a*) a payment made or falling to be made as mentioned in paragraph (*b*) or paragraph (*c*) of section 30(1) of that Act, or

(*b*) a payment in respect of the termination of a person's employment, made in accordance with any provision of the Superannuation Act 1965 or in accordance with **1965 c. 74.** any such arrangements as are mentioned in section 41(3) of the Redundancy Payments Act 1965.

(5) No regulations shall be made under this section unless a draft of the regulations has been laid before Parliament and approved by resolution of each House of Parliament.

151.—(1) The provisions of Schedule 1 to the Contracts of **Period of continuous employment. 1963 c. 49.** Employment Act 1963 (computation of period of employment), and the provisions of any order for the time being in force under section 7 of that Act in so far as it modifies that Schedule, shall have effect for the purposes of this Act in determining for what period an employee has been continuously employed.

(2) For the purposes of any proceedings under this Act a person's employment during any period shall, unless the contrary is shown, be presumed to have been continuous.

(3) Regulations made by the Secretary of State may make provision—

(*a*) for preserving the continuity of a person's period of employment for the purposes of Schedule 1 to the Contracts of Employment Act 1963, or for the purposes **1963 c. 49.** of that Schedule as applied by or under any other enactment specified in the regulations, or

(*b*) for modifying or excluding the operation of section 24 of the Redundancy Payments Act 1965 (which requires **1965 c. 62.** the continuity of the period of employment to be treated as broken for the purposes of that Act where a redundancy payment is paid to an employee and he is subsequently re-engaged), subject to the recovery of any sum which, in accordance with subsection (3) of that section, is treated as payment of a redundancy payment,

in cases where, in consequence of action to which the next following subsection applies, a dismissed employee is re-engaged by his employer or is engaged by a successor of that employer or by an associated employer.

(4) This subsection applies to any action taken in relation to the dismissal of an employee which consists—

(*a*) of the presentation by him of a complaint under section 106 of this Act, or

(*b*) of his making a claim in accordance with the procedure provided for by a procedure agreement designated by an order under section 31 of this Act, or

(*c*) of any action taken by a conciliation officer under section 146(4) of this Act.

Recovery of sums awarded in proceedings involving trade union or employers' association.

153.—(1) Where in any proceedings (whether brought by virtue of this Act or otherwise) an award of compensation or damages, or for the payment of any costs or expenses,—

(*a*) is made against a trade union or an employers' association, or

(*b*) is made against the trustees of a trade union or employers' association in their capacity as such trustees and is not made in respect of a breach of trust on their part, or

(*c*) is made against members or officials of a trade union or employers' association, where the proceedings are brought against them on behalf of themselves and all other members (or, in the case of officials who are not members, on behalf of themselves and all the members) of the trade union or employers' association,

recovery of any such compensation, damages, costs or expenses shall not be enforceable against any property to which this subsection applies.

(2) Subsection (1) of this section applies to any property—

(*a*) belonging to any trustee of the trade union or employers' association otherwise than in his capacity as such a trustee, or

(*b*) belonging to any member of the trade union or employers' association otherwise than jointly or in common with the other members of it, or

(*c*) belonging to any official of the trade union or employers' association who is neither a member nor a trustee of it,

and also applies to any property comprised in any fund belonging to the trade union or employers' association, if under the rules of the trade union or employers' association property which is or has been comprised in that fund is precluded from being used for financing strikes, lock-outs or other industrial action.

(3) Except as provided by subsection (1) of this section, any judgment, order or award which is made against a trade union or an employers' association in any proceedings (whether brought by virtue of this Act or otherwise) shall be enforceable against any property belonging to, or held in trust for, the trade union or employers' association.

(4) In this and the next following section—

(*a*) "property" includes any money, securities or other assets;

(*b*) any reference to a trade union or employers' association shall be construed as including a reference to any organisation which is for the time being entered in the provisional register.

Proceedings against unregistered organisations.

154.—(1) This section applies to any organisation of workers which is not a trade union, and to any organisation of employers which is not an employers' association.

(2) Any civil proceedings (including any proceedings under this Act) may be brought by or against any such organisation in the name of the organisation.

(3) Except as provided by the next following subsection, any judgment, order or award made in any such proceedings against an organisation to which this section applies (including any judgment or order directing the organisation to take, or to refrain or desist from taking, any action) shall be enforceable, by way of execution, diligence, punishment for contempt or otherwise, against any property belonging to, or held in trust for, the organisation, to the like extent and in the like manner as if the organisation were a body corporate.

(4) Recovery of any sum which in any such proceedings is awarded as compensation or damages, or in respect of costs or expenses, against an organisation to which this section applies shall not be enforceable against any property comprised in a fund belonging to or held in trust for the organisation, if under the rules of the organisation property which is or has been

comprised in that fund is precluded from being used for financing strikes, lock-outs or other industrial action.

(5) For the purposes of this section property belonging to the organisation shall not include property belonging to any member of the organisation otherwise than jointly or in common with the other members of the organisation.

Immunity of confidential information.

158.—(1) No employer shall, by virtue of section 56 or section 57 of this Act, be required to disclose—

(*a*) any information the disclosure of which would be against the interests of national security, or

(*b*) any information which he could not disclose without contravening a prohibition imposed by or under an enactment (including any enactment contained in this Act), or

(*c*) any information which has been communicated to the employer in confidence, or which the employer has otherwise obtained in consequence of the confidence reposed in him by another person, or

(*d*) any information relating specifically to an individual, unless he has consented to its being disclosed, or

(*e*) any information the disclosure of which would be seriously prejudicial to the interests of the employer's undertaking for reasons other than its effect on collective bargaining, or

(*f*) any information obtained by the employer for the purpose of bringing, prosecuting or defending any legal proceedings.

(2) In preparing under Part I of this Act so much of any code of practice as relates to disclosure of information, the Secretary of State shall have regard to the provisions of subsection (1) of this section and shall formulate that part of that code in accordance with the like principles.

(3) No information given by any person in evidence before the Industrial Court or an industrial tribunal, at a hearing held in private in accordance with Industrial Court rules or industrial tribunal regulations, shall be disclosed to any other person except with the consent of the person who gave it in evidence.

(4) If any person discloses any information in contravention of subsection (3) of this section, he shall be guilty of an offence and shall be liable on summary conviction to a fine not exceeding £400.

161.—(1) Except as provided by the next following subsection, any provision in an agreement (whether a contract of employment or not) shall be void in so far as it purports— Restrictions on contracting out.

(*a*) to exclude or limit the operation of any enactment contained in this Act, or

(*b*) to preclude any person from presenting a complaint to or bringing any proceedings before the Industrial Court or an industrial tribunal under this Act.

(2) Subsection (1) of this section shall not apply—

(*a*) to any agency shop agreement or any approved closed shop agreement;

(*b*) to any provision contained in an agreement in accordance with section 30(*b*) of this Act;

(*c*) to any provision in a collective agreement excluding rights under section 22 of this Act, if that provision is not to have effect unless an order under section 31 of this Act is for the time being in force in respect of it;

(*d*) to any agreement to refrain from presenting a complaint under section 106 of this Act, where in compliance with a request under subsection (4) of section 146 of this Act a conciliation officer has taken action in accordance with that subsection;

(*e*) to any agreement to refrain from proceeding with a complaint presented under section 106 of this Act, where a conciliation officer has taken action in accordance with subsections (2) and (3) of section 146 of this Act; or

(*f*) to any agreement to refrain from presenting, or from proceeding with, a complaint under section 107 of this Act, where an application under section 81 of this Act has been made to the registrar with respect to the matter to which the complaint relates or, if presented, would relate.

162.—(1) Subject to the following provisions of this section, the provisions of this Act shall have effect in relation to Crown employment and to workers who are Crown employees as they have effect in relation to other employment and to other workers. Employment under the Crown.

(2) In this section (subject to subsection (6)) "Crown employment" means employment under or for the purposes of a government department, otherwise than as a member of the naval, military or air forces of the Crown or of any women's service administered by the Defence Council, and "Crown

employee " means a person who is for the time being in Crown employment or (where it has ceased) was in Crown employment.

(3) For the purposes of the application of the provisions of this Act in relation to Crown employment in accordance with subsection (1) of this section—

(*a*) any reference to an employee shall be construed as a reference to a Crown employee;

(*b*) any reference to dismissal shall be construed as a reference to the termination of Crown employment;

(*c*) any reference to redundancy shall be construed as a reference to the existence of such circumstances as, in accordance with any arrangements for the time being
1965 c. 62. in force as mentioned in section 41(3) of the Redundancy Payments Act 1965, are treated as equivalent to redundancy in relation to Crown employment;

(*d*) the reference in section 158(1)(*e*) of this Act to the interests of the employer's undertaking shall be construed as a reference to the national interest; and

(*e*) any other reference to an undertaking shall be construed, in relation to a Minister of the Crown, as a reference to his functions or (as the context may require) to the department of which he is in charge, and, in relation to a government department, shall be construed as a reference to the functions of the department or (as the context may require) to the department.

(4) On a complaint presented under section 101 or section 102(1) of this Act against a Minister of the Crown or a government department, the only remedies available to the Industrial Court shall be those specified in paragraphs (*a*) and (*b*) of section 101(3) or that specified in section 102(2)(*a*) of this Act, as the case may be:

Provided that, where the complaint relates to an unfair industrial practice under section 55(1) of this Act, the only remedy available to the Industrial Court shall be that specified in section 101(3)(*a*) of this Act.

(5) Subsections (4) and (5) of section 110 of this Act shall not have effect in relation to Crown employment.

(6) For the purposes of this Act—

(*a*) none of the bodies specified in Schedule 3 to the
1965 c. 62. Redundancy Payments Act 1965 (national health service employers) shall be regarded as performing functions on behalf of the Crown, and their employees shall not be regarded as being employed under or for

the purposes of a government department, and accordingly employment by any such body shall not be Crown employment within the meaning of this section;

(*b*) associations established for the purposes of the Auxiliary Forces Act 1953 shall be treated as if they were government departments, and accordingly employment by any such association shall be Crown employment within the meaning of this section; 1953 c. 50.

and for the purposes of this section Crown employment does not include any employment in respect of which a certificate to which the next following subsection applies is for the time being in force.

(7) This subsection applies to any certificate issued by or on behalf of a Minister of the Crown and certifying that employment of a description specified in the certificate, or the employment of a particular person so specified, is (or at a time specified in the certificate was) required to be excepted from subsection (1) of this section for the purpose of safeguarding national security; and any document purporting to be a certificate so issued shall be received in evidence and shall, unless the contrary is proved, be deemed to be such a certificate.

165.—(1) Notwithstanding anything in the Government of Ireland Act 1920, the Parliament of Northern Ireland shall have power to make laws for purposes similar to the purposes of any provisions of this Act, including the provisions of section 162 of this Act; and it shall be within the power of the Parliament of Northern Ireland to impose or confer duties or powers on the Commission or on the Chief Registrar, whether they are duties or powers similar to those imposed or conferred by this Act or not. Northern Ireland. 1920 c. 67.

(2) In sections 121 and 122 of this Act any reference to the Secretary of State, or to a Minister, shall be construed as including a reference to the Minister of Health and Social Services for Northern Ireland (in this section referred to as " the Northern Ireland Minister").

(3) On each occasion when the Commission make a report to the Secretary of State under section 123 of this Act, the Commission shall make a like report to the Northern Ireland Minister; and the Northern Ireland Minister shall lay a copy of every such report before the Senate and House of Commons of Northern Ireland.

(4) Sections 121 and 122 of this Act and subsections (2) and (3) of this section shall be treated for the purposes of section 6 of
1920 c. 67. the Government of Ireland Act 1920 as if they had been passed before the day appointed for that section to come into operation.

S. R. & O. 1922/184. (5) In the Government of Ireland (Companies, Societies etc.) Order 1922, in Article 22 (which provides for reciprocal status in respect of societies registered in Northern Ireland and those registered in other parts of the United Kingdom), after the words " Northern Ireland ", in the first place where they occur, there shall be inserted the words " other than a trade union or a branch of a trade union ".

Meaning of " collective agreement " and " procedure agreement ".

166.—(1) In this Act, subject to the following provisions of this section, " collective agreement " means any agreement or arrangement which is for the time being in force and—

(*a*) is an agreement or arrangement made (in whatever way and in whatever form) by or on behalf of one or more organisations of workers and either one or more employers, one or more organisations of employers, or a combination of one or more employers and one or more organisations of employers, and

(*b*) is either an agreement or arrangement prescribing (wholly or in part) the terms and conditions of employment of workers of one or more descriptions, or an agreement or arrangement relating to one or more of the matters specified in subsection (5) of this section, or both.

(2) Where by virtue of section 35 of this Act a decision of a joint body to which that section applies is presumed to be intended to have effect as a legally enforceable contract, then in this Act—

(*a*) any reference to a collective agreement, or to a collective agreement having effect as a legally enforceable contract, shall include that decision, and

(*b*) any reference to a party to a collective agreement, or to a party to a collective agreement which is a legally enforceable contract, shall be construed, in relation to that decision, as including a reference to any of the constituent parties.

(3) In this Act any reference to a collective agreement shall be construed as including a reference to any provisions which, by virtue of an order under section 41 of this Act which is for the

time being in force, have effect as a legally enforceable contract in accordance with subsection (2) of that section, and any reference to a party to a collective agreement shall be construed accordingly.

(4) Where a collective agreement—

(*a*) is made by representatives either of two or more employers or of one or more organisations of employers or of a combination of one or more employers and one or more organisations of employers, and is so made on behalf of all the parties so represented or on behalf of one or more of them specified in the collective agreement, or

(*b*) is made by representatives of one or more organisations of workers and is made on behalf of those organisations or on behalf of one or more of them specified in the collective agreement,

then for the purposes of this Act each employer, each organisation of employers and each organisation of workers on whose behalf the collective agreement is so made shall be regarded as a party to the collective agreement.

(5) In this Act " procedure agreement " means so much of a collective agreement (as defined by subsections (1) to (3) of this section) as relates to any of the following matters, that is to say—

(*a*) machinery for consultation with regard to, or for the settlement by negotiation or arbitration of, terms and conditions of employment;

(*b*) machinery for consultation with regard to, or for the settlement by negotiation or arbitration of, other questions arising between an employer or group of employers and one or more workers or organisations of workers;

(*c*) negotiating rights;

(*d*) facilities for officials of trade unions or other organisations of workers;

(*e*) procedures relating to dismissal;

(*f*) procedures relating to matters of discipline other than dismissal;

(*g*) procedures relating to grievances of individual workers.

(6) In this section " decision " and " the constituent parties " have the same meanings as in section 35 of this Act.

Interpretation. **167.**—(1) In this Act, except in so far as the context otherwise requires, the following expressions have the meanings hereby assigned to them respectively, that is to say—

"action" includes any refusal or failure to act, and any reference to taking action shall be construed accordingly;

"agency shop agreement" has the meaning assigned to it by section 11(1) of this Act;

"bargaining unit" has the meaning assigned to it by section 44 of this Act;

"the Chief Registrar" means the Chief Registrar of Trade Unions and Employers' Associations;

"collective bargaining" means negotiations with respect to terms and conditions of employment, or with respect to the making, variation or rescission of a procedure agreement, or with respect to any matter to which in accordance with section 166 of this Act a procedure agreement can relate;

"the Commission" means the Commission on Industrial Relations established under this Act;

"conciliation officer" has the meaning assigned to it by section 146 of this Act;

"contract of employment" means a contract of service or of apprenticeship, whether it is express or implied, and (if it is express) whether it is oral or in writing;

"dismiss" and "dismissal" have the meanings assigned to them by section 23 of this Act;

"employee" (subject to subsection (4) of this section) means an individual who has entered into or works under (or, where the employment has ceased, worked under) a contract of employment;

"employer" (subject to subsection (2) of this section)—

(*a*) where the reference is to an employer in relation to an employee, means the person by whom the employee is (or, in a case where the employment has ceased, was) employed, and

(*b*) in any other case, means a person regarded in that person's capacity as one for whom one or more workers work or have worked or normally work or seek to work;

"employers' association" has the meaning assigned to it by section 62(3) of this Act;

"federation of workers' organisations" has the meaning assigned to it by sections 61(2) and 86(1)(*b*) of this Act;

"federation of employers' organisations" has the meaning assigned to it by section 62(2) of this Act;

"independent", in relation to a trade union or other organisation, means not under the domination or control of an employer or of a group of employers or of one or more organisations of employers;

"the Industrial Court" means the National Industrial Relations Court, and "Industrial Court rules" has the meaning assigned to it by section 99(7) of this Act;

"industrial dispute" (subject to subsection (5) of this section) means a dispute between one or more employers or organisations of employers and one or more workers or organisations of workers, where the dispute relates wholly or mainly to any one or more of the following, that is to say—

(*a*) terms and conditions of employment, or the physical conditions in which any workers are required to work;

(*b*) engagement or non-engagement, or termination or suspension of employment, of one or more workers;

(*c*) allocation of work as between workers or groups of workers;

(*d*) a procedure agreement, or any matter to which in accordance with section 166 of this Act a procedure agreement can relate;

"industrial tribunal regulations" has the meaning assigned to it by section 100(3) of this Act;

"industry" means any trade or occupation, and any reference to an industry shall be construed as including a reference to a sector of an industry, and "industrial" shall be construed accordingly;

"irregular industrial action short of a strike" has the meaning assigned to it by section 33(4) of this Act;

"joint negotiating panel" and "joint negotiating panel of trade unions" have the meanings assigned to them by section 44 of this Act;

"lock-out" means action which, in contemplation or furtherance of an industrial dispute, is taken by one or more employers, whether parties to the dispute or not, and which consists of the exclusion of workers from one or more factories, offices or other places of employment or of the suspension of work in one or more such places or of the collective, simultaneous or otherwise connected termination or suspension of employment of a group of workers;

"negotiating rights" has the meaning assigned to it by section 44 of this Act;

"official", in relation to an organisation of workers or an organisation of employers, means any person who is an officer of the organisation or of a branch of the the organisation or who (not being such an officer) is a person elected or appointed in accordance with the rules of the organisation to be a representative of its members or of some of them, including (in the case of an organisation of workers) any person so elected or appointed who is an employee of the same employer as the members, or one or more of the members, whom he is to represent;

"organisation of employers" has the meaning assigned to it by section 62 of this Act;

"organisation of workers" has the meaning assigned to it by sections 61 and 86(1)(*a*) of this Act;

"position", in relation to an employee, means the following matters taken as a whole, that is to say, his status as an employee, the nature of his work and his terms and conditions of employment;

"prescribed" means prescribed by regulations made under this Act;

"the provisional register" has the meaning assigned to it by section 78(1) of this Act;

"the registrar" has the meaning assigned to it by section 63(4) of this Act;

"sole bargaining agent" has the meaning assigned to it by section 44 of this Act;

"the special register" has the meaning assigned to it by section 84 of this Act;

"strike" means a concerted stoppage of work by a group of workers in contemplation or furtherance of an industrial dispute, whether they are parties to the dispute or not, whether (in the case of all or any of those workers) the stoppage is or is not in breach of their terms and conditions of employment, and whether it is carried out during, or on the termination of, their employment;

"terms and conditions of employment" means the terms and conditions on which one or more workers are, or are to be, required to work for their employers;

"trade union" has the meaning assigned to it by section 61(3) of this Act;

"undertaking" includes a business and, in relation to any body of persons (whether corporate or unincorporate) whose activities would not, apart from this provision, be regarded as constituting an undertaking, includes the aggregate of those activities;

"worker" (subject to the following provisions of this section) means an individual regarded in whichever (if any) of the following capacities is applicable to him, that is to say, as a person who works or normally works or seeks to work—

(*a*) under a contract of employment, or

(*b*) under any other contract (whether express or implied, and, if express, whether oral or in writing) whereby he undertakes to perform personally any work or services for another party to the contract who is not a professional client of his, or

(*c*) in employment under or for the purposes of a government department (otherwise than as a member of the naval, military or air forces of the Crown or of any women's service administered by the Defence Council) in so far as any such employment does not fall within either of the preceding paragraphs.

(2) Without prejudice to the generality of the definitions in subsection (1) of this section, in this Act—

(*a*) "worker" includes an individual regarded in his capacity as one who works or normally works or seeks to work as a person providing general medical services, pharmaceutical services, general dental services or general ophthalmic services in accordance with arrangements made by an Executive Council under section 33, section 38, section 40 or section 41 of the National Health Service Act 1946 or under section 34, section 39, section 40 or section 42 of the National Health Service (Scotland) Act 1947; and

1946 c. 81.
1947 c. 27.

(*b*) " employer " includes any Executive Council in accordance with whose arrangements a person provides or has provided or normally provides or seeks to provide any services as mentioned in the preceding paragraph.

(3) The Secretary of State may by order made by statutory instrument provide that in this Act " worker " shall include any individual regarded in his capacity as a person who works or normally works or seeks to work as the holder of an office specified in the order; but no such order shall be made unless a draft of the order has been laid before Parliament and approved by a resolution of each House of Parliament.

(4) Notwithstanding anything in subsection (1) of this section, for the purposes of this Act—

(*a*) service as a member of a police force, or as a special constable or as a member of any constabulary maintained by virtue of an enactment (including any local or private Act), or in any other capacity by virtue of which a person has the powers and privileges of a constable, shall not be regarded as work falling within paragraphs (*a*) to (*c*) of the definition of " worker " in that subsection, and accordingly a person shall not be regarded as a worker by reference to any such service; and

(*b*) in the definition of " employee " in that subsection the reference to a contract of employment does not include a contract to perform any such service as is mentioned in the preceding paragraph.

(5) For the purposes of the definition of " industrial dispute " in subsection (1) of this section, a dispute between a Minister of the Crown and one or more workers or organisations of workers shall, notwithstanding that the Minister is not the employer of any of the workers to whom the dispute relates, be regarded as a dispute between an employer and the worker or workers, or the organisation or organisations, in question if the dispute relates—

(*a*) to matters which have been referred for consideration by a joint body on which, by virtue of any provision made by or under an enactment, that Minister is represented, or

(*b*) to matters in respect of which a settlement cannot take effect without the exercise of a power conferred on that Minister by or under an enactment.

(6) Subject to the next following subsection, in this Act "successor", in relation to the employer of an employee, means a person who, in consequence of a change occurring (whether by virtue of a sale or other disposition or by operation of law) in the ownership of the undertaking or of part of the undertaking for the purposes of which the employee was employed, has become the owner of that undertaking or of that part of it, as the case may be.

(7) Subsection (6) of this section shall have effect (subject to the necessary modifications) in relation to a case where—

(*a*) the person by whom an undertaking or part of an undertaking is owned immediately before a change is one of the persons by whom (whether as partners, trustees or otherwise) it is owned immediately after the change, or

(*b*) the persons by whom an undertaking or part of an undertaking is owned immediately before a change (whether as partners, trustees or otherwise) include the persons by whom, or include one or more of the persons by whom, it is owned immediately after the change,

as that subsection has effect where the previous owner and the new owner are wholly different persons; and any reference in this Act to a successor of an employer shall be construed accordingly.

(8) For the purposes of this Act any two employers are to be treated as associated if one is a company of which the other (directly or indirectly) has control, or if both are companies of which a third person (directly or indirectly) has control; and in this Act "associated employer" shall be construed accordingly.

(9) Any reference in this Act to a person taking any action within the scope of his authority on behalf of an organisation shall be construed as a reference to his taking that action in his capacity as an official or agent of the organisation in circumstances where he is authorised, by or under the rules of the organisation or by virtue of an office in the organisation which he holds or otherwise, to take that action on its behalf.

(10) For the purposes of this Act it is immaterial whether the law which (apart from this Act) governs any person's employment is the law of the United Kingdom, or of a part of the United Kingdom, or not.

(11) Except in so far as the context otherwise requires, any reference in this Act to an enactment shall be construed as a

reference to that enactment as amended or extended by or under any other enactment, including this Act.

Short title, commencement and extent.

170.—(1) This Act may be cited as the Industrial Relations Act 1971.

(2) This Act shall come into operation on such day as the Secretary of State may appoint by order made by statutory instrument, and different days may be so appointed for, or for different purposes of, any one or more of the provisions of this Act (including, in the case of section 169 of this Act, the amendment or repeal of different enactments specified in Schedule 8 or Schedule 9 to this Act or of different provisions of any enactment so specified).

(3) Any reference in any provision of this Act to the commencement of this Act shall be construed as a reference to the day appointed under this section for the coming into operation of that provision.

(4) Any order made under this section may make such transitional provision or savings as appear to the Secretary of State to be necessary or expedient in connection with the provisions of this Act which are thereby brought (wholly or in part) into force, including such adaptations of those provisions or of any provision of this Act then in force as appear to the Secretary of State to be necessary or expedient in consequence of the partial operation of this Act (whether before, on or after the day appointed by the order).

(5) The following provisions of this Act, that is to say—

(*a*) sections 120, 121 and 122;

(*b*) section 165;

(*c*) this section; and

(*d*) so much of Schedule 3 to this Act as relates to the Commission, and so much of that Schedule and of Schedules 8 and 9 to this Act as relate to the House of Commons Disqualification Act 1957 or to the Merchant Shipping Act 1970,

1957 c. 20.
1970 c. 36.

shall extend to Northern Ireland; but with the exception of those provisions, and except so far as it relates to the interpretation of those provisions, this Act shall not extend to Northern Ireland.

SCHEDULES

Section 17.

SCHEDULE 1

SCHEDULE 2

Section 21.

PART I

CONTRACTS OF EMPLOYMENT ACT 1963

1963 c. 49.

Change of name or identity of employer

1.—(1) The provisions of the next following sub-paragraph shall have effect where, after an employer has given to an employee a written statement in accordance with section 4(1) of the Act of 1963,—

(*a*) the name of the employer (whether an individual or a body corporate or partnership) is changed, but without any change in the identity of the employer, or

(*b*) the identity of the employer is changed, in such circumstances that, in accordance with paragraph 10 or paragraph 10A of Schedule 1 to that Act, the continuity of the employee's period of employment is not broken,

and (in either case) the change does not involve any change in the terms (other than the names of the parties) included or referred to in the statement.

(2) Where the preceding sub-paragraph applies, the person who, immediately after the change, is the employer shall not be required to give to the employee a statement in accordance with subsection (1) of section 4 of that Act, but the change shall be treated as a change falling within subsection (4) of that section.

Amendments consequential on ss. 19 *and* 20 *of this Act*

2. In subsections (3) and (4) of section 1 and in subsections (1) and (2) of section 2 of the Act of 1963, for the words "twenty-six weeks", in each place where they occur, there shall be substituted the words "thirteen weeks"

3. In section 4 of the Act of 1963, the following subsections shall be substituted for subsection (8):—

"(7A) In subsections (4) to (6) of this section any reference to that which is, or is to be, included, given or referred to in a statement under subsection (1) of this section shall be construed as including a reference to the note mentioned in section 20(2) of the Industrial Relations Act 1971, and any reference to that which is, or is to be, included, given or referred to in a statement under subsection (4) of this section shall be construed in a corresponding way.

(8) The foregoing provisions of this section shall not apply to an employee if and so long as the conditions specified in the next following subsection are fulfilled in relation to him.

(8A) Those conditions are that—

(*a*) the employee's contract of employment is a contract which has been reduced to writing in one or more documents and which contains express terms affording the particulars to be given under each of the paragraphs in subsection (1) of this section, and under each head of paragraph (*d*) of that subsection ;

(*b*) there has been given to the employee a copy of the contract (with any variations made from time to time), or he has reasonable opportunities of reading such a copy in the course of his employment, or such a copy is made reasonably accessible to him in some other way ; and

(*c*) such a note as is mentioned in section 20(2) of the Industrial Relations Act 1971 has been given to the employee or he has reasonable opportunities of reading such a note in the course of his employment or such a note is made reasonably accessible to him in some other way.

(8B) If at any time after the beginning of an employee's period of employment he ceases to come within the exception in subsection (8) of this section, the employer shall give the employee a written statement under subsection (1) of this section not more than one month after that time."

SCH. 2 4. In section 4A of the Act of 1963, in subsection (7), for the words "Part III of the Redundancy Payments Act 1965" there shall be substituted the words "Schedule 6 to the Industrial Relations Act 1971", and after that subsection there shall be inserted the following subsections:—

"(7A) Subsection (7A) of section 4 of this Act shall have effect in relation to the foregoing provisions of this section as it has effect in relation to subsections (4) to (6) of that section.

(7B) A tribunal shall not entertain a reference under this section in a case where the employment to which the reference relates has ceased unless an application requiring the reference to be made was, in accordance with the regulations referred to in subsection (7) of this section, made before the end of the period of three months beginning with the date on which the employment ceased."

5. In section 8(1) of the Act of 1963, in the definition of "employee", after the words "works under" there shall be inserted the words "(or, where the employment has ceased, worked under)".

6. In Schedule 1 to the Act of 1963, in paragraph 1(1), for the words " two and five years mentioned in section 1 of this Act shall be taken as 104 and 260 weeks respectively " there shall be substituted the words " two, five, ten and fifteen years mentioned in section 1 of this Act shall be taken as 104, 260, 520 and 780 weeks respectively ".

Sickness or injury during period of notice

7. In Schedule 2 to the Act of 1963, after paragraph 3 there shall be inserted the following paragraph:—

" *Sickness or industrial injury benefit*

3A.—(1) The following provisions of this paragraph shall have effect where the arrangements in force relating to the employment are such that—

(*a*) payments by way of sick pay are made by the employer to employees to whom the arrangements apply, in cases where any such employees are incapable of work because of sickness or injury, and

(*b*) in calculating any payment so made to any such employee an amount representing, or treated as representing, sickness benefit or industrial injury benefit is taken into account, whether by way of deduction or by way of calculating the payment as a supplement to that amount.

(2) If during any part of the period of notice the employee is incapable of work because of sickness or injury, and—

(*a*) one or more payments, either by way of sick pay or as amounts required to be paid by virtue of this Schedule, are made to him by the employer in respect of that part of the period of notice, and

(*b*) in calculating any such payment such an amount as is referred to in sub-paragraph (1)(*b*) of this paragraph is taken into account as therein mentioned,

then for the purposes of this Schedule the amount so taken into account shall be treated as having been paid by the employer to the employee by way of sick pay in respect of that part of that period, and shall go towards meeting the liability of the employer under paragraph 2 or paragraph 3 of this Schedule accordingly."

Transitional provisions

8. The amendments made by sections 19 and 20 of this Act, and by paragraphs 2 to 5 of this Schedule, shall not affect the validity of any statement given to an employee before the commencement of this Act ; but (except as provided by the next following paragraph) the coming into operation of those amendments shall be deemed

to be such a change as is mentioned in section 4(4) of the Act of 1963.

9. On the coming into operation of paragraph 3 of this Schedule, an employee shall not be treated as ceasing to come within the exception in subsection (8) of section 4 of the Act of 1963 by reason only that the condition specified in paragraph (*c*) of subsection (8A) of that section is not fulfilled ; but he shall be treated as ceasing to come within that exception unless that condition is fulfilled not more than one month after the coming into operation of paragraph 3 of this Schedule.

Interpretation

1963 c. 49. 10. In this Schedule " the Act of 1963 " means the Contracts of Employment Act 1963.

PART II

SECTION 4(1) TO (9) OF CONTRACTS OF EMPLOYMENT ACT 1963 AS AMENDED

Written particulars of terms of employment.

4.—(1) Not later than thirteen weeks after the beginning of an employee's period of employment with an employer, the employer shall give to the employee a written statement identifying the parties, specifying the date when the employment began, and giving the following particulars of the terms of employment as at a specified date not more than one week before the statement is given, that is—

(*a*) the scale or rate of remuneration, or the method of calculating remuneration,

(*b*) the intervals at which remuneration is paid (that is, whether weekly or monthly or by some other period),

(*c*) any terms and conditions relating to hours of work (including any terms and conditions relating to normal working hours),

(*d*) any terms and conditions relating to—

(i) entitlement to holidays, including public holidays, and holiday pay (the particulars given being sufficient to enable the employee's entitlement, including any entitlement to accrued holiday pay on the termination of employment, to be precisely calculated),

(ii) incapacity for work due to sickness or injury, including any provisions for sick pay,

(iii) pensions and pension schemes, and

(*e*) the length of notice which the employee is obliged to give and entitled to receive to determine his contract of employment :

Provided that paragraph (*d*)(iii) of this subsection shall not apply to the employees of any body or authority if the employees' pension rights depend on the terms of a pension scheme established under any provision contained in or having effect under an Act of Parliament and the body or authority are required by any such provision to give to new employees information concerning their pension rights, or concerning the determination of questions affecting their pension rights.

(2) If there are no particulars to be entered under any of the heads of paragraph (*d*), or under any of the other provisions of the last foregoing subsection, that fact shall be stated.

(3) If the contract is for a fixed term, the date when the contract expires shall be stated.

(4) If after the date to which the statement relates there is a change in the terms to be included, or referred to, in the statement, the employer shall, not more than one month after the change, inform the employee of the nature of the change by a written statement and, if he does not leave a copy of the statement with the employee, shall preserve the statement and ensure that the employee has reasonable opportunities of reading it in the course of his employment, or that it is made reasonably accessible to him in some other way.

(5) A statement under subsection (1) or subsection (4) of this section may, for all or any of the particulars to be given by the statement, refer the employee to some document which the employee has reasonable opportunities of reading in the course of his employment, or which is made reasonably accessible to him in some other way.

(6) If the employer in referring in the statement to any such document indicates to the employee that future changes in the terms the particulars of which are given in the document will be entered up in the document (or recorded by some other means for the information of persons referring to the document) the employer need not under subsection (4) of this section inform the employee of any such change which is duly entered up or recorded not more than one month after the change is made.

(7) If, not more than six months after the termination of an employee's period of employment, a further period of employment is begun with the same employer, and the terms of employment are the same, no statement need be given under subsection (1) of this section in respect of the second period of employment, but without prejudice to the operation of subsection (4) of this section if there is a change in the terms of employment.

(7A) In subsections (4) to (6) of this section any reference to that which is, or is to be, included, given or referred to in a statement under subsection (1) of this section shall be construed as including a reference to the note mentioned in section 20(2) of the Industrial

Relations Act 1971, and any reference to that which is, or is to be, included, given or referred to in a statement under subsection (4) of this section shall be construed in a corresponding way.

(8) The foregoing provisions of this section shall not apply to an employee if and so long as the conditions specified in the next following subsection are fulfilled in relation to him.

(8A) Those conditions are that—

(*a*) the employee's contract of employment is a contract which has been reduced to writing in one or more documents and which contains express terms affording the particulars to be given under each of the paragraphs in subsection (1) of this section, and under each head of paragraph (*d*) of that subsection;

(*b*) there has been given to the employee a copy of the contract (with any variations made from time to time), or he has reasonable opportunities of reading such a copy in the course of his employment, or such a copy is made reasonably accessible to him in some other way; and

(*c*) such a note as is mentioned in section 20(2) of the Industrial Relations Act 1971 has been given to the employee or he has reasonable opportunities of reading such a note in the course of his employment or such a note is made reasonably accessible to him in some other way.

(8B) If at any time after the beginning of an employee's period of employment he ceases to come within the exception in subsection (8) of this section, the employer shall give the employee a written statement under subsection (1) of this section not more than one month after that time.

(9) No account shall be taken under this section of employment during any period when the hours of employment are normally less than twenty-one hours weekly, and this section shall apply to an employee who at any time comes or ceases to come within the exception in this subsection as if a period of employment terminated or began at that time.

Appendix 2

Questionnaire for Managing Directors

THE QUESTIONNAIRE which follows was prepared by a personnel manager of a famous, international company, for presentation to the managing directors of operating companies. From their answers to the questionnaire, the working party set up by the Group formed the policy to be approved by the Executive Committee.

I am very grateful to the Board of Directors (who wish to remain anonymous) for kindly allowing this document to be included in my book.

E.M.

Questionnaire to be Answered by Managing Directors of Operating Companies

Collective Bargaining, Recognition and Representation of Employees

A WORKS EMPLOYEES

Question 1 Would you prefer the works employees in your company to belong to agency shops?

Answer:

Question 2 Do you think it would be better to have a sole bargaining agent for all employees in each branch of your company or would the situation in the company call for separate bargaining units?

Answer:

B STAFF EMPLOYEES

Question 3 The Staff Committee as constituted at present will have no power to act on behalf of the staff under the Act. On this basis, therefore, should your company recommend to all staff employees that the present Staff Committee be formed into a Group Staff Association with rules and regulations acceptable for registration under the Act?

Answer:

Question 4 Do you think the Group Staff Association should become an agency shop to which all staff employees specified in the agreement would have to subscribe?

Answer:

Question 5 If this situation came about, should the Group Staff Association become the sole bargaining agent for staff employees specified in the agreement, or would the situation in your company call for separate bargaining units?

Answer:

Recruitment and Contracts of Employment

A WORKS EMPLOYEES

Question 6 Which members of staff within your company are responsible for recruitment, i.e. in both Personnel Departments and the departments where the vacancies exist? Names and positions please.

Answer:

Question 7 Which members of staff within your company are responsible for dismissal of employees? Names and positions please.

Answer:

Question 8 Do you consider the grievance procedure laid down in the Works Handbook is adequate? If not, what are its main deficiencies?

Answer:

Question 9 Do you make use of the disciplinary action of suspension—with or without pay? If you do, who has the authority to take such action?

Answer:

B STAFF EMPLOYEES

Question 10 Which members of staff within your company are responsible for recruitment both centrally and in the departments where the vacancies exist of:

Answer: (a) weekly staff

(b) monthly staff

Names and positions please.

Question 11 Which members of staff within your company are responsible for dismissal of employees:

Answer: (a) weekly staff

(b) monthly staff

Names and positions please.

Question 12 At the present time there is no established grievance procedure for either weekly or monthly staff and under the Act it will be necessary to lay down such a procedure. The initial stages would normally be dealt with by the relevant levels of management within the department and the final recourse would be to yourself as Managing Director. Who do you think should deal with the grievance at the middle stage?

(a) a senior member of staff at the branch concerned?

(b) your company secretary?

(c) the Group company secretary?

Answer: Weekly staff:

Monthly staff:

A AND B WORKS AND STAFF EMPLOYEES

Question 13 Are all employees of your company sufficiently aware of what constitutes misconduct, i.e. are departmental rules as well as general company rules clearly defined?

Answer: Works employees

Weekly staff employees

Monthly staff employees

Question 14 Should the company wish to dismiss an employee for any reason other than industrial misconduct, it must guard against the possibility of being accused of 'unfair dismissal'. Do you consider that the performance and attendance of every employee of your company is recorded adequately?

Answer: Works employees

Weekly staff employees

Monthly staff employees

Question 15 Are adequate records kept of warnings to employees about misconduct or failure to carry out the job satisfactorily, and do you confirm the warning in writing to the employee concerned, giving details of the misconduct or inadequacy of performance?

Answer: Works employees

Weekly staff employees

Monthly staff employees

Question 16 Is it the practice in your company to confirm dismissal notification in writing?

Answer: Works employees

Weekly staff employees

Monthly staff employees

Question 17 Are job specifications or descriptions available within each branch for all jobs other than those which are defined as national skills, i.e. tool-makers, electricians, lithoprinters, draughtsmen, etc.?

Answer: Works employees

Weekly staff employees

Monthly staff employees

Question 18 If there are, are they used when discussing jobs with employees?

Answer: Works employees

Weekly staff employees

Monthly staff employees

Question 19 Do you give copies to employees' representatives?

Answer: Works employees

Weekly staff employees

Monthly staff employees

APPENDIX 2

Disclosure of Information

A AND B WORKS AND STAFF EMPLOYEES

Question 20 Do you (or would you) discuss departmental or branch changes, redundancy, etc., with employees' representatives?

Answer: Works employees

Weekly staff employees

Monthly staff employees

Question 21 Would such discussions take place before or after decisions had been made?

Answer: Works employees

Weekly staff employees

Monthly staff employees

Question 22 What matters do you discuss with employees' representatives at the present time?

Answer: Works employees

Weekly staff employees

Monthly staff employees

Question 23 What other matters do you think could or should be discussed with employees' representatives?

Answer: Works employees

Weekly staff employees

Monthly staff employees

Facilities for Unions and Employees' Representatives

A AND B WORKS AND STAFF EMPLOYEES

Question 24 What facilities are provided at present by your company for employees' representatives?

Answer: Works employees

Weekly staff employees

Monthly staff employees

Question 25 Would you be prepared to extend these by providing:
(a) accommodation of some kind;
(b) use of office equipment and/or staff;
(c) use of a telephone;
(d) company time to undertake union business?

Answer:

Question 26 In order to encourage all union members to participate in union business (to combat the usual apathy) would you be prepared to allow union meetings:
(a) on the company's premises;
(b) in limited company time?

Answer:

Communication

A AND B WORKS AND STAFF EMPLOYEES

Question 27 Do employees in your company believe that communications between them and the company are good, bad or indifferent?

Answer: Works employees

Weekly staff employees

Monthly staff employees

Question 28 How do you think communication could be improved?

Answer: Works employees

Weekly staff employees

Monthly staff employees

Question 29 If you have works committees in your company do you think they serve any useful purpose or should they be superseded by union committees? If so, what means of communication would you provide for non-union employees?

Answer:

General

Question 30 Have you any specific problems not covered by the questionnaire, or any matters you would like brought to the attention of the working party?

Answer:

Appendix 3

Courts and Tribunals—Forms and Orders

THE INDUSTRIAL COURT reigns in glorious informality. There are no wigs, no gowns, none of the pomp and circumstance of any other branch of the High Court. The presiding judge and his two colleagues sit on a dais raised only about nine inches from floor level. And anyone can address the Court, standing or seated, to suit his fancy.

Outside, there are conference rooms with easy chairs and enormous ashtrays—but no extractor fans. This is the court of the smoke-filled room. In English law, the 'reasonable man' has been described as 'the man on the Clapham omnibus'. This is the industrial omnibus itself.

Just as the procedures are engagingly free of legal formality, so are the 'pleadings'. The *Industrial Court Rules, 1971*, contain a series of forms, ranging from Form 1—workers' notice of application for order declaring pre-entry closed shop agreement to be void—to Form 32—notice of court's decision to consider order for review of ballot.

Here are those forms which are likely to be used most often—Form 21—Notice of complaint of unfair industrial practice; and Form 26—Notice of appeal from decision of Industrial Tribunal.

But please remember that if you are in doubt, you may consult the Secretary of the Court. You may write to him or call at the Court: 5 Chancery Lane, London WC1 L2AX: Telephone (during the day) 01-242 1633—or at night or at a weekend—01-693 9239.

For details of rules and procedures of the Industrial Tribunal, do consult your solicitor—or the Secretary, the Central Office of Industrial Tribunals, 93 Ebury Bridge Road, London SW1 (Telephone: 01-730 9161).

FORM 21 *Rule 20*

National Industrial Relations Court

NOTICE OF COMPLAINT OF UNFAIR INDUSTRIAL PRACTICE PRESENTED UNDER SECTION 101(1)

1. This complaint is presented by [*name and address of complainant*].

2. Any communication for the complainant relating to this complaint may be sent to [*complainant's address for service, including telephone number, if any*].

3. The name(s) and address(es) of the [organisation(s)] [person(s)] against whom the complaint is made are [*name(s) and address(es) of proposed respondent(s)*].

4. The grounds on which this complaint is presented are:
[*here summarise the facts and matters relied on in support of the complaint*].

5. The complainant is seeking the following relief:
[*here specify, in relation to each proposed respondent, the relief under section* 101(3) (*as extended or modified, if appropriate, by section* 105(3) *or* (5)) *of the Industrial Relations Act 1971 sought by the complainant*].

Date *Signed*

FORM 26 *Rule 29*

National Industrial Relations Court

NOTICE OF APPEAL UNDER SECTION 114(1) FROM DECISION OF INDUSTRIAL TRIBUNAL

1. The appellant is [*name and address of appellant*].

2. Any communication relating to this appeal may be sent to the appellant at [*appellant's address for service, including telephone number, if any*].

3. The appellant appeals from
[*here give particulars of the decision of the industrial tribunal from which the appeal is brought*]
on the following question of law:
[*here set out the question of law on which the appeal is brought*].

4. The parties to the proceedings before the industrial tribunal, other than the appellant, were [*names and addresses of other parties to proceedings resulting in decision appealed from*].

5. The appellant's grounds of appeal are:
[*here state the grounds of appeal*].

6. A copy of the industrial tribunal's decision is attached to this notice.

Date *Signed*

SHUT
SHUT
CLOSED

Index